WORK AND LEISURE

THE HUMAN MOVEMENT SERIES
General Editor: H.T.A. Whiting

WORK
AND LEISURE

An inter-disciplinary study
in theory, education and
planning.

Edited by J.T. HAWORTH

Department of Psychology,
University of Manchester.

and M.A. SMITH

Department of Sociology,
University of Salford.

LEPUS BOOKS
London 1975

Standard Book Number 86019 009 9

Computer Typesetting by Print Origination,
Bootle Merseyside, L20 6NS
Printed by Unwin Brothers Limited, Old Woking, Surrey
Bound by Wm. Brendon & Son Ltd., Tiptree, Essex.

FOREWORD

The Human Movement Series to which this text contributes is one of three by the same publishers, the other two being Physical Education and Physical Recreation. A partitioning of this nature has been made necessary by the diversity of material submitted for publication by different authors. While on a broad basis the Human Movement Series publications differ from the other two series in that the focus of attention is on movement *per se* rather than on the activities to which movement contributes, the divisions are to some extent arbitrary and the boundaries between one series and another are blurred. In general the classification of a particular text into one or other of the series is a straightforward matter, but a few texts do pose particular problems for the editors in that they make contributions in two or more of the areas outlined and cannot clearly be seen to be representative of any one.

The present text—Work and Leisure—is a case in point. While the contribution of movement to work and leisure would not be disputed and could form the basis of a text of this nature, the emphasis in this book is not on analyses at the movement level. In a similar way, work and leisure might be topic areas in texts on physical education or physical recreation. The decision to include it within the Human Movement Series is to some extent an arbitrary one and based on the premise that while the material in the book will be of fundamental concern to physical educationists and physical recreationists, its contribution is to a much wider audience. Its scope in this respect is reflected in the three parts into which the book is divided—*Theory, Education* and *Planning*—articles which contribute to both theory and practice through the presentation of psychological, sociological and educational perspectives.

September 1974

H.T.A. Whiting
Series Editor

ACKNOWLEDGEMENTS

This book is based on a series of invited papers presented to a symposium on work and leisure organised by the editors and supported by the British Sociological Association and the British Psychological Society, held at the University of Salford, September 1973.

Contributors were given the opportunity to revise and expand their chapters in the light of the stimulating discussion at the symposium. The editors would like to thank the symposium participants for their invaluable comments and the authors for their diligence.

The series editor and publishers also receive our thanks for their help. Finally we would like to express our gratitude to the people who have read and discussed the book with us. Their advice was most welcome.

SYMPOSIUM PARTICIPANTS

C. Armstrong	Institut Battelle, Geneve, Switzerland
P.A. Arthur-Smith	Civic Trust for the North West, Manchester
R. Austin	University of Keele
Dr. W. Bacon	University of Sheffield
D. Barber	Nelson and Colne College
R.A. Bee	Manchester Corporation Parks Department
K.S. Bibby	Corporat Laboratories, British Steel Corporation, London
Dr. C.C.P. Brooks	Hatfield Polytechnic
Dr. B.J.H. Brown	The Polytechnic, Huddersfield
D. Brown	The Polytechnic, Sheffield
D. Bruce	Wigan Technical College
R.J. Bullas	University of Salford
Miss. R.C.J. Burton	Greater London Council
D.S. Butler	Manchester City Planning Department
Mrs. J. Calder	The Open University, Milton Keyes
R. Carroll	University of Manchester
D.G. Casey	University of Glasgow
A. Clayre	BBC Open University/All Souls College, Oxford
M.E. Collins	The Sports Council, London
Prof. J.T. Coppock	University of Edinburgh
D.K. Cottrell	University of Sheffield
P.S. Cullen	University of Technology, Loughborough
J.P. Dennis	Portsmouth Polytechnic
N.S. Dickinson	Northern Developments Ltd
G. Duce	Parks Department Offices, Bolton
G. Evans	University of Keele
J.J. Foster	Manchester Polytechnic
Mrs. B. Ganley	Wigan Technical College
A. Gibbon	Inner London Education Authority

Miss. J. Glover	Long Range Studies Division, Post Office Telecommunications
B.J.A. Goodchild	Central Lancashire New Town Development Corporation, Preston
D.E. Griffith	Manchester Corporation Parks Department
D.M. Groome	University of Manchester
A.F. Guy	United Kingdom National Documentation Centre for Sport, University of Birmingham
T.J. Hanafin	Directorate of Recreational Studies, London Borough of Greenwich
Dr. D. Hanson	Middleton St George College of Education
D. Healey	Priory School, Bury St Edmonds
L.B. Hendry	University of Aberdeen
Mrs. M. Herrington	Private
S. Hudson	University of Technology, Loughborough
L.J. James	Brunel University, Uxbridge
R.D. James	Polytechnic of North London
C. Jenkins	University of Birmingham
L.W. Jinks	Lancashire Education Committee
Mrs. D. Johnson	Harfield Polytechnic
E. Jones	Teesside Polytechnic, Middlesbrough
T. Keenoy	University College, Cardiff
J. Keiser	Wm. Temple College, Manchester Business School
D. Kidd-Hewitt	City of London Polytechnic
S.J. Kind	University of Lancaster
J. Leigh	Matlock College of Education
Rev. C.P. Lemmon	University of Salford
P.L. Leonard	Countryside Commission, London
K. Lodge	Private
R. Mapes	University of Keele
D. Marsland	Brunel University, Uxbridge
I. Martin	County Planning Department, Ruthin
Mrs. Martin	Private
W.H. Martin	Private
D. McEndoo	Teesside Polytechnic, Middlesbrough
P. McHoy	IPC Magazines Ltd, London
P.C. McIntosh	The Sports Council, London
M.J. McKenzie	Warrington New Town Development Corporation
G.P. McLaughlan	British Waterways Board, London
V.T.C. Middleton	University of Surrey
J.C. Miles	University of Leeds
R.A. Mills	Greater London Council
Mrs. J.C. Moseley	University of South Wales

S.M. Nasir	University of Karachi
T.M. Parker	University of Edinburgh
N.C.A. Parry	Hatfield Polytechnic
Dr. N.H. Perry	S.S.R.C. Survey Unit
J.B. Prince	Bolton College of Education
P. Randall	County Planning Department, Ruthin
J. Richardson	Birmingham Polytechnic
C.S. Riley	University of Lancaster
K. Roberts	University of Liverpool
K. Robinson	Parks Department Offices, Bolton
Florence Sayer	University of Salford
Susan Sayer	University of Salford
S. Sharples	University of Strathclyde
J. Shuttleworth	Liverpool Polytechnic
J.R. Sidwell	J. Roland Sidwell and Associates, Coventry
Mr. G. Smith	University of Salford
Mrs. K.M. Smith	Warrington New Town Development Corporation
J.M. Tait	Parks Department, Edinburgh
M. Thomas	University of Lancaster
W.M. Tidmarsh	Sheffield Polytechnic
K. Turnbull	Warrington New Town Development Corporation
A.J. Veal	University of Birmingham
F. Warner	Polytechnic of Central London
Miss I Waters	City of Newcastle College of Education
D.R. Weeks	City of London Polytechnic
P.R. White	British Waterways Board, Rugby
A. Wiggett	City Planning Department, Leicester
Miss M.B. Willis	Department of the Environment, London
J.C. Wilsher	Lancaster University
E. Wiseman	Lancaster and Morecambe College of Further Education
S. Wood	University of Manchester
I. Wormald	Bertram Ramsey Further Education Centre, Teesside
J.A. Gravell	Building Design Partnership, Preston
J. Curren	Open University, London
C. Jamieson	Royal Institute of British Architecture, London
D. Willey	Polytechnic of North London

CONTENTS

INTRODUCTION

The meanings of work and leisure

We all experience work and leisure, but if we were asked to say what each is, we would find it difficult to come up with any satisfactory definitions. It has been said, for instance, that work is to earn a living, to earn money. Yet this ignores the social aspects of work, the fact that work may be important for many things besides money. Status, prestige, self respect, social interaction and so on, may be provided by some jobs. For some people work offers the opportunity for being creative, involved, achieving some goals they desire, and doing something for its own sake. On these criteria it would be difficult to distinguish work from leisure. And indeed the situation is equally complex when one considers leisure. Residual definitions of leisure, such as time left over from work or after obligations have been met, free time, discretionary time, choice time, time for people to do what they want, are not without difficulties. One can have free time, for instance, but not necessarily have leisure. Leisure, according to functional and normative definitions, is a quality of experience, or is recreative, or recuperative. But, of course, such terms as 'quality of experience' are not easily defined. Much depends on individual attitudes and perceptions.

This concern with the meanings of work and leisure is of both academic and practical importance. If, for instance, a restricted definition of work is used, such as 'to earn a living', this can equally restrict the constructs which are used to study work and thus have important theoretical significance. Practically, it may encourage the attitude in management, trade unions and employees, that work need not be a meaningful experience. Similarly, if leisure is viewed solely as non-work or non-obligated time, a narrow range of methods may be used in its study. And, practically, there would be important questions for policy. For instance, using such a definition of leisure, should a local government department of recreation be concerned with vocational educational activities, or community services, or sponsor craft workshops, for example? If leisure is

1

viewed as discretionary, or choice time, should there be any planning for leisure, or is this permissible if it is attempting to increase the range of choice, and if so, should this include the choice of participating in the planning?

It can thus be seen from examining even briefly just this one aspect of work and leisure that the subject is not simple. But perhaps it is because of the complexity, the differences of opinion, the difficulties of investigation, as well as the important ramifications for theory and policy and for the type of society we wish to aim for, that the subject is so fascinating, challenging and important.

An inter-disciplinary approach

The idea for this book came out of the editors' interest in the study and research of leisure, and this is reflected somewhat in the balance of the book. Recognising, however, the important links between leisure and work, it was decided to have the symposium on which this book is based, on both these areas. It was also decided to adopt an inter-disciplinary approach. A number of factors indicate the importance of such an approach in this area.

Not least important is that many academic subjects and professions have distinctive contributions to make. Sociologists and geographers, psychologists and educationalists, planners, economists, architects, politicians, philosophers, historians, theologians and so on, all have something to say about these areas. In fact, it could be contended that since we all experience work and leisure, the list may be extended almost indefinitely, were it not that, at the moment, not all of us have the opportunity of being explicitly and effectively involved in the provision of these life areas. Yet, for those who have the opportunity, their communication more often than not is with colleagues in their own field, or at best with colleagues in one or two areas. Only rarely have the sociologists, geographers, psychologists, and so forth communicated with each other, and more rarely still has a structured dialogue occurred between members of a range of academic fields on the one hand and professions on the other, such as is presented in this book.

An active view of man

For those involved in particular academic subjects, there is a further pressing reason for inter-disciplinary discourse. A related development is occurring in many subjects which is of profound importance to the way in which we view and study work and leisure, and ultimately to what provision is made. Stated very simply, a more active view of the nature of man is emerging, a view in which consciousness, or brain-function, as it has been called, is seen to have a greater part in the shaping of behaviour and events than has been granted in the past. Man is seen to act on and influence his situation rather than just reacting passively to events.

In psychology, for instance, while it has long been recognised that perception is an active process, one in which 'reality' is interpreted in the light of subjective experience, a greater weight is now being given to the importance of general cognitive factors in determining the outcome of the interplay between man and his environment. Factors such as creativity, spontaneity, curiosity and responsibility are being recognised as important in behaviour. Stimulus response models, portraying behaviour as a simple reaction to stimuli, are increasingly yielding to a broader view, and this is influencing approaches to theory and practice in applied areas, particularly education. Of course, there are different emphases about the degree of importance of consciousness. Some psychologists, drawing on explanations developed by a number of existentialist philosophers and humanists, go further than just stating that it is important and instead view conscious man as a significant source and centre of values, rather than viewing these as being formed primarily by societal or environmental influences. They consider that man has the potential to create his own future, as opposed to just reacting to trends, a view which puts the responsibility on man to question his actions and to ask 'what for?'[1] Other psychologists, drawing on more extreme existentialist standpoints, lay even further stress on consciousness. They emphasise the paramount importance of individual subjective experience. Although there is argument over the relative influence of conscious 'subjective' factors on behaviour, and while this has implications for methodology in the social sciences as will be discussed later, such factors are now becoming more generally accepted as being significant and not to be ignored.

In sociology the structural—functionalist models emphasising the importance of institutional and societal forces in shaping and constraining human behaviour are also being challenged by a more active view of man. The social action approach to behaviour emphasises the importance of subjective factors.[2] The perceptions and meanings which the actor (individual) ascribes to a situation are considered to play a significant part in influencing choice and action options. Norms and values are located in man as well as in the situation. Thus in this case also, man is not seen as just a passive recipient of the external world but as constantly interpreting and shaping its meanings for himself through a universe of symbols. Hence, social interations are affected by background expectancies,

---

[1] See Greening T.C. (Ed.) (1973). *Existential Humanistic Psychology*. Belmont: Brooks/ Cole. Also Huxley, J. (1963). *Evolution the Modern Syntheses,* London: Allen & Unwin. The latter author proposes that we are now in a phase of psychosocial evolution which man must consciously direct.

[2] See Smith M.A. (1972). Perspectives on organisations. In S.R. Parker, R.K. Brown, J. Child & M.A. Smith. (Eds.). *The Sociology of Industry*. London: George Allen & Unwin.

and individuals interact in terms of shared meanings or meanings they attribute to each other's actions. While as in psychology there are different viewpoints as to the extent to which the subjective-conscious factors influence behaviour, depending to some extent upon the existentialist tradition being drawn upon, there is also a growing recognition of the importance of such factors.

In human geography dissatisfaction has been expressed with environmental deterministic models of spatial location and organisation which have attempted to explain the patterning of towns and cities on the basis of the relationship between societies and the physical environment. While one main approach to constructing better models has been an attempt to develop more sophisticated quantitative techniques using statistics and computerisation, another approach has been adopted by some workers which may have important ramifications for planning. Environmental perceptual processes of individuals and groups are being studied, and the process of decision making leading to the creation of new geographical patterns or the modification of existing patterns is also being investigated. Further, not only have the overt factors been studied, but the conceptions of the geographical environment held by the decision makers are becoming admissible evidence.[3]

That this growing recognition of man as an active, creative being is occurring in many different subjects, including others besides those discussed,[4] suggests that inter-disciplinary dialogue in the field of work and leisure is highly desirable. This applies even though it may result in some blurring of traditional divisions between subjects and prompt some re-organisation with all its attendant difficulties.

Change in the planning professions

Developments in other spheres also point to the same conclusion. The change in town and country planning from predominant concern with land use to include, in theory at least, economic and social considerations, can be instanced, as can the initiation of mandatory public participation in this area. The recognition in some local authorities that problems often do not fit neatly into single departments, and the consequent move towards establishing inter-departmental management teams and corporate planning is another example, even though difficulties in overcoming the traditional isolation of different departments are being experienced. The example of corporate planning may be particularly important if, as it has been suggested elsewhere, it is concerned with

---

[3] See Chisholm M. & Rodgers B. (1973). *Studies in Human Geography*. London: Heinemann Educational.

[4] See 'The Social Sciences Today.' A Series in New Society, April–August, 1974.

studying the community as a whole; identifying problems and needs; devising, costing and comparing alternative solutions to decide which gives best value and achieves the best result; and managing the total resources of money, labour, materials and expertise in pursuit of an integrated set of aims.[5] Other developments of importance include the establishment in many local authorities of departments of recreation or leisure services, and the fact of the Minister for Sport becoming the Minister for Sport and Recreation. These changes point up the necessity for evolving appropriate philosophies of leisure, philosophies which are right for the time and the situation. And certainly if such developments are to be widely beneficial, it is arguable that as broad a dialogue as possible is desirable.

Global factors and new directions

Perhaps, however, inter-disciplinary dialogue is not just desirable but is essential. Concern for man's future has been highlighted in recent years by world wide problems of physical and economic resources, pollution and population.[6] The dangers of non-co-operation may be very considerable. Discipline and specialist centred knowledge can result in decisions being taken without adequate appraisal of the causes, nature and consequences of problems. Human and financial costs can be high, especially if decisions become embedded in policies and plans affecting large groups and areas of social life. Imbalances in resources necessary for survival can occur, as is well recognised, and, less serious but still important, opportunities for work and leisure can be greatly restricted.

But it is not only problems of resources, pollution and population which are giving rise to concern. The increasing awareness of ecological factors is resulting in a greater realisation of the complexity of the environment and the inter-relation of this with human society and culture. Not only are the detrimental effects of science and technology being more carefully scrutinised, but the debate has started on the part which these important cultural forces should play in helping to develop society and provide for individual opportunities. In fact, although it is in its infancy in the U.K., the debate on the quality of life has commenced.

---

[5] Ardell J. (1974). *The New Citizens Guide to Town and Country Planning.* London: Charles Knight.

[6] There is a large number of books on these problems. The following give a broad introductory survey. Leach, E. (1967) *A Runaway World.* Reith Lectures. London: Oxford. U.P. Wolstenholme, G. (Ed.). (1963). *Man & His Future.* London: Churchill. Ward B. & Dubos, R. (1972) *Only One Earth.* Harmondsworth: Pelican. Meadows, D.H., Meadows, D.L., Randers, J. & Behrens, W.W. (1972). *Limits to Growth.* London: Earth Island Press. Cole, H.S.D., Freeman, C., Jahoda, M. & Pavitt, K.L.R. (1973). *Malthus with a Computer.* Brighton: Sussex University Press.

Of central importance to these global considerations are individual attitudes and the nature of our idea systems.[7] This has led to the view that it is now essential for man to control his own evolution, to consciously develop his social and physical world, to ask the question 'what for?' An inter-disciplinary approach would seem to be essential to such a task.

Adopting such an approach does not mean, however, that there should not be scope for the pursuit of knowledge for its own sake. Scope for this activity is vital, but such pursuit may be enriched by contributing on a broader front to the society which makes such detachment possible. This contribution can lie in at least the following directions; in relating our enlarged basic stock of knowledge about ourselves and the physical and social world to explorations of the boundaries between the academic and professional frameworks in order to help interpret such knowledge and help to guide further research; in pointing up the political and economic choices to be made and goals to be realised in continually shaping our own evolution; in continually appraising the value systems on which knowledge itself is processed and selected for transmission in the education system and the media in general. There are many areas where theory and practice co-exist well and are of mutual benefit. Work and leisure need not be an exception.

Difficulties

Of course, there are many difficulties in attempting an inter-disciplinary approach. The traditional isolation of many academic fields and professions, and the difficulties of re-organisation have already been mentioned. Other reasons include the reluctance of many people in the academic world to pursue policy-oriented teaching and research. Difficulties can be encountered in obtaining funding for inter-disciplinary projects. The more boundaries a project covers, the greater the number of committees await each other's decisions. The dominance of the professions, with each one believing it has the exclusive right to its chosen field has also been cited.[8] And, of course, even if the previous difficulties could be surmounted, there is still the problem of subject specific language, of understanding people from different fields with their disparate standpoints.

---

[7] See Huxley J. (1963). *Evolution the Modern Syntheses.* London: Allen & Unwin; also Cole, H.S.D., Freeman, C., Jahoda, M. & Pavitt, K.L.R. (1973). *Malthus with a Computor.* Brighton: Sussex University Press.

[8] See Eversley D. (1969). A Question of Scale. Talk given at a Conference on The New Planning Courses. London: Newscombe House, 45, Notting Hill Gate. Regional Studies Association.

This book is no exception to the difficulties facing an inter-disciplinary approach. It has many shortcomings, not least of which is its incomplete coverage. Your views are not presented and they could well be of significance. Whole disciplines are not represented, even though many are. Many relevant issues in work and leisure are not mentioned. The contributors do not all focus on the same issues, and even when they do this can be from widely different standpoints which are not always easily related. The problem of setting aside one's own values is also particularly difficult. Nevertheless, it is an attempt at an inter-disciplinary approach. Perhaps as a result of such ventures theorists will come to appreciate more fully some of the difficulties of the practitioners and examine carefully their plea for constructive, clearly communicated knowledge. Perhaps practitioners will become more sophisticated in their appreciation of academic inquiry and not demand overly simplistic models, explanations or briefs.[9]

Dialogue themes

The contents of the book divide into three parts: theory, work and leisure; education, work and leisure; and planning work and leisure. The term theory is used in a broad sense and encompasses philosophical as well as empirically based views and models of the nature of man, work and leisure. Perhaps this is only reasonable. Certainly science has no unique claim to knowledge in these areas. In fact, some would argue that it makes the smaller contribution. However, there is no doubt that science plays a part. Models of man and society present in science are used, even if not always deliberately, to underpin decisions about work and leisure.

The first part of the book considers a number of broad but related issues in work and leisure. One of these is whether or not we are a work or leisure centred society and the implications for policy. A second is the associated issue of what aims society will wish to plan for, and what goals and needs it will try to meet. The problem of what methodologies will be used in the investigation of these areas, where there exists such a high degree of uncertainty, is the third major theme.

The other two parts of the book develop further some aspects of these themes. The education, work and leisure part examines the role of education in a changing society in relation to both schools and community. The inter-relation of culture and class is a linking theme in this second part. The

---

[9] Since this symposium, it is pleasing to see the formation of an inter-disciplinary Leisure Studies Association, and also inter-disciplinary working parties on selected topics, such as community needs & provision. However, the approach is in its infancy. For it to be fruitful it will require a sustained and sincere attempt at co-operation.

planning work and leisure part looks at some of the problems associated with the formulation of objectives in planning and examines a number of factors which affect both provision and implementation in the public and private areas.

The three parts of the book do not, then, correspond directly to the major themes, which tend to cross cut and interpenetrate the different contributions. In order to make the dialogue more fruitful, the major themes are now briefly pinpointed and discussed.

What kind of society: work or leisure centred?

The new active view of man as the choice maker, thrusts upon him the responsibility of asking 'what for?', of questioning the reasons for his decisions, and of consciously deciding what kind of society to aim for. However, this process does not occur in a vacuum. Central to a discussion of what we want to become is a consideration of what we are, and pertinent to this is the issue of whether or not society is work or leisure centred.

Central life interest. Since the industrial revolution the predominant view has been that work and economic activity in general is the main focus of life, the principal organising force, the main provider of satisfactions and dissatisfactions. Leisure has been considered to have a more peripheral function. Its role has been seen to be essentially one of recreation and recuperation, with entertainment subserving these functions. Recently, however, this view has been challenged. It has been suggested that there has been a decline in work as a 'central life interest' and that increasingly significance and meaning are being sought in leisure. Leisure, it is suggested, is crucial to the development of self-identity, and self realisation. There is a quest for new sensations, new experiences and fulfilment through fun. The fashion revolution, the growth of minority cultures, the cult of the eccentric and the exotic, the acceptance of revolution as a way of life, have all been cited as examples of the rejection of work as a central organising force and the pivotal link between the self and society.[10]

This debate on the centrality of work or leisure is reviewed by Stanley Parker in Section 1. Recent writings are cited which support both standpoints. Parker presents data, however, to show that as far as leisure time is concerned there has not been a great increase. The average working week has not been significantly reduced in the post-war period mainly because whilst normal working hours have been reduced, there has been a tendency towards a corresponding increase in overtime. Holidays have increased, three weeks becoming the norm, and a

---

[10] See the general introduction in Smith M.A. Parker S.R. & Smith C.S. (1974). *Leisure and Society in Britain.* London: Allen Lane.

number of unions have adopted the fourth week as a target. There has also been a longer expectancy of life in retirement. Parker concludes that while there has been some decline in work centrality, and an increase in leisure centred attitudes, we are certainly not yet a leisure centred society. With regard to policy, Parker considers that we must concentrate on improving both work and leisure.

Glasser also touches on this debate in Section 2. He considers that a technology based society has organised work in such a way as to force man to abandon hope of fulfilment during his working hours and instead to seek it in his leisure. But, he considers that potentially work is a significant integrating force. Like Parker, he concludes that we must improve both work and leisure.

In Section 3, Dower and Downing, the leisure researchers and planners, wonder whether or not we should be looking with more wholeness at life satisfaction, at how activities and facilities can better serve human need. They query whether or not leisure is the right concept to pursue.

Haworth, in Section 4, considers that in our present society many jobs may well provide satisfactions and serve purposes other than the provision of income, some of which are not realisable at all or to the same extent if one has total spare time. He quotes authors who claim that work may give people a recognised place in the community; confer status and self respect; give a sense of usefulness; help people to structure their time and be important for identity; help in the retention of mental health; satisfy a need for stability, predictability and control; and help to satisfy a need for psychological growth, the need to discover, actualise, progress and add to one's existence. Of course, many of these factors may rise from work centred values, from people conforming to the puritan ethic that work is to be glorified and that leisure has to be earned. But such values may only change slowly, and while leisure may provide many satisfactions, the quality of life in the work sphere cannot be neglected.

Basini in Section 7, in the education section, takes a more extreme view. He considers that leisure is a non-issue. Like Parker he questions the idea that there has been a significant increase in leisure time, stating that many obligations have to be fulfilled during non-work time. Professional classes may read for profit, lunch for contracts; many classes have household repairs to do. Family obligations may be extensive. Basini believes that the obligations of work and ancillary roles still tightly circumscribe man's life. The so-called leisure problem has arisen, he considers, because it has been defined as such, institutionalised and hence perpetuated.

However, Basini's thesis does not lead him to conclude that leisure should be ignored. Rather he is concerned that within education there is an attempt to impose a curriculum and culture which may bring about an inappropriate leisure centred society for the lower socio-economic groups, and that this will be at the expense of a proper concern for the quality of work, its experiences, expectations and rewards.

Class. This issue of class, and its bearing on the centrality of either work or leisure is also considered by Murdock in Section 8. He examines and refutes the proposition that generations are replacing classes as the decisive determinants of life styles and social consciousness, and that the generational consciousness of youth is expressed and sustained by their participation in the symbols and meanings provided by parts of the leisure industries, particularly the pop music industry. His research shows that youth culture is heterogeneous, and that the different types may be recognised on a class basis. Class based, rather than leisure based, meaning systems are important in structuring life styles. He suggests that this requires the rejection of the youth culture notion (the predominance of meaning for youth through leisure) and the revival of a class analysis. He also indicates that there is considerable evidence against the related embourgeoisement thesis that the working man, preoccupied with home and family, sees his work 'instrumentally' as a means of acquiring the income necessary to support his leisure time life style.

Work and leisure centred. The general issue then of whether we are now a leisure centred society is not given much support by the contributors to the book. This is a conclusion with which we, as editors, would agree. This does not mean that leisure is not important, or not a priority. As is concluded by many of the authors in this book, both work and leisure need to exist in balance. Perhaps such a consideration will lead to a greater appreciation of the potential of leisure for self expression and individuated self-awareness, and also to the importance of the quality of life at work. These considerations, however, bring us even more into the realm of the aims and goals of society, which is the next major theme to be considered.

What kind of society: aims, goals and human needs.

Quality of life. The essence of being human is defining goals and pursuing them. This view which, as suggested earlier, would receive some support from developments in science, is outlined by Glasser. In his chapter he makes a challenging analysis of a number of approaches used in leisure assessment and provision. The marketing and related demand and supply approaches to leisure provision, which purport to determine and satisfy perceived demand, are criticised on the grounds that not all demands are desirable. Some balance is required between the demands of individuals and those of society. Therefore, one must consciously define goals. The recreational approach, a variant of the demand and supply school, is equally criticised on the grounds that it views man as a battery which can be recharged by physical recreation. The social therapy approach is also criticised for its simplistic view that provision of leisure facilities will reduce frustration and give a purpose to life. So-called education for leisure is seen as education for the use of facilities, and the provision of knowledge to enable one to use leisure more knowledgeably, an objective which, without considering the quality of life, Glasser feels is like being urged to step on a mental treadmill. The expression of the personality approach is also considered to be no answer unless one defines personality, and also recognises the need to compromise between free expression of the individual will and the needs of society.

Glasser considers that these approaches are detrimental because they encourage people to use leisure as a means of ignoring the causes of stress and thus create the conditions in which stress will become socially destructive. Further, they encourage people to retreat from the basic question of whether or not the purpose of leisure is different from the goal of life itself.

A crucial goal in life, according to Glasser, is the need to establish an identity as close as possible to that which society sets up as a standard for emulation. He believes that society is only presenting transitory and unsatisfactory models for emulation in terms of the life styles of the folk heroes of pop culture, sport and the business world. The models are transitory because of the requirements of business to sell fashion and change. Hence, individuals are being frustrated in their search for a model identity.

Glasser sees the foremost problem of society as one of restoring the authority of a common code of ethics and social discipline, a model of the ideal identity maintained until recent times by religion. Education in the schools, he believes, should play an important part, and the mass media should also be utilized by the state in a holding operation until a revival occurs of moral authority as exercised by the great religions.

These prescriptions have not been without their critics, and in an appendix to his article Glasser replies.

Perhaps the major criticism has been concerned with the idea of a model identity, some sort of value consensus, which has been interpreted by some as meaning a single optimum identity. If by this is meant a detailed blueprint for behaviour, then criticism would indeed be justified. In a pluralistic society, as Glasser recognises, many variations exist. But perhaps society does require some shared frame of reference, if change is not to become anarchistic and self destructive. Whether or not the frame of reference should be concerned with individual fulfilment and the values of freedom, toleration, fairness or justice, and respect for reasoning, values which are seen by some as essential to political debate in a liberal democracy, is obviously open to question. But whatever is proposed, it would seem to be important that the debate is widespread if the imposition of values is to be avoided.

The criticism that leisure policy has ignored man and has concentrated too much on the provision of facilities is also made by Dower and Downing in Section 3. They consider that the 'providers', the Sports Council, Countryside Commission, local authorities and so on, have been concerned in the main with the efficient use of scarce resources. In attempting to satisfy imputed demand, or demand which it was felt desirable to encourage, they have been preoccupied with questions of quantity, deficiency and imbalance rather than with the quality of provision. They have not been concerned with what leisure means to man. Yet the production of facilities is not an end in itself, but is for the 'personal fulfilment of the populace,' and this, Dower and Downing suggest, should provoke the question why do people do things?

Like Glasser, Dower and Downing consider that not all demands must be satisfied. Many demands, they believe, are interchangeable. Instead, they suggest that the main aims should be satisfaction of underlying needs (in work and leisure), and they call on the help of the man oriented researchers to aid in clarifying these.

Such aims as the satisfaction of basic needs, fulfilment, enhancing the quality of life, and related aims are put forward by many of the contributors. Haworth, for instance, considers that there should be a greater recognition of the active nature of man, with creativity, curiosity and exploratory behaviour being seen to be not just the prerogative of the few. These and other components of what has been termed an innate potential for psychological growth should, he believes, be nurtured in work, leisure and education. Crompton too, in discussing the provision of leisure facilities in Section 12, says that quality has been neglected and this is echoed by Gillinson in Section 13 on designing for leisure. In both these sections the concepts of quality, while being related to some extent to the management of facilities, appears to be viewed primarily in terms of decor and the physical atmosphere it produces. Perhaps this is understandable. Nevertheless, it does illustrate the lack of precision and the uncertainty of such concepts, and highlights the difficulties in using them.

Uncertainty. Yet conceivably, this uncertainty is a basic feature of the situation of attempting to define societal aims and goals and individual human needs. As Haworth points out in outlining various theories of human needs, the status of some as learned or innate is uncertain. While investigations of human needs may provide insights of value, ready tailored definitive check lists of innate or enduring human needs cannot be provided. In such a situation of inbuilt uncertainty, perhaps it is still of some value to use such concepts as needs, fulfilment, quality and so on, providing we constantly review them and assess the effects of any action we take in connection with them. Maybe if questions of 'meaning' and 'significance' were taken as admissible and treated seriously in planning, as Melville requests in Section 10, then a great advance would be made, even if there are difficulties of definition. And perhaps the enquiry and search themselves are important.

Culture. The issue of quality of life and societal aims overlaps with the analysis of culture and the implicit judgements of better or worse which are often assigned to different types of culture. Mass culture has received its share of criticism in the past. In Section 6 Peterson criticises the search for a fun identity on the grounds of its concern with immediacy, a cult which he says, has its root in the nihilist tradition, and as such is a destructive force. Education, he considers, should act as a countervailing force to fashion change. It should be concerned with activities which take some time and effort extended over time, such as the traditional arts. This is especially the case, he believes, in view of the possible increase in leisure time.

Other criticisms of mass culture have been that it provides spurious gratification, reduces the level of cultural quality and civilisation and encourages totalitarianism by creating a passive public particularly responsive to the techniques of mass persuasion. But, as Basini notes, many authors argue that there is little supporting evidence for such claims.

High culture is often viewed as the alternative to mass culture; Glasser is a critic of high culture, at least in so far as it is purported to be a remedy for the ills of society. High culture, he considers, does not make a person better in the sense of more mature and morally and socially responsible as, he says, is claimed.

But perhaps high culture receives its severest criticism not so much on account of its content, although the immediate relevance of much of this for some groups has been questioned, but because of the values and behaviour expectations which may have become associated with this type of culture. Education is a particularly sensitive area in this respect. Schools have been viewed as the keepers of high culture and middle class values. Murdock points out that schools are organised on the middle class values of individual achievement, rational calculations, forward planning, and deferment of immediate gratification in favour of long term gains. Working class children are expected to identify with these values and adopt behaviour patterns which are geared to middle class careers while being in the main excluded from the rewards of the system. Rennie in Section 9 also refers to what has become known as the hidden curriculum. Streaming, he points out, can be an education for failure. House systems, prefect systems, assemblies, and the way teachers speak to their pupils, carry an implicit (middle class) message to children. Basini points to authors who claim that education for the so called 'less able', a group which overlaps considerably with the poor, is a social control process, an inculcation of appropriate standards and values; also that education is geared to predisposing some people to accept failure and lack of self-fulfilment in work. Education processes knowledge as well as people, and educational aims, he claims, may be elite oriented and reflect the norms and values of those holding economic and political power within society. Peterson also makes an important point. While supporting the liberal arts tradition, he distinguishes between content and method in education. The content he sees as a leisure activity, but the method he sees as predominantly an education for work, a conditioning for the pattern of working life, including for many, a certain amount of drudgery.

Education for leisure. Dangers in liberal education for the masses, so-called education for leisure, are most clearly recognised by Basini. Such education can be used to attempt to offset unrewarding work experiences with the implication that these need not therefore be rectified. Basini considers that this type of education, particularly the humanities programmes, will give pupils a false sense of satisfaction with their situation and lead them to accept the inequality present in society. Such education as proposed will, he believes, effectively restrict access to high status knowledge and occupations. Basini's alternative policy suggestions in the educational sphere are implicit in his analysis of the situation. In essence he believes that education should be for both satisfactory work and leisure for all children and not just for an elite.

Rennie's solution is community education. He considers that it is essential for teachers to change their role from information givers and disciplinarians to that of senior colleagues working with junior colleagues where communal decisions are taken. Education, he believes, should recognise an explicit social purpose for the school in enabling children to live fully, rather than conditioning them to be conforming acceptors of what is provided for them. This approach, he believes, should be linked on the one hand with curriculum development in which problems of relevance to the students are studied, and on the other with community development and adult education. Thus, in discussing how home and school links can be improved, he cites happenings and carnival events which involve teachers, pupils and parents. Other activities which extend the concept of education into leisure and life generally are coffee mornings at the school, parent run tuck shops, after school play centres, and the fact that parents can also mix freely with children during lessons. This approach to education, culture and life is, as Rennie notes, still in its infancy. High culture need not be excluded, even though many of the supporters of the community approach advocate initially a critical evaluation of other cultural forms on the grounds of relevancy. The approach obviously cuts across traditional boundaries. Theory, particularly critical philosophical analysis, education, planning and design are all involved as well as the need for carefully detailed investigations.[11] This, of course, raises the issue of the methodology for exploring and testing questions of relevance to society. This is the issue to which attention now turns.

What kind of society: methodological considerations

Theoretical issues. It was stated at the beginning of this introduction that a point of view is emerging in many subjects in which human consciousness and choice is seen to have a greater role in the shaping of behaviour and events than has been granted in the past. It was also noted that there are different degrees of

---

[11] Some other community projects illustrating the interrelationship of theory, education, planning and design are discussed by Haworth, J. (1974). *Leisure & Involvement*. P.T.R.C. Summer Annual Meeting. University of Warwick.

emphasis on the extent to which conscious or 'subjective' factors influence behaviour, depending to some extent upon the academic and philosophical tradition being drawn upon, and that this has implications for methodology. Some phenomenological philosophers, for instance, place such an emphasis on subjective factors that they would denounce the possibility of objective social reality and hence of objective research in the social sciences. In a similar tradition, although not quite as extreme, are those theorists who, while rejecting a science of detached observation, support an experiential approach, believing that insights can be gained from experience. Participant observation is the most accepted method of enquiry. Other investigators in the social sciences support a still less extreme existentialist viewpoint while at the same time rejecting the main tenets of logical positivism. They believe that the importance of subjective factors means that the methodological procedures of the natural sciences are not appropriate to the social sciences. Abstraction by either experimentation or surveys, to produce laws or law-like generalisations is eschewed. However, the possibility of some generalisation is accepted. Norms, values and shared meanings, for example, are recognised. On this view, the technique of detached observation is considered permissible, although participant observation is often used. The ethnomethodological tradition in sociology is akin to this.

The recognition that subjective factors are important is not taken by all investigators as a reason for denigrating the influence of general social factors. Goldthorpe,[12] for instance, considers that situations may be structured by the differential control people have over economic and political resources as well as symbolic factors which participants may bring to their interaction. Thus 'class', for example, still seems to be an important influence on behaviour. Emmett, in Section 5, also points to the importance of considering the factor of power and its differential control, if a realistic analysis of behaviour is to be made, particularly in the leisure sphere. But she also recognises the need for more in-depth studies using observational methods in order to learn the 'language', tease out the complexities of the situation and think about the matter.

In line with this broader approach is the view that research surveys and different observational techniques, can all be of value, given cognizance of ethical problems, even though at times they may deal with different levels of reality. In this book Dower and Downing point to the fact that surveys in the leisure sphere have produced basic factual information of value. However, like Emmett, they also say the time is now ripe for in-depth studies. Statistical surveys can tell us about quantity, but not, they consider, about quality.

Another factor of importance which directly affects the generality of findings, is the recognition of the uncertainty in the nature and relationship between elements which underpin human behaviour. There is uncertainty

---

[12] Goldthorpe, J.H. (1973). A revolution in sociology. *Sociology* V.7. No. 3.

surrounding some 'human needs'. The extent to which 'needs' are determined by culture, the degree to which behaviour is a reaction to norms, values and ethics, some of which may change rapidly, is hard to determine. Similarly, the effect which the creative, active nature of man will have on expectations and aspirations is also hard, if not impossible to estimate. It may bear repetition that while investigations of human needs may well provide insights of value, insights which may be given additional support if statistical procedures can isolate clustering domains of needs,[13] definitive check lists of enduring human needs cannot be provided. Emmett makes a similar point in relation to forecasting needs and demands. She considers that the planners' and decision makers' desire to know what people want and what they will want in 25 years time, cannot be realised. Several reasons for this are given. People's wants conflict. People do not know what is possible now. People's attitudes and values are not homogeneous. Demand is dynamic and is affected by unpredictable fashion change. In addition, much of the complexity of the situation is ignored because of the methodology used to examine leisure, particularly its social dimensions.

Yet, perhaps recognition of this uncertainty concerning human needs and interests could prove to be of value. Emmett considers that the 'providers' delude themselves into believing that they will satisfy our needs (if only they knew them). But if in reply to questionnaires we asked for bingo, old films or television, to get drunk, smoke pot, or watch soccer rather than play it, we would not, she states, get more facilities for these. They would not be viewed as good for us! Perhaps demonstration of the uncertainty concerning needs and what is good or bad for us will make providers more flexible.

Research strategies and public participation. Recognition of uncertainty also has implications for research strategies used in planning for work and leisure. Haworth, while indicating that many methods may have to be used, considers that more emphasis should be placed on both assessing the effectiveness of projects and on authentic public participation. Such a combined course of action could, he argues, result in mutual education of the providers and users, and overcome to some extent the arguments in environmental planning that people are not educated enough to participate, that generally they do not know what they want, and if they do, it is detrimental to society in the long term. Such proposals emphasise, of course, the potentially important role of each individual in helping to define and construct a satisfactory reality. Other contributors also follow a similar view. Rennie, for instance, in the description of the work of a community education project, indicates that in the process of people meeting and discussing things with the staff of the centre, their needs may be discovered. He also stresses the importance of finding ways of enabling people to organise

---

[13] See Miles I. (1974). Social Forecasting: from Impressions to Investigation. In S. Encel, P. Marstrand & W. Page (Eds.). *The Art of Anticipation.* London: Martin Robson.

the centre and give to it their talents and skills. An adult education tutor is used to work in the pubs and clubs, and through informal discussion, to help people formulate their own conclusions on their needs and interests. Approaches like this, following on from the educational priority area experiments, have similarities with the community development projects. These neighbourhood based schemes, aimed at finding new ways of helping people living in areas of multiple deprivation, also lay special emphasis on citizen involvement and self help. Housing, social services and welfare matters, planning law, and citizens rights are all matters of concern.

Public participation is also, of course, part of the methodology of large scale assessment of goals and needs and is particularly important now that it is mandatory in the preparation of structure plans. Melville makes a strong case for the exercise to be treated seriously. But he also considers that it will only be successful if it is politicised. Recreation planning, he argues, is based essentially on measuring and forecasting demand trends, and then assuming that one must attempt to satisfy them, with little thought for the consequences. Yet many of these consequences may be detrimental. A still greater imbalance in provision favouring those that have transport may occur, to cite but one example. Melville considers that planners and other 'providers' in the community fail to consider what sort of community we want. But at the same time he also points out that only a limited amount can be done from within the bureacracy. Pressure from outside the administrative machine will be all important, he considers, in determining the output of our bureaucracies.

However, as is now recognised, public participation at whatever scale conducted is not without its difficulties. Boaden in Section 11 considers that the 'where', 'when' and 'how' of participation must be taken into account. It is important to know where to participate, i.e. at what level of decision making, and also when to participate, i.e. at what point in the process, which can extend over a considerable time, if frustrations are to be avoided. It is also important for people to know how to participate, or to ensure that the system is altered to fit in with their capabilities. Effective communication, not only among the public and the decision makers, but also among the public themselves and the decision makers themselves is, Boaden argues, central to the where, when and how. But he also points out that more than dialogue is needed. Influence is also vital. Without influence, public participation may just be used to legitimise the decisions of those in authority and make it even more difficult for objections to be made at a later date.

Crompton also points to the difficulties of public participation in practice. If large samples are studied, a project could, he considers, be delayed for a considerable time. With costs rapidly escalating there would effectively be less money to spend on a project. This could entail curtailment of facilities or even abandonment of the project. He considers that the sort of public participation achievable in connection with the provision of leisure facilities is little more than information dissemination and public relations. Although he recognises that some background data must be researched and calls for this to be clearly communicated, he nevertheless proposes that much still depends upon the empathy of the recreation planner. Gillinson also considers that perhaps the architect will have to continue to rely on an intuitive approach to designing facilities, but with an evaluation of projects to check out assumptions. He hopes that social scientists will make a creative contribution.

The complaint that public participation decreases efficiency excessively is not unique to the field of leisure provision. It has also been claimed by the authors of some of the recent structure plans submitted for government approval. Ministers too have also made a point of saying that participation in depth must not mean participation at length. Planning, it is felt, must not be made impotent by prolonged delays in the participation and objection stages.[14] Yet time is not the only difficulty. Planners have pointed to the large numbers of conflicting pressure groups at local and national level and the unrepresentativeness of 'fly by night' social science leaders of communities.[15]

But despite these and other difficulties faced by planners concerned with public participation it has not deterred some planners at least from preferring it to what they call the untenable theory that council committees and their advisers know what is best for the individual and the community.[16]

Action research. Finally, brief mention should be made of a research approach likely to develop, viz, action research or collaborative research as it is viewed by some. In this approach the knowledge and research techniques of social science are combined to both plan and promote change. The approach has been used with some success in the work sphere, although there have been calls for caution.[17] In the broader community sphere, the educational priority projects and the community development projects are examples of its use.

In the broader community spheres, however, there has been considerable difficulty in planning and co-ordinating change. The projects have also been criticised on the grounds that evaluation of action to produce findings for general policy formation is very difficult, if not impossible; and further, that if the design of the projects were to permit evaluation, it is questionable whether it could be

---

[14] Ardell J. (1974). *The New Citizens Guide to Town and Country Planning.* London: Charles Knight.

[15] Eversley D. (1973) *The Planner & Society:* the changing role of a profession. London: Faber & Faber.

[16] Battey R.W. & Givilliam M.C. (1974). *Public Participation in Structure Planning.* P.T.R.C. Summer Annual Meeting. University of Warwick.

[17] Cherns A.B. (1974). Work or Life? *S.S.R.C. Newsletter,* 21st January.

done adequately by researchers involved in planning and implementing action.[18] The latter criticism obviously has some substance, but objectivity in any type of research has to be striven for. As for producing findings, for general policy formation, this may not be the aim of the researcher. Findings of some possible value in similar situations may be the more modest and realistic objective.

Some critics of action research have proposed alternatives. Surveys, it has been suggested, should be more closely tied to policy making.[19] But this approach does not tackle the difficult problem of implementation of policy. In many cases policy may emerge as research and action continues.

Perhaps the latter point indicates a fundamental issue concerning both action research and policy oriented survey research. Who will be involved in formulating the goals? This, of course, is a central issue, albeit an implicit one, in this book.

Manchester 1974

J.T. Haworth
M.A. Smith

---

[18] Town S.W. (1973). Action Research and Social Policy: Some Recent British Experience *Sociol. Rev.* Nov.

[19] Abrams M. (1974). Social Surveys. Social Theory and Social Policy. *S.S.R.C. Newsletter*, 24 January.

1

THEORY

THEORY

WORK AND LEISURE: THEORY AND FACT

by S. R. PARKER Principal Research Officer,
Office of Population, Census and Surveys, London.

In this paper I want to make a critical analysis of contributions in recent years to the study, both empirical and theoretical, of the relationship between work and leisure. In this context the term 'theory' should be defined loosely to mean theoretical propositions and hypotheses, since theory in the full sociological sense has scarcely started to be developed in this field. My treatment will be primarily sociological, emphasising the social nature of behaviour and relationships, but psychological considerations are also relevant. The theme of work and leisure may be broken down into a number of sub-themes, and of these I shall not be reviewing data on the leisure industries, or the sociology of occupations in the leisure industries. I shall refer to a fairly large number of authors and publications, but my review is not intended to be exhaustive: further references may be found in Parker (1972) and Smith (1973).

A double purpose may be served by examining work and leisure in this way. Academically, the time seems ripe to review the progress that has been made and to suggest directions of future development. But there is also the more practical question of how planning and policies for leisure may be framed in the light of existing or possible future research. In other words, leisure may be seen as an area where academics and practitioners may learn from each other and contribute to what each group is trying to achieve, without sacrificing relevant professional interests or standards.

The facts of work and leisure

I propose first briefly to review the data available on time left over after work and available for leisure. These residual blocks of time are not necessarily *spent* on leisure, because they may have to be used for work-related purposes such as travelling to work or non-work obligations such as self-maintenance or duties to others. Nevertheless, time nominally free for leisure is a useful and reasonably objective starting point for analysis. The following is a summary of a longer article on the subject (Parker 1974).

Work time (i.e. average hours of employment) may be considered by the day, the week, the year and the whole life. Although the work day and the work week are conceptually different, it is not realistic to separate the two. In 1972 male manual workers in Britain had, on average, a working week of just over 40 hours and female manual workers one of just under 39 hours. Non-manual workers usually had shorter normal hours as one of the benefits of staff status. There tends to be a broader spread in the range of normal hours worked by non-manual employees, with no particular range being dominant, but the average for both men and women was about 36-37 hours.

As normal working hours have been reduced over the years, there has been a tendency towards a corresponding increase in overtime. In 1972 actual hours for manual workers were 5 hours above normal hours. On the subject of double-jobbing ('moonlighting'), reliable information is difficult to obtain. About 7% of the working population have second jobs at some time over a period, but the proportion who have a second job in any given week is probably no more than 3-4%.

So far as the work year is concerned, the position has been changing rapidly in the last few years, and the most recently available data are likely to be out of date. If a 5-day week is assumed, then 20% of men manual workers and almost 15% of women manual workers had 1970 holiday entitlements in excess of three weeks; 4% of both men and women manual workers exceeded 4 weeks' entitlement. The comparable figures for non-manual workers were: 66% of men and 51% of women entitled to more than three weeks, 31% of men and 24% of women entitled to more than four weeks. Agreements covering some 5 million manual workers conceded a fourth week of annual holiday to come into effect during 1973 or 1974, and a number of unions have adopted the fourth week as a target.

Estimates of the current average length of work life are difficult to make. Several factors are tending to shorten the work life: young people are remaining in full-time education for longer periods, and the age at which employees are retired from work has been lowered. But the greater expectation of life due to improved medical and welfare services is probably having a small effect in the opposite direction, i.e. fewer people are having their work life cut short by death. A more significant effect of longer life is, however, a longer expectation of life in retirement.

To sum up on time available for leisure, the working week has in recent years not decreased markedly for most people—an increase in overtime and double-jobbing has very largely eaten into time gained by a reduction in normal hours. The length of holidays, however, has certainly been increasing and is continuing to do so. A longer expectation of life in retirement is the other major gain in time nominally free for leisure.

Let us now look at the efforts of those researchers whose contributions have taken the form primarily of reporting on some facts of work and leisure rather than of any theoretical discussion of the issues and values involved. I do not want to imply that these contributions are less valid or valuable than others, nor that their authors are without theoretical ideas. It is simply that these contributions take the form of telling us about what people actually do or say rather than suggesting to us what the relationship between work and leisure is or should be. Almost all the items deal with the work and leisure lives of people in different occupations.

Child and Macmillan (1973) have taken a comparative look at the leisure lives of managers in Britain and other countries, notably America. Results from several surveys suggest that for British managers work-related activities do not take up a major part of their leisure time. Managers generally spend most of their leisure time at home, and share with other occupational groups in Britain a propensity to watch sport on Saturday afternoon. Few British managers devote any appreciable part of their leisure time to activities that in any way directly further their work and career. Furthermore, these managers prefer to compartmentalize their lives so that the job is forgotten during leisure hours. The picture emerging from surveys of American managers, however, is quite different. Many of them are completely job-oriented, intellectually narrow and uninterested in the humanities or liberal arts. The evidence is that the typical American executive enjoys his work and that his way of life permits no clear-cut distinction between work and leisure.

Several British studies throw light on aspects of the work and leisure lives of manual workers. Brown and his colleagues (1973) show that, while home- and family-based activities predominate in the leisure of shipbuilding workers, some of their leisure activities take place in work time. Very often the social meeting places at work are more fixed and permanent than the places in the yard where the work is actually done, and shipyard workers talk about their 'leisure-at-work'. Mott (1973) traces the historical association between miners and weavers and pigeon racing and breeding. Drawing on research carried out by French sociologists in a mining area, he suggests that the complex business of pigeon racing provides individual and social compensations and the opportunity to exercise many kinds of skill, lacking in the often coercive, fragmented and repetitive work in the mine. Tunstall (1962) describes a different kind of compensatory leisure behaviour indulged in by some distant-water fishermen: the hard-drinking, 'living it up' and status-seeking activities of people who are ashore for only three months in the year.

Some types of worker tend to carry work attitudes over into the week-end in spite of fatigue and often an expressed desire to get away from work and everything it stands for. Blum (1953) discusses the relation between work and leisure experienced by the typical packing-house worker. Since it is almost impossible to work eight hours intensively and switch over suddenly to a new, creative way of life, these workers are pushed into some kind of activity which keeps them occupied without reminding them of their work. Fishing is one of their favourite pastimes. It has some elements which are just the opposite of work—relaxing outdoors 'away from it all'—yet it is in other ways continuous with work and requires no basic change of attitude. Also, the *style* of a particular type of leisure activity may be related to work experience. Thus Etzkorn (1964) notes that 'public campground' camping, which is routinized, is practised more by individuals with routinized jobs, while 'wilderness' camping is preferred by individuals in more creative occupations.

Several studies have sought to establish a connection between type of occupation and choice of leisure activity. Reisman (1954) found that people in higher class positions were more active and diverse in their social and leisure participation than those in lower classes. This finding has been confirmed in a number of other studies, including the two British national recreation surveys (British Travel Association, 1967, and Sillitoe, 1969). Sometimes occupational 'prestige' is taken to be the variable, as with the studies of Clarke (1956) and Burdge (1969). The general conclusion is that people in the higher prestige classes participate in a greater variety of leisure activities than do people in the lower classes, although a few pursuits, such as bowling and gardening, are more favoured by the lower classes. One wonders whether the fairly gross categories of 'prestige level 1' etc conceal more specific differences in occupations which may be linked with characteristic forms of leisure behaviour.

The examples of work-leisure relationships considered so far have been British or American, but the cross-cultural nature of these relationships is illustrated by Vogel's (1963) study of middle-class Japan. The Japanese businessman, like the American, finds it difficult to distinguish working time from leisure time, and often entertains his clients with a trip to the golf course or a party with entertainment by geisha girls. Like successful businessmen, doctors rarely make a sharp separation between work and leisure, partly because to some extent working hours are determined by the arrival of patients. It is the salaried man who makes the sharpest distinction between working time and free time. In contrast to the businessman who mixes business with leisure, and to the doctor whose leisure is determined by the absence of patients, the salaried man generally has set hours so that he can plan certain hours of the day and certain days of the week for himself and his family.

All the above studies are reports on static situations. What happens to leisure when work routines change? Meyersohn (1963) describes the consequences for leisure of an American aircraft factory giving its employees a 3-day weekend every month without a reduction in total weekly hours worked. At first the general attitude to the change was favourable, but after a while more people became dissatisfied with the 3-day weekend and fewer made definite plans about how to spend such future weekends. The findings of that particular survey may be biased because it took place at a time of economic recession. A report by Miller (1972) indicates that, while only a very few firms in Britain operate a 4-day week, their employees seem generally well satisfied with the arrangement.

The bunching of free time is said to be more beneficial to certain forms of leisure, but so far the evidence seems inconclusive.

To evaluate briefly the present state of purely empirical research on work and leisure: a fair number of studies have been carried out concerning the work and leisure lives of people in different occupations, but progress has been uneven. We know more about managers' leisure than about ordinary employees' leisure, and more about the 'exotic' patterns (perhaps because they are more interesting to research?) than about the more everyday patterns. Perhaps what we need is a more concerted approach—fewer projects but each of them more comprehensive and comparative.

The theory of work and leisure

The second group of studies I want to look at are those which have made some contribution to the theoretical study of work and leisure, but based on sociological imagination or secondary analysis rather than on original data. These theoretical contributions take three major forms: an analysis of work and leisure in the context of the present state of society (including its legacy from the past); the various possible types of relationship between work and leisure; and the particular question of whether work and leisure are becoming more alike or less alike (the 'fusion versus polarity' debate).

Several writers have sought to trace the ways in which the development of the social and economic processes of industrialism have influenced the relationship between work and leisure. Burns (1973) argues that the swamping of everyday life by industrialism has not been succeeded by a mere ebbing or forcing back of the flood. Social life outside the work situation has not re-emerged; it has been created afresh, in forms which are themselves the creatures of industrialism. He maintains that the way in which people spend their disposable money and time is a mode of organising their lives, and that the concept of 'style of life' is more than a variable which is dependent upon class or occupational status.

Roberts (1970) has put forward the thesis that, along with other modern industrial societies, Britain has become a society of leisure, in that the activities in which people participate during their free time play a significant part in the development of their sense of self-identity. He claims that it is only in their leisure lives that individuals feel they are expressing their real personalities. Furthermore, he believes that leisure-based values and attitudes are necessary to explain people's conduct in other spheres. Roberts also claims that Britain is now a 'leisure democracy'. Using data from surveys of the length of the working week for employees at different levels, he concludes that the extent of an individual's social obligations outside work makes more difference to the amount of free time he has than his employment does. He also suggests that there are no sharp cleavages distinguishing the leisure activities of one stratum of society from another.

While Roberts believes that the 'society of leisure' is already here, others see it as only a promise. Bacon (1972b) maintains that the technological basis exists to build a society of leisure, but regrets that most people still structure the whole of their lives around the world of work. Cultural norms, inherited from the past, socialize us into the belief that work is good and idleness reprehensible. So the long-term unemployed and the retired, who ought to be able to adjust to a life of total leisure, in fact mostly find this extremely difficult. They cannot envisage leisure as an autonomous sphere of activity enjoyed for its own sake. Instead, they—and most others—see leisure as a marginal period of recreational time, which can only be legitimately enjoyed in conjunction with the experience of work.

The theme of cultural influences on work and leisure is also apparent in the writings of some European theorists. For example, Matejko (1971) notes the attitude to work and leisure of people in countries under foreign domination where individuals have been socially downgraded: they work slowly or not at all, but as long as they are not educated and their cultural expectations are modest, they will not do much about their situation. On the other hand, in rapidly industrializing countries young people reject the conditions which were acceptable to older generations: they experience a separation of work from the rest of life which liberates them from control by family and community, but denies them an occupational identity and intrinsic satisfaction in their work. Separation of work and leisure is thus closely related to the separation of work and pleasure.

A second major concern of theoretical studies is the various possible types of relationship between work and leisure. Gross (1961) has adopted a functional approach to leisure analysis, part of which includes an attempt to demonstrate the functional role of leisure behaviour in work situations. In terms of Parsons' four functional problems of social systems, Gross points to (1) the *pattern maintenance and tension management* functions of colleague groups of 'mutually trusting equals who drink coffee or play cards together', (2) the *adaptation* functions of recreation and creative leisure in compensating for the fatiguing or deadening effect of some forms of work, (3) the *goal attainment* functions which are served by assigning differential access to leisure and consumption opportunities (allegedly helping to solve the problem of allocating people to appropriate and needed positions), and (4) the *integration* functions of sociability and horsing around at work. This whole analysis seems very strained, and though I have summarized its main features I do not think the detailed statements add very much to our understanding of the relationship between work and leisure.

Although attempts to *define* leisure in terms of its relationship (or lack of relationship) to work constitute a somewhat limited theoretical endeavour, they seem to have been more successful in contributing to our understanding of behaviour and situations than such ambitious aims as those of Gross. Thus DeGrazia (1962) draws a distinction between free time and leisure:-

> Work is the antonym of free time. But not of leisure. Leisure and free time live in two different worlds. We have got in the habit of thinking them the same. Anybody can have free time. Free time is a realizable idea of democracy. Leisure is not fully realizable, and hence an ideal not alone an idea. Free time refers to a special way of calculating a special kind of time. Leisure refers to a state of being, a condition of man, which few desire and fewer achieve.

To say that leisure and free time live in two different worlds is another way of saying that they are not measurable by the same criteria. It is a plea against treating them as interchangeable concepts. But the distinction is not confined to the area of non-work. It applies also in the work sphere. *Some* working time is paid time, but you do not have to be an employee in order to do work, and in that sense 'anyone can have working time'. Yet work as a certain kind of activity, a productive relationship between man and his environment, may, like leisure, be something which few desire and fewer achieve. I maintain that the two worlds of time and activity are thus not the domains of work and leisure respectively, but are both *dimensions* of work *and* leisure.

In a thoughtful and critical review of the main concepts employed in contemporary research, Bacon (1972a) insists that leisure should not be studied as a residual sphere of activity independent of other important and characterizing elements such as work. He also proposes that leisure be conceptualized on both behavioural and normative dimensions, since it is composed of many complex elements. With the behavioural dimension, an examination of work-leisure relationships would be concerned with the degree of fusion or polarity between the component elements, and with the normative dimension the concern would be with the degree to which values found in work complement or oppose those found in leisure. Bacon suggests that such a conceptual scheme could be used as a base for a systematic examination of leisure in industrial society.

A third major concern of theoretical studies is the question of whether work and leisure are becoming fused or polarized. I shall not attempt to summarize all the contributions to this debate, but shall give two examples of each point of view. First the 'fusionists'. Kaplan (1960) writes:-

> ... we are heading, by and large, toward a kind of work that we cannot arbitrarily, by hours, divide from the rest of our lives. It is not enough to say that we work harder at our play or that work is becoming more like play. This is only roughly true. We must begin to think of a society in

which the lines between such concepts as work, play, family, individual, group, state, religion, education, and entertainment have faded.

In the same vein Wilensky (1964) cites as evidence of work-leisure fusion the long coffee break among white-collar girls, the lunch 'hour' among top business and professional people, card games among night shift employees; and, off work, the do-it-yourself movement, spare-time jobs, 'customers' golf' for sales executives, and commuter-train conferences for account executives.

Against all this, the supporters of polarity cite other evidence. Greenberg (1958) maintains that work has become more concentratedly and actively work, and that its present standards of efficiency require one to key oneself to a higher pitch of nervous and mental effort. The implication is that such work has become less like leisure. Also, Green (1964) believes that the 'break in consciousness' between work and socialised play, begun during the Industrial Revolution, has now been completed.

To assess the current state of the theory of work and leisure: my impression is that its sense of history and philosophy is reasonably good, but its compatibility with mainstream sociological theory and with the rules of evidence is not so good. The 'society of leisure' is a gross oversimplification of what is happening in our society, and the advocates of fusion and polarity should realise that their evidence concerns sub-cultural and occupational-cultural levels rather than whole societal trends and that there is some truth in both positions. Attempts to apply functional theory to work and leisure will appeal only to fans of structural-functionalism, though one is left with a vague feeling that someone ought by now to have developed work and leisure in an action frame of reference.[1] There is much to be said for dimensional analyses of the complex relationship between work and leisure, and I believe that most progress has been and can be made along these lines.

Theory and fact

The third group of contributions I want to review are those which use original data to formulate or test theoretical propositions. Again, three major themes may be discerned: how empirical studies can contribute to sociological theory; the evaluation of evidence about the extent to which work and leisure are central life interests of groups of people in particular circumstances; and the

---

[1] The action frame of reference is based upon the individual or role player's definition of meaning, i.e. his perceptual and motivational perspective. This contrasts with the structural—functionalist approach which stresses the institutional—system level of analysis. See M.A. Smith, chapter 7 in S.R. Parker et al. *The Sociology of Industry*. Allen and Unwin. 1972.

evaluation of evidence for the compensation/spillover and derivative theories of leisure in relation to work.

I can find only one published study which attempts to link explicitly an empirical investigation into work and leisure with classic sociological theory. Blakelock (1961) examined the effect of rotating shift work on leisure activities, and concluded that such workers were generally less active in their leisure and tended to spend more time around the house than did other workers. He links these findings to Durkheimian propositions about the effects on the individual of transition from consensus-based to division-of-labour-based social integration, and draws a somewhat tenuous analogy between such a transition and the restricted leisure opportunities of shift workers. A more obvious and simple explanation of Blakelock's findings is that rotating shift workers have less of their leisure time when most people are having theirs.

The French sociologist Dumazedier (1967-1972) has done as much as anyone to develop both the theory of, and empirical research into, leisure, but his theory is not of any sociological school and is fairly restricted in scope. He uses the results of his own empirical investigations and those of others to argue that decisions such as where to work and live will be taken with an eye on the scope of leisure facilities available in a particular district. He sees leisure emerging as the main institution in modern society, and maintains that it is leisure that is shaping the whole style of life of the modern family. I agree with Roberts that these views should be treated as hypotheses requiring further investigation rather than as definite conclusions.

A good deal of research effort has gone into testing propositions about work and leisure as sources of central life interest. Dubin (1956) coined the term 'central life interest' to a significant area of social experience. Assuming that social participation in a particular sphere may be necessary but not important to an individual, he classified replies by industrial workers to a series of three-choice questions as job-oriented, non-job-oriented or indifferent. The results showed that by a majority of three to one work was not in general a central life interest for the industrial workers sampled. Orzack (1959) gave an amended version of Dubin's schedule to a sample of professional nurses and found that nearly four to one of them gave overall 'work' replies.

Studies of manual workers in several countries generally confirm Dubin's findings, and my own survey of business and service workers (Parker, 1972) is consistent with the findings of both Dubin and Orzack. Where I differ from Dubin is in the evaluation of these results in terms of social policies. Whereas he maintains that since most workers obviously don't want to be involved in their work we should abandon attempts to get them so involved and instead concentrate on improving things for them in non-work life, I argue that the forced choice of central life interest doesn't adequately allow for what seems to me to be the preferable pattern: the integration of work and leisure and the rest of life, with the corollary that we should seek improvements in *all* spheres.

I have left until last the empirically-based theories which seek to explain the nature of the work-leisure relationship. In this field Wilensky (1960, 1961, 1964) is an outstanding contributor, despite the failure of his long-awaited book on work and leisure to appear. He puts forward two alternative hypotheses to explain leisure behaviour in terms of work experience and attitudes: it is 'compensatory' if it seeks to make up for dissatisfactions felt in work, and it is 'spillover' if it is the continuation of work experiences and attitudes. My own threefold typology of work-leisure relationships (extension, opposition, neutrality) owes much to Wilensky's ideas and especially those in his 1960 article.

Two further recent contributions are worth noting. Salaman (1971) investigated work-leisure relationships among samples of two occupational communities: London architects and Cambridge railway men. Both groups had a high level of work-leisure fusion, and Salaman suggests that this is due to three inter-related elements: self-image or identity, values, and relationships. The causal factors responsible for the type of work-leisure relationship were shown to be involvement in work and work tasks and a type of inclusivity (features of a job which affect non-work life).

The study by Young & Willmott (1973) of family, work and leisure confirms the findings of previous research that professional and managerial people have a wider range of leisure activities (including work-related activities) than do other employees. But the authors go beyond this to suggest how people with absorbing work and varied leisure interests try to prevent both from undermining their family relationships. They comment on how their case-study findings on the functions of leisure in relation to work compare with my modification of Dumazedier's linkages (extension and continuation of personal development, neutrality and entertainment, opposition and recuperation). They 'would rather say that the people whose work extends outwards are those who most loudly voice the need for recuperation'. I think we need to look more closely at the concept of 'recuperation' in this context. Their book should stimulate plenty of thought and debate.

Conclusion

In recent years a good deal of research effort has been put into the study of various aspects of work and leisure. But much more remains to be done before we can speak with any confidence about patterns of relationship, prediction from one sphere to the other, or any real 'theory' of work and leisure. The progress that has been made has been somewhat diffuse and patchy, and it seems that theory has sometimes gone in one direction and the data in another, that is, the ideologies associated with the evaluation of work and leisure have not always been consistent with the facts about how much 'free' time people have and how they spend it.

There has been much talk about a 'society of leisure', which allegedly has already arrived or at least is imminent. This view is sometimes accompanied by a claim that the salience of work has declined, the two views coming together in the composite assertion that we have moved from a work-centred to a leisure-centred society. As with most generalisations, there is more than a germ of truth in all this. The nature of modern work has, as Mills (1956) among others has pointed out, become less satisfying and creative for many employees than formerly, because of a loss of skill and more dehumanised working conditions. On the other hand, leisure undoubtedly features more prominently in the lives of ordinary people than in the past, and this is especially evident in the case of holidays. However, such trends as these hardly add up to a 'leisure revolution'. The fact that such a revolution is widely thought to be happening or imminent may indicate that what people *think* is happening to work and leisure is just as significant in explaining attitudes and behaviour as what is demonstrably happening.

References

BACON, A.W. (1972a). Leisure and research: a critical review of the main concepts employed in contemporary research. *Society and Leisure*, 2.

BACON, A.W. (1972b). The embarrased self: some reflections upon attitudes to work and idleness in a prosperous industrial society. *Society and Leisure*, 4.

BLAKELOCK, E.H. (1961). A Durkheimian approach to some temporal problems of leisure. *Social Problems*, Summer.

BLUM, F.H. (1953). *Towards a Democratic Work Process*. New York: Harper.

BRITISH TRAVEL ASSOCIATION—University of Keele (1967). *Pilot National Recreation Survey*.

BROWN, R., BRANNER, P., COUSINS, J. & SAMPHIER, M. (1973). Leisure in work: the "occupational culture" of shipbuilding. In M.A. Smith, S.R. Parker & C.S. Smith (Eds.). *Leisure and Society in Britain*. London: Allen Lane.

BURDGE, R.J. (1969). Levels of occupational prestige and leisure activity. *Journal of Leisure Research*, Summer.

BURNS, T. (1973). Leisure in industrial society. In M.A. Smith, S.R. Parker & C.S. Smith (Eds.). *Leisure and Society in Britain*. London: Allen Lane.

CHILD, J. & MACMILLAN, B. (1973). Managers and their leisure. In M.A. Smith, S.R. Parker & C.S. Smith (Eds.). *Leisure and Society in Britain*. London: Allen Lane.

CLARKE, A.C. (1956). The use of leisure and its relation to levels of occupational prestige. *Am. Soc. Rev.*, June.

DEGRAZIA, S. (1962). *Of Time, Work and Leisure.* New York: Twentieth Century Fund.

DUBIN, R. (1956). Industrial workers' worlds. *Social Problems,* January.

DUMAZEDIER, J. (1967). *Towards a Society of Leisure.* London: Collier-MacMillan.

DUMAZEDIER, J. (1972). The dynamics of free time or leisure in advanced industrial societies. *Lo Spettacolo,* September.

ETZKORN, K.P. (1964). Leisure and camping: the social meaning of a form of public recreation. *Sociology and Social Research,* October.

GREEN, A.W. (1964). *Recreation, Leisure and Politics.* New York: McGraw-Hill.

GREENBERG, C. (1958). Work and leisure under industrialism. In E. Larrabee & R. Meyersohn (Eds.). *Mass Leisure.* Glencoe: Free Press.

GROSS, E. (1961). A functional approach to leisure analysis. *Social Problems,* Summer.

KAPLAN, M. (1960). *Leisure in America.* New York: Wiley.

MATEJKO, A. (1971). Culture, work and leisure. *Society and Leisure,* 2.

MEYERSOHN, R. (1963). Changing work and leisure routines. In E.O. Smigel (Ed.). *Work and Leisure.* New Haven: College and University Press.

MILLER, R. (1972). The four day week. *Guardian Newspaper,* February 28th.

MILLS, C.W. (1956). *White Collar.* New York: Oxford University Press.

MOTT, J. (1973). Miners, weavers and pigeon racing. In M.A. Smith, S.R. Parker & C. Smith (Eds.). *Leisure and Society in Britain.* London: Allen Lane.

ORZACK, L. (1959). Work as a "central life interest" of professionals. *Social Problems,* Fall.

PARKER, S.R. (1972). *The Future of Work and Leisure.* London: Paladin.

PARKER, S.R. (1974). Evolution and trends in work and non-work time: Great Britain. *Society and Leisure,* (in press).

REISMAN, L. (1954). Class, leisure and social participation. *Am. Soc. Rev.,* February.

ROBERTS, K. (1970). *Leisure.* London: Longman.

SALAMAN, G. (1971). Two occupational communities, examples of a remarkable convergence of work and non-work. *Soc. Rev.,* 2.

SILLITOE, K.K. (1969). *Planning for Leisure.* London: H.M.S.O.

SMITH, M.A. (1972). The sociology of industry. In S.R. Parker, R.K. Brown, J. Child & M.A. Smith (Eds.). *The Sociology of Industry.* London: Allen & Unwin.

SMITH, M.A., PARKER, S.R. & SMITH, C.S. (Eds.) (1973). *Leisure and Society in Britain.* London: Allen Lane.

TUNSTALL, J. (1962). *The Fisherman.* London: MacGibbon & Kee.

VOGEL, E.F. (1963). *Japan's New Middle-class.* Berkeley: University of California Press.

WILENSKY, H.L. (1960). Work, careers and social integration. *Int. Soc. Sci. J.*, 4.

WILENSKY, H.L. (1961). The uneven distribution of leisure. *Social Problems*, Summer.

WILENSKY, H.L. (1964). Mass society and mass culture, interdependence or independence. *Am. Soc. Rev.*, April.

YOUNG, M. & WILMOTT, P. (1973). *The Symmetrical Family: a Study of work and Leisure in the London Region.* London: Routledge.

THEORY

LEISURE POLICY, IDENTITY AND WORK

by R. GLASSER Management and Development Consultant, London.

I must begin by correcting some current misconceptions about leisure. Some of them follow Romantic thinking so far that they lose touch with reality. Others take a mechanistic approach to man's nature that virtually destroys his humanity. As I explain in my recent book (Glasser 1970) *Leisure–Penalty or Prize*? society is attempting to treat leisure as a *residual* instead of as an integral part of life. In fact the technology-based society is steadily forcing man to abandon any hope of fulfilment through his working hours and to seek it instead in his leisure. In effect this attitude represents a retreat from the task of defining goals and pursuing them, the essence of the human situation. Yet this task is all the more urgent and dangerous because of our transition from a craft-based society disciplined by religion, to one based on technology in which religion is weak and moral goals are indistinct. Accordingly there is a predominant inclination for everybody, sociologists included, to turn aside from these questions of 'Total' goals and to treat leisure purely as a demand for facilities without pausing to examine the nature and the merits of the desires that produce the demand.

Such an attitude reflects the Romantic belief in a Natural Man whose nature would always steer his efforts in the right direction, morally right for himself and for society. This demand for facilities is to be met in the same non-normative manner as any other in our rational society, by counting heads, by the marketing approach, a view that regards the leisure phenomenon in the same way as the demand for sewage disposal, for water supplies, for roads to drive upon, for tranquiliser pills or beer, cinemas or contraceptives. This view of leisure sees only the time to be filled, not why the demand presents itself in certain forms, whether all these forms are equally valid according to some accepted standard of moral value, or whether they may be evidence of deeper needs that are not being satisfied by the conditions and policies of modern society. This demand and supply view of leisure policy-making takes a simplistic view of man. It says merely that demand exists and that society should arrange to supply it, because not to do so would result in greater social stress than

36

already exists. There is no disposition to examine the emotional sources of the demand or the anxieties associated with it. We should not be surprised at this, for to supply demands uncritically is usually a profitable and popular occupation, whereas analysing them is painful. Yet it is surely amazing that the fruits of the Age of Progress should be a state of affairs in which the much sought relief from long hours of work should produce anxiety about how to fill one's leisure, so much so that leisure itself became a problem demanding a cure. The social reformers of the early nineteenth century did not envisage the possibility that anyone could have more leisure than he knew how to use, or that one needed a policy for it. Children of the Romantic movement, they believed that each person possessed an automatic guidance system which, once the burden of labour was lightened, would steer him infallibly to a fulfilment that would be correct for him and for society and would make him a better person and society a better place for that reason.

That this belief was sadly mistaken is only grudgingly being accepted. The accompanying disappointment is one of the main psychological reasons for the present moral gloom in Western society, whose peoples, obtaining more and more leisure, are suffering more, not less stress. While the causes of this stress are complex, it is becoming uncomfortably clear that leisure is not in itself the automatically fulfilling influence the reformers assumed it to be. Unfortunately this naïve view of the human spirit and its requirements is now being replaced by another, equally superficial, namely that the answer to the needs of the human condition is to organize an unlimited supply of distraction and forgetfulness. It is on this view that the *demand and supply school* of leisure thinking takes its stand. Boredom is a crime. We must fill every moment of leisure time. Eradicate unfulfilled desire at any price. On the surface at least, let there be no feeling of deprivation. Longing must be stilled. In social affairs and in business it is pleasant and profitable to follow a trend, however deluding it is, for there are markets to be exploited, leisure complexes to be built, contracts to be won and much easy popularity. Let it be sufficient, therefore, to remove symptoms of discontent by means of organised leisure distraction. When, for example, advertising advises us to take a certain brand of aspirin to cure a headache, what we will remove is only the symptom of some deeper condition. Medical science tells us that the headache might well be a signal of a condition that we would be unwise to ignore. However the aspirin blots out the signal. It is forgotten and it may be, after all, that forgetfulness is all we really want. If we can blot out the signal long enough maybe the deeper cause will also go away without our having to take any fundamental action. The line of least resistance is always the most attractive because it appears to demand the least immediate rearrangement of our basic attitudes. So it is with boredom and stress, the twin syndromes of life in the high consumption society and the most destructive, personally and socially. People in the advanced countries are massive consumers of tranquilisers, as I shall show by example in a moment. A tranquiliser may be regarded as merely a different route to forgetting certain conditions that produce pain, and friction with the environment. If forgetfulness is a sufficient answer to the pains of the human condition why indeed look further? The demand and supply school of thought, in philosophical terms, is really treating leisure as merely a *different kind of tranquiliser*. A tranquiliser may crush the more obvious symptoms of inner stress and so lead us to believe that we can function for a time as if the stress no longer existed. Yet in some part of the mind we know it does exist. It remains and grows. It works its corrosive damage beneath the surface where the emotional needs clamour for understanding and fulfilment.

The demand and supply school have another thesis, not in fact so very different, based upon the literal meaning of the word recreation. Leisure, they say, should be occupied with activities that *re-create* a person from the wear-and-tear of life. But re-creation of what? This is not made clear. One is left to assume a mechanistic view of man, to the effect that the stresses of work and the human situation in general create a need, as with machinery, for maintenance, to restore the machine to its normal working capacity. With man, as with machines, this view seems to say there is a pristine state which the business of living corrodes, and so we need leisure to re-create us in that ideal state over and over again, just as we send a car to be serviced, the cylinders de-carbonised, the battery recharged. In fact some such assumption has crept into our everyday speech. We hear people talking of a holiday as being for the purpose of re-charging our batteries. When Charles Kingsley wrote about man's divine discontent did he have in mind merely a symptom of overheating in our engines, something to be cured by a ski-ing holiday or a session at the swimming pool or the discotheque?

This mechanistic approach to the human situation was taken to one type of extreme in Karel Câpek's (1936) satirical, apocalyptic play, *R.U.R.* His artificially produced work-force the Robots, made in man's image but without a soul, fell victim to a state of extreme stress he called 'Robot's cramp', a completely disabling condition for which there was no cure. It sounds, one might think, not unlike some extreme conditions of stress occurring among human beings today. In the play, Dr. Helman, Psychologist-in-Chief to the Robot manufacturers, Rossum's Universal Robots, describes the condition:-

> ... Occasionally they seem to go off their heads... We call it Robot's cramp. They'll suddenly sling down everything they're holding, stand still, gnash their teeth—and then they have to go into the stamping-mill. It's evidently some breakdown in the mechanism.

In our society we have various equivalents of Robot's cramp. We may call it emotional fatigue, depression, a nervous breakdown, neurosis. Contemporary society treats Robot's cramp in various palliative or indirect ways, more or less unsuccessfully. In the United Kingdom, for instance, more than 24 million prescriptions for tranquilisers and anti-depressants are consumed in a year, and the rate is on a steady increase. This figure has more impact if we make the reasonable assumption that in general the consumers of these drugs are adults or at least adolescents, let us say the over-fifteens; this gives us a figure of 42 million people consuming 24 million prescriptions a year, a melancholy comment on the stress of life in the contemporary high consumption society. The picture is worse still if we remember that this figure of 24 million prescriptions is additional to the astronomical quantities of other drugs of various kinds that are also used in the hope of combatting stress, the pain-killers, sleep-inducers, indigestion mixtures, placebos. And in addition to these, there are the oceans of alcohol consumed each year, perhaps man's oldest method of seeking release, the illusion of fulfilment, or at least a pleasant forgetfulness.

Such figures might be thought to indicate that access to leisure is not the automatic key to fulfilment. The demand and supply school appear to argue that Robot's cramp will be cured if the right kind of leisure facilities are provided and if people are given the right education to enable them to use leisure correctly. The words, right and correctly, beg a number of important questions, and assume the acceptance of certain dogma about how people should be made to use leisure, and about the better claims of some leisure activities over others, for example, classical music as opposed to pop or Racine as opposed to Walt Disney. That this assumption is not borne out by experience is shown, for example, by the high incidence of stress and related problems among people with a high culture. But a prime question whose answer is also assumed but never explained is the most important of all in terms of social policy: what is the purpose of leisure? The demand and supply school appears to assume that the goal is a frictionless or stress-less condition of which the test is: does it keep the individual contented and working at optimum efficiency? The same view is often presented in lofty language, such as to say that the aim of leisure is the expression of the personality. Such a statement propounds a dogma about the purpose of life which, apart from being highly ambiguous, appears to exclude the need for that compromise between free expression of the individual will and the needs of society which is the essence of the human condition. Expression of the personality at once says too much and too little. In this it has the meretricious attractiveness of most emotive slogans; in seeming to answer every person's secret wish it deters too close an examination. Societies in every age have had to set limits to the individual expression of the personality. With deep experience of the moral discipline required by these compromises, man has built up through the ages an ideal image of the kind of person that is acceptable and the behaviour code that is desirable—in a sense the same thing. One might say that human maturity is the resultant of an acceptance of the moral imperatives implied. The mature person, working with the materials of his life as he finds them, and within the necessary social constraints and obligations, constitutes the model in all the great cultures. As I show later in this paper, it is in the emulation of this archetypal model of a desirable identity that the individual conceives his goals, which he attempts to realise in his way of life and which will condition his attempts at fulfilment in his freely disposable time. This in my view is a practical approach to man's needs in seeking to define the proper goals of a leisure policy.

Again the uncritical provision of leisure facilities is often advocated on the ground of what must be termed crude social therapy: leisure facilities will reduce people's frustration with their lives, give them a purpose they do not otherwise feel, alleviate their sense of friction with their emotional environment. Such statements must be interpreted in terms of economic costs and benefits, the need to suppress anxiety in the work force so that motivation and productivity may be stimulated and maintained, once again a tranquiliser for the Robots. While the economic issues are real and serious, it is sad that leisure is being sold to the masses as a convenient opiate. Such a policy earns easy popularity and status for the practitioners, but it encourages people to retreat from two basic questions: firstly, what causes the stress and the declining motivation to work and to be socially constructive? Secondly, is the purpose of leisure different from the goal of life itself? It is strange that this school of thought has not paused to test their view by the simple method of examining the incidence of stress, frustration etc. among the upper income groups of society who possess uninhibited access to leisure facilities and to education. There is no evidence whatever that these more privileged people are any less prone to the chagrins of the human condition than anyone else. If leisure does not bring such benefits to them, why should it do so for the masses?

Both the adherents of the demand and supply approach as well as of the re-creation school base their position to some extent on education, knowledge of how to use the various facilities for filling up leisure time. The word usefully is usually added. Useful for what is never made clear. Useful for increasing knowledge that will improve one's skill at the leisure pursuit itself, at chess, or gardening, at swimming or sailing a boat? The reasoning here is, as usual, circular. Knowledge will enable you to use your leisure more knowledgeably. This sounds very much like being urged to step on to a mental treadmill, on much the same principle as physical labour was once used in mental asylums to produce so much fatigue in the patient that he had too little energy left with which to feel stress. Again, as with the use of leisure by the more privileged members of society, there is no evidence that education *per se* causes people to live a life with lower stress than the less educated. In fact there is a good deal of evidence showing that more highly educated people make at least as much if not more use of aids to forgetfulness, tranquilisers, self-administered placebos, and alcohol as the less educated. This emphasis on education often contains yet another, even more misleading assumption, namely that there is a hierarchy among recreational interests in which some, like music and the arts, rank much higher than, say, billiards or cards, in short that the higher a person's cultural interests the better the person he will be and the better will be the society he lives in. High culture, on this thesis, provides an elevating, humanising influence that makes the individual more mature, moral and socially responsible. One has merely to look at the example of Nazi Germany, a country that inherited a high culture, where education had taught respect for it and yet whose moral ethos was certainly no better, and some would say far worse, than in many contemporary societies where respect for high culture was far from general. Similarly, if one takes a university community as representing high education and culture, and a group of unskilled workers in the same country representing low educational attainment, one finds that in terms of the relative incidence of stress, boredom and frustration, there is little to choose between them.

The cachet attached to education derives from associations of ideas dating from the pre-industrial age. The preserve of an élite concerned with government and its associated power the Church, education became identified in the popular mind with access to control of events and so with personal volition. Later, by a related association of ideas, education became identified as the key to control of nature and therefore, by what now seems a pathetic optimism, as the key to the mysteries of the human condition, providing the individual with a chart for steering his personal journey through them. Ironically this rationalist vision originated in the educated élite and was fostered by them, unconsciously perhaps, in the interests of maintaining their position of privileged leadership. In the movement of social reform, access to education became a major goal partly because of its identification with privilege, partly because it was recognised, in the dawn of the technological age, as a means of personal economic advancement and social mobility. In the present day, the belief in education as a humane influence is an extension, by a confused association of ideas, from its recognition as a key to the use of technology. This is the real reason why national education budgets are now expanding so rapidly. Man has a great aptitude for making a virtue out of necessity. The present surge of expansion in education follows the recognition that, in the super-technological age we have entered, more extensive education is needed. Yet this is presented not as an economic requirement but as a move forward in social progress, a term incidentally that is as seldom subjected to strict definition as is the purpose of leisure or for that matter of education.

I have devoted space to the foregoing analysis of the received ideas about leisure policy because they are not only mistaken and harmful in themselves but their vogue impedes acceptance of realistic policies. On the analogy of aspirins and headaches such misconceptions do harm in two ways: firstly because they direct people's aspirations away from their true goals; secondly, by encouraging people to use leisure as a means of ignoring the causes of stress, they create the conditions in which stress will become socially destructive.

The realistic route is to look for empirical evidence of the basis of goal-formation in the unconscious motivations people reveal in day-to-day behaviour. In doing so I must refer here to my identity theory of leisure, which I have already discussed in my book, (Glasser 1970). Briefly its origins were in some motivation studies into shopping habits. Contrary to conventional thinking, these revealed that the primary purpose of a shopping expedition was to reaffirm the person's perception of his identity and to compare this with an ideal identity that was the goal, and only secondarily to make purchases. Further studies led to the conclusion, which I summarise here, that the over-riding compulsion on the individual, governing *all* his actions and attitudes is to pursue a desired identity. People have a basic need to attain an identity that is as close as possible to that which society and the inherited culture sets up as a standard for emulation. The desirable identity is a compound of ideas about behaviour, ethical standards, physical appearance and life-style, and achievement. Even though this identity may seem to be expressed in superficial ways, by dress, possessions, etc., essentially it is the view the person has formed of the closest copy he can achieve at that moment of the model identity or ideal person *as he perceives him.* Each person is engaged, unconsciously, in a continued quest, firstly to perceive clearly what this desirable identity is, secondly to achieve it within himself, and thirdly to display it. Its display and its approval by others is a necessary part of the process. The whole emulation and its confirmation, is the means whereby he measures his success in life. Each purchase he makes is in some way an affirmation of his perception, at that moment, of his desired identity. Unfortunately our perceptions of identity, both of the ideal and of the one we have attained, fade rapidly and need constant renewal. In earlier times this frequency of renewal was facilitated by bringing people together in religious observances, often powerfully reinforced by association with the forces of nature through fertility rites and sympathetic magic. This still happens in the less 'developed' societies. Periodically, in consort with the seasons, the routines of life changed with the ritual, and with these changes the individual was brought to feel closely attuned to the model identity, and helped to feel that he was 'on the beam' towards it. Religion itself, in whatever form it is found, is essentially concerned with communicating the *idea* of the model identity, and in obtaining acceptance by the individual of a discipline, personal and social, by which he can consistently emulate it.

Psychological depth research thus confirms, as if that were necessary, the essential social role of religion—however we define it. It shows that the goal of life is unconsciously perceived as the constant refinement of the identity to bring it as near as possible to a commonly desired one. I make no assertions here about a transcendental identity. It is not necessary here to debate whether because mankind has, in many cultures, come to broadly similar conclusions about what the model identity should be that this is proof of its divine origin. The fact of the broad unanimity in the great cultures should be sufficient. It can be no accident that this identity is one which is conducive to social responsibility. Apart from anything else, it is by observing his interactions with the environment, his culture, that the individual monitors his identity and attempts to bring it nearer to the accepted ideal. Emotional fulfilment is in the achievement of an identity close to the ideal one. With the erosion of the influence of religion, it is becoming more and more difficult for people to renew their perception of the ideal identity; its image is no longer being projected with its old emotional force. One recognises of course that the great religions were by no means fully effective in imposing moral discipline, in convincing people to emulate the ideal identity. The Age of Faith was no golden age. Nevertheless the individual, even in deviating from the ideal, perceived what he was deviating from, in the same way as we are aware that we are telling a falsehood only if we perceive what the truth is! In modern society the old moral consensus is much weakened and its voices are confused. The culture of high consumption presents purely transient models for emulation in terms of the life-styles of the new synthetic aristocracy, the folk-heroes of pop-culture, sport, the business world, even of the criminal world. The marketing of goods, and the persuasion process that bends consumer demand to buy them, use this emulative need to achieve their sales targets. The persuasion practitioners, by a skilful deflection of thought, lead people to behave as if the ownership of products, and the life-styles these products symbolise, constitute a desirable identity. Thus consumption patterns are formed that fulfil business strategies. The practitioners of the marketing process now exercise the leadership function of the high priests of old.[1] However, business policy demands changes in the themes of selling, and in the products being sold, almost as often as the folk-heroes come and go in popularity. There is, accordingly, a sense of impermanence in the certainties that the persuasion process sells to the consumer. Changes in marketing policies, planned obsolescence, variety reduction, product differentiation, model changes and so forth compel the high priests to make frequent changes in their gospel. While the high priests of old aimed at an unchanging model of an ideal identity, the new high priesthood aims to mould an *ideal consumer,* one who willingly makes the changes in his life-style demanded by competing marketing policies, accepting too the idea that his immediate anxieties can be assuaged by buying new and more products, imagining that each piece of emotional comfort so obtained will be long-lasting. The only test of the new high priests' gospel is that it sells products successfully in the quantities and at the profit desired. Therefore in business terms the ethical content of their message is irrelevant, subject of course to any public relations repercussions that might harm sales or goodwill in the long-term. In other words the true test of the message is: can we get away with it? This cynical philosophy cannot fail to be transmitted together with the selling message. If the consumer is swayed by the message to buy the product, he buys the philosophy too. There is a tragic irony here. The *raison d'être* of the high priesthood of marketing is to sell a kind of certainty. Yet because they

---

[1] cf. the author's *The New High Priesthood*—the social and political implications of a marketing orientated society (Glasser 1967).

must also sell fashion and change they are also transmitting *uncertainty*. Consequently the individual's need for a secure model of identity to emulate is being inescapably frustrated by the most potent leadership force in society. It is hardly surprising that stress is the prime characteristic of the modern high-consumption society.

Against this background of shifting certainties, one of the most important methods of pursuing identity, emotional involvement in work, has steadily withered, because of the ways in which technology has been used to reorganise work. In the old craft-based economy the individual could be emotionally involved in the conversion of materials and could identify himself not only in the work process but in the finished product. He could feel, therefore, potent and creative in his own right. Instead he is now being converted into an anonymous component of an aloof technology. In social and economic terms the loss might be critical. With increasing affluence, financial incentives are losing their former power in work motivation. The divorce of management from the ownership of big companies is placing the control of business in the hands of salaried people who, as Galbraith rightly says, do not get the profit they are supposed to maximise. And yet it is one of management's prime tasks to motivate the work force. With management's money rewards thus not directly related to profit performance, its motivation must slacken and the general social problem of maintaining productivity become greater. The prospect of attaining power remains a management incentive of a kind, but the power struggle in business is punishingly stressful, and recent studies have shown it to be a situation out of which management personnel are increasingly trying to opt (Mellor 1973). The result of these combined influences is a growing tendency for the business environment to be heavily structured to minimise risk-taking, leading to increased rigidity, less creativity and lower emotional involvement throughout.

Up and down society, therefore, people's expectation of emotional fulfilment in work is becoming attenuated and they are turning *faute de mieux* to leisure to find it. This means, of course, that leisure must carry an additional burden, to supply the social motivation for high productivity that work as at present organised is ceasing to do.

If in their leisure time too, people feel the absence of certainty about the identity to emulate, this basic emotional need will obviously be totally frustrated, leading to still greater insecurity and greater stress. People confronted by intolerable stress stop trying, and attempt to opt out of responsibility. The result, as we see today, is a steep rise in social irresponsibility and in destructive behaviour. An analogy can be seen in the behaviour of children. The greater their feeling of insecurity the more destructive and violent they become. A recent study in Britain shows a strong correlation between parents' permissiveness towards their children and child violence in schools (Lowenstein 1972). Permissiveness here means absence of clear leadership. Adults who lack security about the identity model they should follow are obviously unable to offer coherent and strong leadership to their children, who thus have to bear the distressing burden of their parents' perplexity as well as their own. In the conditions of social stress I am discussing, these influences making for socially disruptive behaviour can only increase. The insecure and violent children of today are the even more insecure and stressful adults of tomorrow. Signs of this are already apparent in all the advanced societies. Present day conventions about behaviour, responsibility, respect for one's neighbour, honest dealing, all considerably eroded already, retain what adherence they still possess merely as a survival from the social ethics of the past. These conventions, in spite of all the modish criticisms, constitute the mortar holding the bricks of society together. If they are eroded still further, the mortar will crumble away and the basic liberties of the citizen, which social institutions protect, will become very flimsy indeed. Man's increasing dependence on interlocking technology makes it relatively easy to bring society to the edge of chaos, as the recurrent strikes in the power and communications industries have shown. The individual's increasing sense of frustration in his identity search is likely to cause society to suffer a series of dangerous breakdowns, in which it will seem that the only cure for chaos is to take refuge in the discipline of authoritarian rule, harsh but at least predictable. By an old paradox of his nature, man's insecurity can be temporarily comforted by the apparent certainties conveyed by dictatorship. Certainty, even a cruel certainty, is a form of emotional security for which he seems prepared to pay a heavy price.

Society's foremost problem, therefore, is to restore the authority of a common code of ethics and social discipline, in other words of a model of the ideal identity, maintained until recent times by religion. That mankind failed to translate the code into universal behaviour more successfully is a problem in political philosophy that does not invalidate the point I am making. My thesis is that the code did exist as a standard. At least there was a consensus about what was normally desirable. At least one knew with some certainty what one deviated from. Now there is no such certainty, or at least very little. To have a consensus is basic. Without it social policy has no confident foundation on which to build. A consensus, of some kind, must be created first. There are few people in the advanced countries who, however much they may hope for a religious revival, really believe that the great religions will recapture the dominant ethical influence they once possessed. I am among those who still hope, but I do not see it happening soon enough to arrest the processes I am describing. The tide of rationalism has swept so far that even the nuclear family, that keystone of the social arch and powerful engine for transmitting attitudes and ethics, is also under attack. The two-adult family is becoming accepted, from which children will be sent, virtually from birth, to be nurtured until adult age in a series of institutional substitutes for parental care. What we still refer to as the family environment is becoming an archaic survival. In due course such two-adult households will not trouble to maintain even the vestigial continuity with ethical tradition which the civil marriage ceremony still provides. Man in the advanced societies is becoming *déraciné* in every sense.

In recent decades the main *educative* force in society has become the persuasion process in the service of business, conditioning people to see fulfilment and identity solely in consumption terms. But as I have already mentioned, the underlying ethical message is the amoral one: the only test of a statement or action is, does it achieve its purpose, not: is it right or wrong. Consequently people are being educated in the dismal ethic of expediency as the sole guide to action or judgment, so attacking the last attachment to an inherited ethic of responsibility. To the extent that there still remains enough social discipline to preserve the fabric of society, we are living on the ethical capital of the past, maintained as it has been by religious influence. With religion a waning force, our ethical capital is dwindling fast too, and it is not being replenished. In the resulting vacuum of belief that he has entered, man is turning, albeit unsuccessfully, to new but transient fashions in his anxiety to fill the vacuum with something that is 'sold' to him as a secure model of identity. In obedience to marketing policy, he shifts repeatedly to new fashions in products and in life-styles, each gospel supposedly the true one while it lasts. All the contemporary protest movements, for example, share one principal characteristic, a desperate desire to believe in something, a longing for emotional security in the form of a stable model of identity to emulate. Society's primary task, then, is to provide this firm basis for identity development so that, in leisure as in the rest of life, people can feel a sense of continuity and therefore of emotional security in forming their personal goals. How are we to achieve this?

Whether man can ever be morally disciplined by any secular religion must remain an open question until we have longer experience of such attempts, for example, in Russia and China. By definition such efforts do not set out to fulfil man's evident need for an emotional identification with a transcendental model, wherein lay the supreme civilising contribution of the great religions. For this reason such experiments cannot in my opinion succeed for very long, and to the extent that they do, it will only be by subsisting on the inherited ethical capital. One cannot exclude a slender hope that they can do so long enough—provided man escapes self destruction—until a new wave of spiritual fervour arises to rescue him from his present empty rationalism and spiritual loneliness. Meanwhile the only constructive policy that I can discern as a practical possibility is along the following lines. Before proceeding let me make my reservations quite clear. Having just expressed my scepticism about the efficacy of a secular religion, what I propose may seem an attempt at one. If so, and I can only sketch the outlines of my proposals here, then I freely acknowledge that they constitute a *pis aller,* a holding operation only, not an ultimate solution. That I can see no alternative but this, except an acceleration of the present decline, underlines the critical nature of man's predicament. It is a race against time. If we lose we either destroy ourselves or descend into another age of barbarism. My purpose is to compel greater recognition of urgency in the hope that growth points of change will result. Greater awareness may increase the hope of a new emotional consensus. Meanwhile, recognising the limitations, I believe that practical policy must proceed as follows. We must use modern persuasion techniques to organise belief in social responsibility, building upon the foundation of the ethical capital we still retain. We must appeal to self-interest. In blunt terms our message could be: it is in your own selfish interest to follow the code of moral behaviour and social responsibility. We should use all the subtle power of the persuasion process to sell a canon of socially desirable behaviour, an identity for people to emulate in terms of the goals they individually pursue in work and leisure. Society will have to draw lines beyond which anarchic permissiveness, disguised as rationalism, will not be permitted to destroy the remaining frail consensus about socially desirable behaviour. The State will have to intervene, for example, to prevent the marketing and persuasion process from purveying its ethic of expediency still further. A basic step towards this, for instance, would be to prohibit marketing themes that present the goals of life purely in consumption terms. However reluctant one may be to allow the State to use the persuasion process to promote norms of behaviour at all, the real choice is between the use of these methods responsibly by society or irresponsibly by business. Society is already exposed to this form of persuasion by the marketing process. It sells patterns of behaviour and goals of achievement as the means of selling products. It thus wields great power to shape the behaviour of people, yet without any social accountability in the ordinary course of events. This indiscriminate use of power should be curbed in such a manner that normative influence is exercised by consensus under the democratic process. The persuasion process was used in this way in war time, for example, in Britain in such aspects of conduct as encouraging domestic food growing, waste prevention, and taking holidays at home. The principle could safely be extended in the way I suggest.

If I have appeared to exclude the great religions from these proposals, it is because their former pivotal influence over behaviour has largely gone. I believe that a spiritual revival—a new birth rather than a re-birth—is possible but it is a very long way off. I do not think it likely, however, unless the great religions can learn a new appeal to the emotions as powerful as that of the old prophets. Meanwhile the secular approach I suggest seems to me the only slender hope.

The major aspects of this policy can only be indicated here in general terms. Obviously it would have to be subject to democratic safeguards. Methods of implementation would naturally vary from country to country. However since history has shown us the broad unanimity that man reaches on the subject of the ideal identity in ethical terms, the pattern is not likely to differ in fundamentals. Education, of course, should transmit a socialising ethos much more strongly than it does at present. Reinforcing this, there should be a period of two years compulsory social service for all young people between leaving school and proceeding either to further education or into a job, at approximately 17½-18 years of age. At this most perceptive and formative age, on the threshold of adult participation in society, the period of active work in social service would provide an integrating experience. It would be emotionally constructive in providing immediate involvement in dealing with the pains and problems of life in all their multiplicity and, through them, some understanding of the interactions between the pursuit of personal goals and social ends. This disciplined service should be individually supervised by people qualified to understand, and advise upon, the emotional and career problems that will arise. The young person would thus be led to understand at each step the problems and the rewards, of translating ideals of fulfilment into terms of service to the community as well as in the development of his own personality. The aim would be to bring him to perceive his position as one of total responsibility, which is after all the goal of maturity.

In sum, the criteria for a leisure policy are inseparable from those governing behaviour in general. Any other view leads one into the position of treating leisure as a form of tranquiliser, a therapy to compensate for the frustration of living, an expression of the moral bankruptcy that seems to be prevalent at the present time. The tranquiliser approach to leisure is negative and therefore self-defeating. To be truly life-enhancing, leisure must take its place as only one of the sum of activities whereby inseparably, the goals of identity achievement are pursued. In the absence of consensus about them, leisure can have no positive purpose on its own. In saying this I am far from dismissing leisure as irrelevant. If, as I hope, opinion can be mobilised to reconstruct a consensus about the goals of responsible life in society, we shall in doing so convert leisure into a positive activity. It is a serious mistake to suppose, as many people do in their attempts to compromise with technology, that the hours of work and other necessary but perhaps frustrating relationships can be somehow hermetically sealed away, leaving leisure to fulfil the full objectives of living. Life is psychologically total, and any thinking about leisure must begin with this obvious truth.

We must remember, after all, that leisure is not simply wasted time as many people define it. Leisure is any activity other than time one is absolutely compelled to spend in earning one's living or carrying out other inescapable responsibilities like those of a housewife and mother. In other words leisure must be equated with *choice of activity*. If society can achieve, one way or another, a revival of consensus about the desirable identity, leisure would not be restricted to the role of a mere antidote to frustration, a kind of mass leucotomy, but could be part of a continuum of responsible life from one sphere of activity to another. Leisure would then have its due place in making choices that answer particular identity needs.

On the subject of the diminished emotional rewards of work, there may be a slight hope of making it once more fulfilling. It is a modest hope but worth pursuing. It is based on two grounds. Firstly, the world energy shortage may compel man to reorganise work so as to substitute more human energy and skill for the dwindling, non-renewable, fossil energy the use of which has been deemed inseparable from high technology. This forced shift may result from the slowly growing recognition that our technology is still a very long way indeed from being able to tap nuclear energy in sufficient quantity and in safety. Work could be reorganized, without loss of productivity, so as to eliminate the worker's present sense of isolation, of being excluded by technology from emotional involvement. If this were to be done it could open up once again a normal prospect of identity fulfilment in work. Secondly, there is a movement in business management to rejuvenate worker motivation by re-integrating tasks, as opposed to conventional methods of splitting them up into minute repetive segments in the interests of mass production. This movement, called job enrichment, seeks to re-involve the worker in the making of judgements and in identifying himself emotionally both with the task and the end-product. Unfortunately there is such a weight of commitment to the substitution of technology for human skill that only an enforced reversal of policy could bring about such a life-enhancing change in the emotional content of work.

Nevertheless society's over-riding task, critical because the alternative is disintegration, remains that of creating the mental climate of social responsibility that will instil into work and all other activities a commitment to the development of identity in emotionally constructive ways, and in conformity to an accepted ethical model. Only then can leisure become what it should be, a positive extension of life instead of a tranquiliser attempting to cancel out its increasing stress.

Appendix

The following notes deal with various comments and criticisms of the author's viewpoint:

1 Many critics appear to shrink from my integral view of leisure. They apparently feel it more comfortable to view leisure as a beguiling anodyne for life's stresses, and prefer to carry examination of its functions no deeper. Most of the criticisms of my identity theory of leisure can be described, in psychological terms, as 'screen evasions'. Since I present leisure as an integral part of the pursuit of a desirable identity, and since most people are dissatisfied with the identity they have achieved, my critics are understandably reluctant to bring an open mind to bear on this central point of my argument. Yet the proof is there for those who are willing to see it (Glasser, 1970). People demonstrate by their choices, in clothes, furniture, speech, manners, leisure activities, friends, and as far as possible work, their individual

interpretation of the ideal identity they are pursuing. The goals of leisure and of life are inseparable, as are the means of achieving them. Leisure is not a residual, to be viewed on criteria different from those we must employ in choosing the attitudes, directions, behaviour we adopt in life as a whole. When I say that we reach out towards fulfilment through the pursuit of an ideal identity, to which the *totality* of our actions and attitudes is intended to contribute, I am simply making an empirical statement. Whether the ethical discipline that sustains us in this quest is contained in a religion of the great theological type or in one of the Chairman Mao type is from some points of view irrelevant—except to those innocents who may imagine themselves moved by no 'religion' at all!

2 Surprisingly, some people have been troubled by my use of the word 'discipline'—when I talk of ethical discipline for example. If I argued for a stronger ethical discipline in our society, one critic wanted to know, how did I propose to punish deviations from it! How do we 'punish' those who violate the Ten Commandments? The best answer probably is that life itself punishes, one way or another, though unfortunately this retribution is not always perceptible in its certainty *nor* without cost to society. All societies rest upon an ethical discipline, or frame of reference, about behaviour and standards of personal valuation, which favours one type of behaviour such as driving on the stipulated side of the road or not spitting on the floor, and deplores others such as obtaining sexual pleasure by rape or money by fraud. The type of identity that results from the favoured attitudes and avoiding the proscribed ones will be the socially desirable one, the result of following the *ethical discipline* predominantly influential in that society. As T.S. Eliot once said: 'All desires are not desirable'. The great religions say the same thing in their various ways. To the extent that we in our present society can still walk in the street at night without falling victim to the leisure demands of people who happen to obtain satisfaction from violence, it is because such an ethical discipline survives. And to the extent that it does survive, though it is getting steadily weaker, we are drawing dividend from the ethical capital of the past. The present confusion about leisure goals is because, with that ethical capital not being replenished, there is confusion about the goals of life as a whole.

3 Another 'screen evasion' takes the form of interpreting my identity theory as a wish on my part to abolish all diversity of values, to press everyone out of the same Robot mould. No one who reads my work attentively, especially perhaps Para 5 of my present paper, where I use the Robot analogy to state precisely the opposite view, could reasonably sustain this criticism. Again to avoid repetition, I appeal to the reader to reflect on the implications of my thesis that leisure aims

and behaviour are inseparable from the fulfilment aims of life as a whole. How people design their leisure depends on their strategy in emulating the 'ideal' identity *as they perceive it* contained in the ethical discipline of their society. Indeed, in my total view, leisure is differentiated from work only by the degree of choice available to the individual. Nothing I have said denies diversity among individual interpretations of the 'ideal' identity. To take a very crude example, let us imagine any collection of people wearing the same fashion in clothes. Because of differences in build, posture, appearance, way of moving and so on, the myriad differences in personality, each person will present his own special variation on the identity theme contained in the fashion as such. The same degree of diversity in interpretation must necessarily emerge in every other type of activity. The ideal identity, to use an analogy from music, can be likened to a theme on which each person composes his own variation. It must be understood, of course, that although I use the example of clothes and fashion to illustrate the point, it applies equally, *mutatis mutandis,* to all attitudes and situations. It must be admitted that as high technology in manufacture increasingly pushes to the wall the craft industries—which hitherto catered for individual and minority attitudes to life, clothes, furniture, etc.—the expression of personal variations on the ideal identity theme will become more and more difficult. Even so, considering the quite high degree of standardised production already practised, domestic interiors for example are still highly individual. A sitting room, a kitchen, a bedroom, still show unmistakeably the occupant's personal attitudes, *his* particular variation on an identity theme. One of the features of industrial standardisation is the fact that, by a kind of counter-stimulus, institutions spring up to help people find ways of defeating the steam-roller of uniformity. The electronics industry is an interesting example, with its specialised Hi-fi shops, the small firms offering particular designs, the magazines giving advice on the vast number of component permutations available to improve the range of choice. Equally, then, there will always be scope, in the general conduct of life, for individual variations.

4 Again, some critics are unhappy about my attack upon the received ideas that suggest a hierarchy of leisure pursuits, which would have us believe that, for example, Bingo stands lower than Bach of Hatha Joga. Most discussions on this topic do assume, though seldom state, that the so-called higher pursuits produce a 'better', that is more moral, person. This amounts to a belief that high culture is, in ethical terms, a better religion! If the aim of leisure is mere diversion, a tranquiliser, then the only criterion we need is its effectiveness in this regard. If, however, the criterion is that leisure choices should produce a benevolent, stable

personality, a 'good' man, there is no evidence whatever to favour the Bach addict against the Bingo player. In fact experience, past and present, supplies plenty of evidence to the contrary. In this area of discussion one feels the influence of *the Great Rationalist Confidence Trick*:-

> Throw out your old religion! Buy culture instead! Culture makes you a superior person; it fills up your time and your thoughts more beguilingly than gloomy old religion and what is more you won't be troubled by your soul!

As all confidence tricks must be, it is a pleasant fiction, a flattering anodyne, a comforting belief that high sensibility and/or good muscle tone are satisfactory substitutes for ethical awareness. Probably the heart of my critics' unease is that total responsibility is irksome. And it is hard for people to write off their emotional investment in the 'progressive' belief in the supposed moral uplift to be won by addiction to high culture. How can they dare to throw that religion overboard? Was that not what Progress with a capital 'P' was all about?

References

CAPEK, K. (1936). *R.U.R.* Oxford: University Press.
GLASSER, R. (1967). *The New High Priesthood—The Social and Political Implications of a Marketing Orientated Society.* London: MacMillan.
GLASSER, R. (1970). *Leisure, Penalty or Prize?* London: MacMillan.
LOWENSTEIN, L.F. (1972). *Violence in Schools and its Treatment.* National Association of Schoolmasters.
MELLOR, M. (1973). The reasons for those drop-out executives. *Business Administration,* March.

THEORY

ATTITUDES TO MAN, LAND AND LEISURE

by M. DOWER & P. DOWNING
Dartington Amenity and Research Trust.

Introduction

We have been encouraged to take a provocative look at some of the assumptions about man and the land which appear to underlie current thought and action in the field of provision for leisure, particularly in the countryside.

Before appearing to criticise others, may we disarmingly admit the beam in our own eye. DART's current research programme is concerned mainly with recreation and tourism and their place in and impact on the countryside.[1] We are in the 'middle ground' of that subject, in the sense that we do not specialise on demand (what people want) or supply (what resources exist) but rather on the point where people and resources meet, and the practical issues of planning and management and interpretation. Our small team is inter-disciplinary—planner, surveyor, geographer/economist, natural scientist, sociologist.

We might therefore seem to be bringing man and the land into some sort of balance in our thinking. Certainly our studies, for example, of water recreation or of second homes, do deal (in a mainly statistical way) with people and their activity as well as with the places they use. But we are acutely aware that our work has been more concerned with the place than with the visitor, with the land rather than man. We have kept our eye more on what we think the land can do and can sustain (the ecology of leisure activity) than on what people want to do or to experience (the sociology—or psychology—of leisure). We have tended to take leisure 'demands' for granted, but also to assume that what is good for the land is good for (or at least will be accepted by) man.

Nor are we alone in this. The bodies we advise and work for—Sports Council, Countryside Commission, Tourist Boards, local authorities, landowners—are not, in general, actively concerned with what leisure is doing to man, what it means to him. Their interest has been mainly in the efficient—and environmentally

---

[1] DART: Dartington Amenity Research Trust.

cautious—use of scarce resources of land and money to meet those 'demands' for leisure which are apparent or which it is felt desirable to encourage. They have been pre-occupied with questions of quantity, of deficiency and imbalance. In general, they have not sought to probe the motives which underlie leisure demands, the springs of human action; nor to question the many assumptions which underlie their major programmes of research and action.

It may be that little harm has resulted from our own, and others', outlook. One could argue that the demands are so palpable, and the supply of facilities so limited, that no harm can come from pressing ahead with provision of a range of leisure facilities of types which are already familiar, and in which we are 'behind' some countries in Europe and elsewhere. But awareness is growing that these facilities are posited on assumptions which may or may not be right, may or may not be the really significant assumptions. With the first spurt of activity now behind them, the official bodies set up 5 years or so ago (Sports Council, Countryside Commission, Tourist Boards) are beginning to question their own assumptions. It may therefore be timely, and not too presumptuous, for us to try some such questioning. We should record in doing so that we are beholden to a number of people, notably Robert and Rhona Rapoport of the Institute of Family and Environmental Research, for illumination in this; and that we have drawn on a provocative paper 'Cultural "Fogweed" and Outdoor Recreation Research' by Wilbur F. La Page (1971).

Some assumptions

There are many assumptions in the field of leisure provision. Here, we simply probe a handful of them:

— that *mass surveys* provide a sure base for action
— that *leisure activity is 'caused'* by factors such as growth in income
— that people have *equal opportunities and needs*
— that *'demands' for leisure* must be met
— that *mass usage* equals successful provision
— that *outdoor recreation* is good for you
— that *leisure is a distinct part of life* and of land use
— that *resources must be used* because they are there
— that managers must state, and can enforce, clear limits on *man's impact on the environment*.

Mass surveys. The relatively sudden emergence of mass leisure activity over the last two decades, the relative lack of information on the subject, the preoccupation with basic questions of supply and demand—these have naturally prompted official bodies to get as much standardised, basic information, mainly statistics, as their finances appeared to permit. A body of such information is certainly needed, for reasons political (e.g. to convince Government there is a problem) as well as technical. But basic, standardised information *is* basic and standardised. It does not illuminate the enormous variations in human condition and attitude, indeed it may actually blind one to the existence of such variations. For example, the familiar splitting into age cohorts (45 to 65, 65+) ignores the great variation in actual age of retirement, never mind the emotions and needs associated with the long and often agonizing transition into retirement.

Statistics may describe, very inadequately; but they do not *explain*. Why, for example, has cycling apparently dropped in popularity, despite the sale of over 20 million cycles in this country since the war? The statistics of demand will not tell you that the probable reason is a plain shortage of safe and attractive routes to cycle on. Mass surveys, however carefully done (oh! the joys of 'statistical significance') do not tell you why things happen, what people want in quality rather than quantity, what the real alternatives are. To understand these, one needs direct human contact, not with people in the mass through questionnaire surveys, but with individuals and small groups in a more open and probing way. There are welcome recent examples of this in work by Rapoport and Rapoport (1973); by Young and Willmott (1973) and by the Young Tourism study group of the English Tourist Board (1972).

'Causes' of leisure activity. Report after report on leisure over the last decade (including 'The Challenge of Leisure' by one of us) has implied that leisure activity is *caused* by certain familiar factors—population, personal income, education levels, car ownership. This has become the most luxuriant example in our field of what La Page calls 'cultural fogweed'. There is no doubt that certain socio-economic patterns are associated with certain activity pattern: they correlate, if you like. But correlates are not necessarily causes. The more accurate view must surely be that these familiar factors are, at most, serving to *release* demands which are caused by something much more fundamental—namely the impulses, or motives, or preoccupations which people have or feel.

Now, it is understandable that administrators and planners, who are asked to produce leisure facilities, should seek shorthand guides to questions of demand. But they know that this work, the production of facilities, is not an end in itself—but rather a means to a greater end, namely the personal fulfilment or satisfaction of the populace. And this ought to provoke the question—*why* do people fish, or dance, or go on a camping holiday? The answer is not 'because they earn £2,000 a year': but rather 'because they need to fulfil themselves in some way'—and this is where we look to the fields of sociology and psychology to help us. We land-oriented researchers may guess that the basic impulses and pre-occupations have to do with questions of personal identity, of social reassurance, of escape or fantasy, of rootedness in natural things, of wholeness or integration in personal life—and we may believe it is important to probe these things, in order that physical provision may most closely satisfy these impulses. But we need the man-oriented researchers to bore a tunnel towards us from the other side of the hill.

Equal opportunities and needs. The statistical assessment of demand, which we have had to develop as a blunt first tool of planning, treats people as digits, as components within blocks of demand. We speak of age cohorts, of socio-economic groups, of geographical units, as if each person within such chunks would behave the same. To an extent, of course, they will behave the same—impelled to do so by sheer limitations in supply of facilities, by cultural norms and personal inhibitions. But, if we are really concerned with the human need, such conformity should not blind us to the wide variety of condition and of impulse. This variety can range from the obvious (but often overlooked) point that millions of people still have no car to use for leisure activity, to subtle differences in attitude to gregariousness, privacy and being alone. People's impulses can vary widely within a single age or socio-economic group; indeed a single person can swing from passivity to activity, from gregariousness to isolation, within short periods of time. Moreover, a host of factors—family commitments, personal health or disability, disposable income, home environment, public transport patterns—affect the opportunity which people have to turn their impulses into activity.

Demands and needs. This complexity means, in particular, that the idea of 'demand' should be handled with great care. We have, quite properly, qualified the concept by adding words like 'expressed' 'deferred', 'latent' or 'potential'. As entrepreneurs, public or private, we need the idea. But just as activities are the superficial expression of impulses, so demands are the surface appearance of needs—and needs should be our concern if human fulfilment is our purpose.

We should also beware of seeing 'demands' as an imperative, of feeling that all demands must necessarily be met. Such a feeling undeniably animates much of the pressure by Countryside commissions, Sports Councils and Tourist Boards upon Government and local authorities to release money and to create facilities. We do not deny the need for action, nor that many facilities are clearly adding to human enjoyment and fulfilment. But the world went round, with a fair sum of human happiness, before the great expenditure of the last 5 years: and there is a touch of irony in the fact that the Sports Council, in order to activate greater supply of facilities, launched a 'Sport for All' campaign to activate greater demand—while the Tourist Boards have launched major marketing campaigns to generate demand while arguing the need for more facilities.

We make no plea for less active planning, or for disregarding of demand—rather we urge a realisation that *needs* are the basic thing; that needs can be met in various ways; that demands for one thing may thus be readily transumutable into another; and that (though we must not abuse this attribute) people are, at root, resourceful and adaptable, so that they don't *have* to be satisfied in the most obvious way. Moreover, as scarcely requires to be said to most public bodies, each measure taken to satisfy a demand has a cost to the community, to the environment, to other people's satisfaction. In a thickly populated island, we are concerned all the time with balance between multifarious needs: no one demand can be seen as absolute or imperative.

Mass usage and success. The entrepreneurial concern with supply and demand, with efficient use of resources, and with maintaining political support and the flow of funds—these understandably lead to heavy emphasis on numbers as a criterion of success. 'Overseas tourists 12% up', 'historic house tops ¼ million visitors', 'sports hall used 7 days a week, 14 hours a day'—are accepted as quick, but sure, guides to the rightness of policy and the success of its execution. But let us remember that every digit is a *person,* to whom that holiday, that visit, that game of squash is an event important to his senses and emotions, either enhancing or diminishing or neutral to the pattern of his life. The other million people also on that trip are not irrelevant to his satisfaction, but they can as readily diminish as enhance it—and certainly an entrepreneur preoccupied with the number of visitors is not necessarily so concerned with the quality of the experience offered.

Numbers alone should therefore never be used as a measure of success, if indeed one should use the word 'success' at all. A sure guide, but one less easily measured, would be the sum of life-enhancement achieved. A neat example is the approach taken by John Barrett at the Pembrokeshire Countryside Unit, whose eye is not on the numbers of people who join his guided walks, but on what real contact he can make with them and they with the countryside.

Out-door recreation is good for you. A major, but usually unspoken, assumption behind much of the research and action in our field is that outdoor recreation is good for you; that contact with nature is life-enhancing; that city man should re-find his rural origins—an expression of Arcadia regained. Cert-ainly, the superficial evidence suggests a mass human quest for contact with natural, and even with elemental forces—witness the mass movement to the coast, the country excursions at the weekend, the visits to farm and wildlife parks, the desire for a 'village' home. On such indications, public bodies base their country parks, their marketing of inland tourism, their Goyt Valley experiments—or rather they assume that provisions which are good for the countryside (e.g. traffic controls, economic return from tourism) will be good for, and even meet some deep need in, the consumer.

It may be so. But we see the necessity for deeper probing. How real, and how deep, is the desire for contact with nature? Is it the appearance or the reality that people want? Do they seek the village or the garden-suburb 'village'? Is it the countryside they seek, or simply a change of scene? Do they seek communion with nature, or to reassure their sense of man's dominion over it? These questions may seem esoteric, but they have a very practical importance to us in judging how best to deploy 50 million people on a still-mainly-rural island.

The separateness of leisure. Just as we use statistics to help our decisions, so we chop up life and human affairs to ease our administration. Housing, transport, education, health are parcelled off for purposes of government—and, when leisure (or rather communal leisure activity) grows to the point of needing government attention, so it becomes another parcel. In order not only to administer, but also to understand, it, we then apply the parcelling to our analysis of life itself—and we define leisure as the time left over after work and personal chores. We identify chunks of time—evenings, weekend, annual holidays—as being 'leisure', the rest as being something else, with the implication that the fulfilments which leisure can bring are sought exclusively within the leisure time.

We claim no special insight in saying that life is not like that. For a start, work and leisure interpenetrate in many subtle ways. Voluntary overtime, second jobs, do-it-yourself, evening education are all familiar examples of work-in-leisure. The professor who chops wood at weekends, and the forest worker who reads in his spare time, show how things can stand on their head. But more important than this is that life is, or people wish it to be, integral. Life-satisfaction is to be gained from all parts of it, from 'work' and 'personal chores' as much as from leisure. The human need may be, not for a white (leisure) patch to cancel out the black (work), but for a rich fabric with the life thread running through the weft of alternating activity.

This takes us back to the need to understand human impulses or pre-occupations; but, more immediate, it throws a sharp light on our physical provisions for leisure. The main emphasis in current policy is on facilities specifically designed for leisure, set apart from other activities and land uses, and so located as to be usable during the distinguishable chunks of 'leisure' time. Examples are the sports halls, swimming pools and golf courses which dominate the Sports Council's campaign: the country parks of the Countryside Commission's programme: the hotels, youth tourism centres and caravan sites of the Tourist Boards. This separateness is neat in administrative terms: it avoids the complexities of multiple activity and conflicting interest. But does it reflect the realities of life for the consumer? Should we not, in addition to (perhaps, to a degree, in place of) these separate facilities, be seeking to integrate our 'leisure' facilities more closely into our housing areas, our offices and shops, our farms and forests? More fundamentally, should we not be looking, with more wholeness, at life-satisfaction—at how all activities and facilities can better serve human need? Is leisure itself really the right concept to pursue?

Use of resources. Switching now to the land itself, we detect in ourselves and others a strong (often unspoken) feeling that physical resources should be used—and should be protected—because they are there. This applies particularly to human artifacts inherited from the past—historic buildings, footpaths, disused railways, canals. This feeling goes deeper than a rational concern to get a continuing return from capital and labour invested: it calls also upon instincts of continuity in a changing world, of respect for our ancestors, of man-made things in a machine-ridden environment. To those who have such feelings, and who seek to defend such resources against decay and destruction, a potential new use for leisure is a godsend, a bright new sword 'Don't sell off that railway or fill in that canal: it is needed for recreation and tourism.'

Undeniably, many such features can serve as platforms for leisure activity. But we risk distorting both our use of communal resources and our provision for leisure activity if we overplay the point. In this field, we need a little more rationale and a little less emotion. An example from our own work is the study commissioned from DART by (courageously) the Exmoor Society into the implications of converting 44 miles of disused railway line into a 'greenway' for walking, horse-riding and cycling. We showed it could be done, but we also showed that it might cost up to £1,500 per mile per year (including loan charges on capital) to convert and run the greenway, assuming British Rail gave it free to the sponsors. The scheme did not go ahead.

Clearly, we should respect what we inherit, from nature and from our ancestors: moreover, we should take thought about what we leave to our successors. But what man has made, man can change. Each generation has to adjust the pattern of resources to meet its perceived needs—including those of leisure, observed with clarity and not distorted to meet some other sentiment.

Man's impact on the environment. Clear thinking is also needed about the meeting between man (in leisure activity) and the land. Since Cyril Joad's cry about 'the untutored townsman's invasion of the countryside', indeed further back to the likes of Wordsworth and Ruskin, those who care for the land have expressed dismay at the impact of human leisure. Litter, pollution, noise, erosion of dunes and mountainsides, compacting of soil, destruction of trees, traffic congestion and resulting roadworks—all these have undeniably occurred and been deplored. The natural result has been a call to limit the numbers of people, of cars or boats or caravans, to state and to enforce a 'recreational capacity'.

We have ourselves pressed for this idea, and have been striving to clarify what capacity should mean in a practical way. It is easy to state, in principle, that a wood or a dune can only take so much use if it is to remain 'stable', to suffer no 'unacceptable change', to have a 'sustained yield'. But why should it be stable? Why should it not change? Is there any magic about the present state of a habitat, particularly one already much-influenced by human activity (which applies to most of the surface of Britain)? And, if one states a limit to what the land can sustain, how should we set this against what the people may need or can tolerate? How should one reconcile the 'ecological' and the 'psychological' aspects of capacity? And can the land be protected unless the people accept the need for discipline? Perhaps a sociologist or psychologist among you might apply his mind to this field, before the ecologists run away with it or drop it in disgust.

Conclusion

So much for the provocative probing of our own and other people's assumptions. We hope it may throw light not just on what we all do, but may suggest we should do some things differently. Four positive conclusions might be drawn:

- that we should look more closely at the human impulses and preoccupations which appear to animate leisure activity
- that we should seek, in our provision for leisure, to give as much weight to what people need as to what the land can sustain or what is convenient to manage
- that we should seek to soften the hard outlines and separateness of leisure time and leisure provision, and to integrate it more into the full fabric of life and land use
- that we who study leisure should recognise how little we know about people, and should temper our activity somewhat to that realisation.

References

ENGLISH TOURIST BOARD (1972). *Young Tourists in England.* A report to the E.T.B. Young Tourism Study Group.

LA PLAGE, W.F. (1971). Cultural 'fogweed' and outdoor recreation research. In Recreation Symposium Proceedings, State University of New York, College of Forestry, Syracuse. Washington: U.S. Government printing office.

RAPOPORT, R. & RAPOPORT, R.N. (1973). Leisure and the family life cycle. Unpublished report, Human Resources Centre, The Tavistock Institute of Human Relations.

YOUNG, M. & WILLMOTT, P. (1973). *The Symmetrical Family* (Reports of the Institute of Community Studies). London: Routledge & Kegan Paul.

THEORY

HUMAN NEEDS, WORK AND LEISURE

by J. T. HAWORTH Lecturer,
Department of Psychology, University of Manchester.

Introduction

With the increasing trends towards educating and planning for leisure, the topic of human needs is becoming more important. It is a topic which cannot be fully considered, however, without some reference to work, since many studies on human needs have been conducted in this context. In addition, developments in the work sphere may have implications for planning for human needs: automation may possibly cause a decreased availability of jobs in the future. While its economic benefits may ensure an adequate income for all, possibly certain jobs give satisfactions and serve purposes other than providing income.[1]

Although there have been a number of valuable studies of work and leisure,[2] they have in general neglected the study of human needs. Possibly this is because the concept of basic human needs has been severely criticised by some workers. For instance, the sociologist Cohen (1966) has claimed, in essence, that apart from physiological considerations the concept is unproductive. However, the sociologist Etzioni (1968) has presented a strong case in reply for its usefulness. Certainly in psychology the concept of basic, as well as learned human needs, is important. This chapter includes a consideration of both basic and learned

---

[1] There are many predictions concerning the potential effects of automation on working time, including those by Gabor (1963), Clark (1966), Neuloh (1967), Kaplan (1968), Boston (1968), Kahn (1969), Polak (1973) and Szalai (1973). While they conflict in many aspects and conclusions are by no means certain, it may be that, unless the future is planned, leisure time, or at least non-work time, may greatly increase, and many more people than at present may not have jobs for large parts of their potential working life. This may especially be so if one takes into account the trend towards increasing longevity with the consequent increase in time spent in retirement.

[2] See, for example, Parker (1972), De Grazia (1962) and Anderson (1961).

human needs, though other approaches used in explaining how behaviour is directed are also touched upon.[3]

The chapter commences with a review of a number of claims for satisfactions provided and purposes served by some jobs, along with associated need systems which have been postulated. From this review it is concluded that although uncertainty exists as to the status of some of these needs, evidence shows that man has innate potentiality to fulfil, and that a broader view of his nature should be accepted; also that in our present type of society, many jobs may well provide satisfactions and serve purposes other than the provision of income, some of which are not realisable at all, or to the same extent, if one has total spare time. A case for an education for living is then presented, laying emphasis on the development of potentiality, in particular creativity and curiosity. These factors are then considered in relation to provision for leisure. Finally, they are also considered, along with the fact of uncertainty surrounding some human needs, in relation to research strategies used in planning for work and leisure; and it is concluded that, while various methods may have to be used, more emphasis should be placed on a self-correcting (cybernetic) approach, and that increasingly individuals may demand greater participation and involvement.

Work and human needs

In an important article on concepts of work, Shimmin (1966) indicates that some jobs may give people a recognised place in the community, that they can confer status and self respect, though this may carry over to retirement since people may be accorded the status and self respect of their former occupation. Argyle (1972) notes that jobs may give a sense of usefulness. Berne (1968) points out that work is extremely important in helping people to structure their time. It may fill vacant spaces or even possibly, in Sartre's terminology, avoid the risk of encountering one's inner self caught between 'being' and 'nothing-ness'. Work may thus be involved in 'being' and 'identity', and hence have an

---

[3] The selection for main consideration of the concept of needs of individuals from the considerable number of approaches to explaining how behaviour is directed is not meant to imply any criticism of other approaches. Many others are also important, including structural-functional, organisational and social action approaches, Silverman (1970); personal construct theory, Bannister (1966), which like the social action approach emphasises expectations; morphogenic psychology, Allport (1970), concerned with the uniqueness in form, pattern and growth of the whole individual; incentive approaches, Bolles (1967), and behaviourist models, Krasner, (1971). It is also noted that the different approaches can be interrelated. Thus it is pointed out later in the chapter that the recognition that man has potentiality and a need for psychological growth has implications for social action theory and similar ones, in that satisfying such a need may well generate new expectations, aspirations and so on, factors of considerable importance in work and leisure.

existential significance. Jaques (1965), making an analysis of the mental processes involved in work, in fact concluded that working, especially for a living, can be a fundamental activity in a person's retention of mental health. Not unrelated to this is the article by Williams & Blackler (1971) indicating that people find role ambiguity and role conflict stressful, and that they have a need for stability and predictability; that people like to be able to predict the development of personally important events and that they like to have some control of relevant variables. They further consider that some major factors in our society relevant to our ability to predict are the abilities to maintain income and to preserve and develop status with others, and that a job is central to this.

Herzberg (1968), in a review of his own and related studies, considers that many jobs not only help man directly or indirectly to avoid hunger, pain, loss of life and various learned fears that may become associated, but that they can also help him to satisfy the need to discover, to achieve, to actualise, to progress, to add to his existence. Recapitulating on his motivation-hygiene two-factor theory of need satisfaction he proposes that job satisfaction is not on the same continuum as job dissatisfaction and that each is affected primarily by different factors. He considers that job satisfaction is closely related to psychological growth and that these occur when certain motivators are present, especially opportunities for achievement, recognition and responsibility. Although the absence of these may in some cases cause job dissatisfaction, this is mainly produced by a different cluster of so-called hygiene factors such as company policy, working conditions, supervision and salary. Alleviation of unsatisfactory hygiene factors may at the time cause some job satisfaction but this he considers to be of only a short term variety and not to be equated with that derived from the motivators. This two-factor theory is extended to the area of mental health and mental ill-health, which he considers to be closely related to job satisfaction and job dissatisfaction.

Another empirically based global theory of man's needs which is relevant is the hierarchical model proposed and reviewed by Maslow (1968). In this model the most urgent needs are the lowest needs, those of the body, the physiological needs for e.g. food, water, warmth and sleep. Second are the safety needs for protection and security. Third are the social needs for belongingness, as in a family, a clan, a community (or working group?). Here he also places needs for friendship, affection and love. Fourth are the needs for esteem, approval, dignity and self respect. Finally come the needs for self-actualisation, freedom for the fullest development of one's talents and capacities, the need to fulfil one's potential. The model is hierarchical in that when lower needs are satisfied higher ones may come into being. It also makes the point that people can't be pushed into growth, and that it must be based upon a baseline of safety and security.

A certain approximate correspondence can readily be recognised between the theories of Herzberg and Maslow. The motivator factors of Herzberg may be equated to some extent with the 'higher' growth needs of Maslow, and the hygiene factors with Maslow's 'lower' 'survival' needs.

Herzberg and Maslow are not alone in stressing that man has a need for what has been called self-actualisation. Cofer and Appley (1967) review the theories of a number of people, including the theory of 'existential being' by May and 'creative becoming' by Allport. Shaw (1972) has also recently reviewed the position.

Innate or learned needs

Although the previous claims cited are impressive in their scope, there is still, of course, the question of their status. For instance, are the needs referred to innate or learned? Are there basic criticisms of the theories?[4] These queries are particularly important for the more global theories with their wide ranging implications for the mental health of society and even for its survival. It is the status of these global theories which will now be considered.

Experimental work done on the Herzberg theory is much more extensive than work done on any other 'self-actualisation' theory. While initial work was confined to a sample of engineers and accountants, this has now been extended to a wide range of occupational groups including unskilled workers, with essentially the same results. Both similar and different methodologies have been used indicating, Herzberg claims, that the findings are not a product of the methodology, as some workers had suggested. Furthermore, during these studies it has been found that factors such as the age of the subject are not significant. Herzberg also reports that similar results have been obtained from a study conducted in Hungary, and that the 'motivators' (or at least job content) are the key factors found in a Russian study. This may not, however, mean that one can

---

[4] For some workers these two queries are intimately connected. Maslow (1959) considers that the fundamental point concerning his type of theory is that it is referring to an inner core of innate needs. The charge that the needs are culturally determined would then be the most important criticism. To some extent the search for basic human needs is understandable. As Etzioni (1968) considers, if man does possess basic needs over and above the physiological ones, such as hunger and thirst, then his behaviour may not be as malleable as would be inferred from a consideration of some 'social' approaches to the study of behaviour. Also, even if man does adapt, it may, as Maslow and others consider, involve considerable stress, anxiety and frustration. This may be detrimental to the individual and also to society if in fact it results in vandalism, strikes and so on. This is not to imply though, that the investigation of learned needs cannot be useful. It may well be so, especially if in some cases the situation in which they arose continues to exist. In such cases it would indicate the necessity for decisions concerning whether to satisfy these needs or not; and if the decision is not to satisfy them, what actions to take concerning the situation generating them.

conclude that such factors as 'the need for achievement' and the 'need for responsibility' are innate needs and not culturally determined to a greater or lesser extent. The similarities of advanced industrial systems in different cultures may require some similar patterns of behaviour to maintain themselves, and these 'motivator' factors may be to some extent trans-culturally determined. Certainly there is plenty of evidence to suggest that this is so in the case of the need for achievement. (Cofer and Appley 1967). It has also been claimed that the self-actualising needs suggested by Maslow and others are culturally determined. Maslow, for instance, analysed the peak experiences of a very small sample of older self-actualising Americans. Although he claims that the essential higher values in his model are found to be present in many religions throughout the world, this certainly does not prove that they are innate. Other criticisms have also been made of Maslow's theory. For instance, it has been claimed that it is a value laden approach and that there is very little substantive evidence for the concept of hierarchies of needs, especially in relation to higher needs. There is, therefore, uncertainty surrounding the status of some suggested human needs.

It is thus apparent that while these global theories may give important insights and ideas as to the possible nature of man, they cannot be used as ready made check lists of unchanging human needs. This uncertainty and the difficulties of resolving it have implications for research strategies used in planning for work and leisure, and will be discussed later.

The fact that there are uncertainties on critical issues does not, however, have to lead to the conclusion that man does not possess some form of innate psychological growth need, or that he has no potentiality to fulfil, or that he is just a creature of comfort. Rather work from a variety of sources indicates the contrary. Thus, studies on creativity (Torrance 1964) show that it is not just a prerogative of the few. Work done on sensory deprivation indicates that a lack of stimulation can have a disturbing effect, even producing hallucinations in some cases. Both physiological and psychological studies show the importance of variety. These studies, coupled with the work done on exploratory drives (Berlyne 1960) indicate a more active view of the nature of man. They show that he has needs beyond tension reduction and comfort, that he naturally seeks stimulation, explores, investigates, and influences situations rather than just passively reacting to events. In fact, work from all these areas indicates that a broader view of the nature of man should be accepted than has traditionally been the case for the majority of people in industrial societies.[5] This key subject of potentiality will also be returned to in later sections.

---

[5] Herzberg (1968) indicates that myths concerning the nature of man which have been accepted and propagated are those which are best suited for the requirements of industrial organisations. He also points out how some sections of social science have been used to bolster the prevailing myth.

Work centred values

The fact that there are uncertainties concerning some human needs may only mean that some aspects of a need for psychological growth may be culturally determined, and that the satisfaction of, for example, the need for achievement by work may in part be due to people conforming to prevailing cultural norms, values and ethics. However, this may also apply to a range of other satisfactions attributed to jobs. Thus the Puritan Ethic, The Gospel of Work, glorifying work and implying that leisure time has got to be earned and re-earned, except for the old, is still to some extent part of our present cultural values. As Galbraith asserts in the 'Affluent Society', to be idle is no longer rewarding or even entirely respectable. Shimmin (1966) also points out that work provides a standard by which to judge and be judged by others. She says that 'What is his job?' or 'What do you do?' are regarded as normal questions surrounding introductions to which the expected reply is a specific occupation. Thus jobs are often an important topic for social interaction, and at times people may even be defined by their jobs. Obviously, then, the cultural aspects associated with work can be very important. But, even if a considerable amount of satisfaction and use does come from conforming to cultural values, and even if many needs are learned, this does not necessarily reduce the potential importance of jobs for people. Work centred values may possibly change only slowly, even if rapid change occurs in others, and this might still be so even if an anti-work education were introduced.

The prevalence of work centred values in our society is also relevant to two further issues related to the question of the importance of jobs. The *first* is the one raised by Frazer (1962) of whether or not there are different basic types of person who obtain satisfaction of needs either mainly in work or in leisure. The prevalence of work centred values would tend to indicate that if there are different types, it would not be to any considerable extent. Lancashire (1971) also indicates that there is no unanimity amongst psychologists concerning whether job abilities and desires are fixed or whether they can develop through life. The *second* issue is the claim made by Havighurst (1961) that there may be a general principle of the equivalence of work and play. In coming to this conclusion he equated the studies of Donald and Havighurst (1959) on satisfactions gained from a favourite leisure activity with the study of Friedmann and Havighurst (1954) on the satisfactions gained from work. The satisfactions common to both were contact with friends, chance to achieve something, making time pass, chance to be creative, benefitting society, helping financially, and conferring self respect, standing and popularity. The samples of subjects were different for the two studies, however, and Havighurst recognised that there are severe limitations to the equivalence of work and play. Thus he said that 'they are not identical . . . and the most one can say is that equivalent satisfactions may be obtained from the two forms of activity by some people in some situations'. In addition, the studies did not explicitly investigate questions of identity and place in the community. Klapp (1969) and Smith (1973) may well be right in suggesting that leisure is becoming increasingly important for identity, though the studies cited previously would indicate that work is very important. A more significant drawback in the Havighurst studies is that the strength of different satisfactions was not compared within or across spheres of work and leisure. Thus while the studies show that leisure may play a part in providing many satisfactions, and while they may also indicate possibilities for the equivalence of work and leisure in the long term, in the present work centred society it may not always be easy to substitute adequately in leisure for activities lost through not having work, even if activities may be theoretically inter-changeable. Further, even if work only provided a small number of satisfactions and served only a few non-economic purposes for many people, these could be crucial ones, and full-time leisure may not suffice to satisfy.

There is further evidence to support this position. Neuloh (1967) reports that when staff and workers in industry in the Federal German Republic were asked whether or not they would continue working if financially independent only 12% said that they would not. I put the same question to a group of people with a range of jobs who were attending an extramural class at Manchester University. Anonymity of answers was ensured and only 25% said that they would not continue working if financially independent. The strength of feeling of some individuals on this matter can be gauged from an answer which said 'Work is my whole life and when I can't I'm dead'.

In view of the previous discussions, therefore, it would seem reasonable to conclude that, in our present type of society, some jobs may well provide satisfactions and serve purposes other than the provisions of income, some of which are not realisable at all or to the same extent if one has total spare time. This may well apply to many jobs.

Work and psychological growth

This conclusion concerning the importance of jobs is obviously of relevance to the debate about the potential effects of automation on job availability. If, in fact, for economic and other reasons, automation is widely introduced, and if it has the potentiality to result in total spare time for many, then it could well be the case, as Gabor (1963) has said, that a period of unnecessary work will be needed with jobs having to be created. In view of the difficulties of defining work, the sort of jobs created may not necessarily be based solely on existing types. Whatever the sort, however, the point made earlier, that man has a need for psychological growth, should be taken into account.

Taking account of the need for psychological growth is also important in relation to present jobs, of course, especially for some. For a number of jobs some of the previously discussed satisfactions may be minimal and instead boredom, alienation and depersonalisation may occur. While the degree of individual work centrality may be one variable in the extent to which these factors are experienced (Smith 1969), such attitudes may be with us generally for a while. In fact aspirations for 'better' jobs may well increase. By job enrichment, job enlargement, job rotation and so on, it may prove possible to remove or reduce, in many cases, factors such as alienation. But the way these changes are at present implemented is not always successful or even welcomed by some workers. Possibly, effective participation in decision making by workers may be of use and, as discussed later, it would seem essential to use this. Automation itself may also eliminate a number of jobs which are considered detrimental. It must still be recognised, though, that for certain jobs considerable routine and boredom may still exist, at least for the near future. This, of course, poses the problem of the effect of this on a person's life. For instance, can apathy at work cause apathy in leisure time, or can satisfactory leisure time compensate for dull boring jobs? However, this problem of the interrelationship between work and leisure is complex, as is illustrated by Wilensky (1962), and can only be touched on here; suffice it to say that, depending upon the population studied, there appears to be some evidence to support both alternatives.[6]

Education and human needs

Although the problem of the interrelationship between work and leisure is complex, the fact that satisfactory leisure seems to compensate for dull work in some cases does have implications for education. It supports the case for education to be for living, for both leisure and work rather than just for the latter, as it still tends to be in many cases, despite contrary theoretical statements as to its purpose; in fact for education to be for the development of the full human being whatever the difficulties of definition may be.[7] There are many other reasons for education to be for living and some of these are now presented, since the subject is intimately concerned with the topics of innate human potentiality and its realisation, the formulation of norms and values and hence learned needs, and also the generation of expectancies and aspirations,

---

[6] See, for example, Parker (1972), who tends to favour the proposition that dissatisfaction at work can produce dissatisfaction in leisure, and Zwieg (1952), who considers that satisfactory leisure can compensate for dull repetitive jobs.

[7] While the subject of an education for living is concerned primarily with breadth of education and individual development, it is recognised that it is intimately related to the organisation of education. However, space prevents a discussion of such topics as comprehensive versus selective education though the topic of examinations will be raised in the context of factors affecting the realisation of an education for living.

factors which are also of considerable importance in work and leisure.

Rogers (1967), in the Pilot National Recreation Survey of Britain, shows that some retired people want less leisure time and that a significant proportion of people with jobs are satisfied with the amount they have, especially the lower paid. Yet in the future it is likely that there will be more people in the retired category, and if automation spreads, possibly more non-work time for some categories of workers, especially the lower paid. Of course, more leisure time may be welcomed to some extent if real incomes greatly increase, but initially at least, this may not be the case. Again more leisure time may be welcomed as increased facilities are provided, and the proper provision of these is important. But it could be that the provision of facilities will not be enough. Martin (1960), Chairman of the American Psychiatric Association's Committee on Leisure Time and its Uses, instances Sunday Neuroses and various other psychosomatic phenomena that occur during holidays and vacations as illustrative of a present day leisure problem, and considers that the mere provision of external resources, facilities and opportunities for leisure does not suffice.[8] Martin claims that the beneficial use of leisure time has subjective determinants and depends upon certain personality characteristics which, he says, have been loosely referred to as the inner capacity and the inner resources for leisure. These essential inner qualities, he says, have been neglected, restricted and undeveloped. Martin is, of course, distinguishing between leisure time and leisure. Leisure time, he says, is that period when we have no outer compulsion to work. Leisure on the other hand he sees as a psychobiological phenomenon, an internal state of affairs, an internal quality of being. Possibly an increase of opportunities for education in its broadest sense may be of value if leisure time increases. Maybe the mass media have a greater role to play. Perhaps the developments in community education, which tend to feature fairly unstructured activities, participation and involvement may also prove important in this context. Possibly such developments could even help the sort of people Drucker (1969) has called 'knowledge workers', if they have to retire: people who work in the knowledge, ideas and information industries in the U.S., of whom he has said that only jobs will satisfy.

Although the provision of leisure facilities may not suffice on its own, they are important, as stated previously. However, an education for living is also needed in relation to this in order to inform people of choices and opportunities. Likewise it is also needed for environmental planning in general. Thus the Skeffington (1969) report 'People and Planning', acknowledges that the growing interest in public participation is a valuable new development. But they say that only if participation is constructive and informed will there be the fullest realisation of the opportunities that are now open to local planning authorities and the

---

[8] See also Glasser (1973). His criticism of the 'educational model' is really a criticism of an education for living being one solely for the use of facilities.

people they represent. They also say that the education of school children about aspects of community life offers the best foundation for worthwhile participation in years to come. Other parts of the report stress that the public at large should be informed.

A broad education is also necessary to support public participation on much wider issues than those discussed in the Skeffington report. On the world stage there is the plight of the underdeveloped nations, (Ward & Dubos 1972). There is concern for pollution, population growth, resources and so on, (Meadows et al 1972). Yet many of these problems, the severity of which may require us to attempt to control our own future, could possibly be prevented by changing individual attitudes. (Cole et al 1973).

Attitudes are also relevant to the question of satisfaction in leisure raised earlier, and to the topic of education and the development of individual potential. Martin (1960) discusses various attitude patterns which he considers may interfere with the use of leisure, as he defines it. Amongst these he includes the compulsive pattern where people are driven by the imperatives 'I must' 'I should' 'I ought', and he maintains that of all compulsions in our culture the inner compulsion to work predominates and is glorified by the culture as a great virtue. But, he says, sustained effort under such compulsion blocks all leisure and creative growth. Work can be overdone! An education for leisure as well as for work may help. Martin also discusses and deprecates the superintellectual pattern, where the intellect is encouraged and developed at the expense of the emotional. This theme also receives support from Cohen (1963), who considers that man is essentially a creature of imagination rather than of intellect, and that contemporary education is out of joint for overemphasising the latter. He also points out that one should not try to direct pupils' energies in advance but rather that we should aim to nourish each individual's potentialities.

In the wake of 'The Plowden Report' (1967), education in some primary schools in Britain is, in fact, becoming more child centred with children being taught as individuals. The assumptions concerning the uniformity of human nature at set ages and the related values adopted in order to underpin an authoritarian approach are being challenged. Exploratory behaviour, curiosity and creativity are being allowed to become manifest alongside the more structured activities. The approach is beginning to be felt in some secondary schools. However, it needs to be considerably extended. It also needs to be coupled with the broad education referred to earlier. Interestingly, it is an approach which could well affect people's aspirations in work and leisure.

Although an education for living is beginning, and there are some pointers to what the content should be, considerable debate is obviously still needed on this and other aspects. There are also a number of factors delaying its expansion. These include some organisational aspects of education, specialisation of many teachers, attitudes of some teachers and parents, finance and so on. One which is central to many of these is the examination system in Britain, which encourages early specialisation. While the Briault Report (1973) shows that attempts are being made to change this, it would seem that it could be a very slow process, and that the general introduction of an education for living is not yet forthcoming. Ironically, it seems from this report that the Universities must bear a considerable part of the blame on account of their systems of selection emphasising high grades in a few subjects. Possibly, as further ideas on work and leisure are disseminated, these restrictions may be overcome.

Leisure provision and human needs

Education is not the only sphere in which it can be said that too little attention has been paid to creativity, curiosity and exploratory behaviour. This is also the case in provision for leisure. Certainly leisure may serve many purposes. A number have been listed previously, and Dumazedier (1967) indicates that it serves the purpose of rest, recreation and entertainment. However, he also indicates that it can serve the purpose of self-development. Yet the majority of planning schemes and the projects of many architects focus almost exclusively on the rest, recreation and entertainment aspects. Even the latest D.o.E. design guide on children's play, (D.o.E. (1973) Design Bulletin No. 27) focuses principally on these aspects. It concentrates on the design of conventional playground equipment with just a little additional on adventure playgrounds. Some planning decisions may even be impeding the development of creativity and curiosity. Many small fields and wooded areas are disappearing in towns under the pressure of development. Yet these areas can provide for many inventive games, unstructured activities, and manipulation of the enviroment, in fact for greater involvement. They could be particularly important as even streets become impossible to play in.

Perhaps as the inquisitive, creative characteristics of human nature are accepted, increasing attention will be paid to them, permitting greater involvement, as well as catering for the more passive characteristics. Certainly the objective is feasible. Gaskell and Pearton (1973) refer to a much appreciated park scheme where passive enjoyment from strolling can be coupled with more active participation by familiarising oneself with the names of shrubs and trees and afterwards answering a quiz, satisfaction coming from enquiring about and mastering the environment. Some education-community approaches, such as that at Dartington, combine both aspects with education and the provision of jobs. Conceivably, collation of information on projects in these and other areas would be fruitful, especially if the difficulties involved in implementation were also determined.

Research strategies and planning

Finally the question of research strategies used in planning for work and leisure must be discussed. In outlining various theories of human needs it became apparent that the status of some 'needs' is uncertain. The extent of cultural determinism, the degree to which behaviour is a reaction to norms, values and ethics, some of which may rapidly change, is hard to determine. Similarly the effect on expectations and aspirations of the development of creativity and curiosity will also be hard, if not impossible, to estimate. In fact, it is now becoming recognised in many areas of the social sciences that it is difficult to substantiate global theories in detail, and that it is difficult to make general predictions with any great accuracy.[9]

In such a situation of uncertainty it would seem that while various methods may have to be used in planning for work and leisure, more emphasis should be placed on a self-correcting (cybernetic) approach, so that the system can try to adjust continually to people's changing needs and aspirations. Thus, despite the cost, time involved and difficulty, much more should be done than at present on assessing the effectiveness of projects. This should be done in a positive manner, rather than solely relying on complaints that manage to filter through, as is often the case.

Operational schemes, whether in work or leisure, should be evaluated in terms of the benefits and harm they are producing and could produce if extended. Suggestions from users should be obtained as well as complaints. Although the methods available for doing this need improvement and continual appraisal, the knowledge obtained by them would still be valuable. Such knowledge should be used with other forms of public participation in reassessing human needs and aspirations; in reformulating goals, objectives and values; and in deciding on new courses of action from the many which could be available.

In environmental planning such a method could possibly overcome, to some extent, the argument that the mass of people are not educated enough to participate, that generally they don't know what they want, and if they do it is detrimental in the long term. If planners, designers, and social scientists discussed with people their needs and aspirations while informing them of alternative choices and the likely consequence of selecting some of these, then mutual education could occur, and joint decisions could possibly be taken which

---

[9] Recognition of uncertainty in science is not new, of course. Some existentialists extend this to man claiming that he is basically irrational and that a rationally ordered society is not possible, or even desirable. This school of thought is tied in with views on the individual and self-actualisation. However, it may not be realistic to follow the implications of the societal suggestions. A minimum of planning would seem to be essential, even if only to handle side effects of science and technology such as pollution, over population and so on! In practice even more planning is likely.

actually reflect people's desires and which would benefit all, or as many as possible.

Such an approach presumes, of course, that people will want to become involved and participate. But this could well be the case, providing it is genuine participation. Further, as creativity and curiosity develop and as a broader education is introduced, participation, and in fact involvement in general, may be increasingly demanded.

Although some participation is occurring now in industry and also in environmental planning, it is only in its infancy. Considerable research is needed into the complexities involved if it is to become more than just a novelty. The methods used, the areas of greatest applicability, the extent advisable, the process of decision making, all need further investigation. There could, however, be a much greater difficulty in extending public participation. The fact that some participation is occurring may not be indicative of an authentic society, one which is responsive to human needs. Rather, as Etzioni (1968) has pointed out, it may be that much of what passes for participation is in fact not so. An inauthentic society may, in fact, be the case, one in which there is a front of 'participation', but where the underlying reality for many is alienative. If such is the case, whole value systems would have to change for participation to become widespread.

In the end of course some value system will be used. Ongoing studies may help in its formulation. But it may still to some extent be based on myth. If it is, and one has to pick one's myth, it would seem as well to pick a generous one!

References

ALLPORT, G.W. (1970). *Pattern and Growth in Personality*. New York: Holt, Rinehart and Winston.

ANDERSON, N. (1961). *Work and Leisure*. London: Routledge and Kegan Paul.

ARGYLE, M. (1972). *The Social Psychology of Work*. London: Lane.

BANNISTER, D. (1966). A new theory of personality. In B.M. Foss (Ed) *New Horizons in Psychology*. 1. Harmondsworth: Penguin.

BERLYNE, D.E. (1960). *Conflict, Arousal and Curiosity*. New York: McGraw-Hill.

BERNE, E.L. (1968). *Games People Play: the Psychology of Human Relations*. London: Deutsch.

BOLLES, R.C. (1967). *Theory of Motivation*. New York: Harper and Row.

BOSTON, R. (1968). What leisure? *New Society* 26th Dec. London.

BRIAULT REPORT (1973). 16-19: *Growth and Response. 2. Examination struc-*

ture. Schools Council Working Paper 46. London: Evans—Methuen Educational.

CLARK, F. LeGros (1966). *Work, Age and Leisure.* London: Michael Joseph.

COFER, C.N. & APPLEY, M.H. (1967). *Motivation: Theory and Research.* New York: Wiley.

COHEN, A.K. (1966). *Deviance and Control.* Englewood Cliffs NJ: Prentice-Hall.

COHEN, J. (1963). The scientific revolution and leisure. *Nature,* **198,** 1028-1033.

COLE, H.S.D., FREEMAN, C., JAHODA, M. & PAVITT, K.L.R. (1973). *Malthus with a Computer.* Sussex: University Press.

DE GRAZIA, S. (1962). *Of Time Work and Leisure.* New York: Twentieth Century Fund.

DEPARTMENT OF THE ENVIRONMENT, (1973). *Children at Play.* Design Bulletin No. 27. London: HMSO

DONALD M.N. & HAVIGHURST, R.J. (1959). The meanings of leisure. *Social Forces,* **37,** 357-360.

DRUCKER, P.F. (1969). *The Age of Discontinuity.* London: Heinemann.

DUMAZEDIER, J. (1967). *Towards a Society of Leisure.* New York: The Free Press.

ETZIONI, A. (1968). Basic human needs, alienation and inauthenticity. *Am.J. Sociol.* 33, 870-885.

FRAZER, J.M. (1962). *Industrial Psychology.* Oxford: Pergamon Press.

FRIEDMANN, E. & HAVIGHURST, R.J. (1954). *The Meaning of Work and Retirement.* Chicago: University Press.

GABOR, D. (1963). *Inventing the Future.* London: Secker & Warburg.

GASKELL, G. & PEARTON, R. (1973). New rules in the leisure game. *Design,* May, 41-43.

GLASSER, R. (1973). Criteria for a leisure policy in conditions of declining work motivation, social fragmentation, and the energy gap. Paper presented at the International Congress: Leisure Activities in the Industrial Society. Van Cle Foundation, Brussels.

HAVIGHURST, R.J. (1961). The nature and values of meaningful free-time activity. In R.W. Kleemier (Ed.) *Ageing and Leisure,* Oxford: University Press.

HERZBERG, F. (1968). *Work and the Nature of Man.* London: Staples Press.

JACQUES, E. (1965). The mental processes in work. In *Glacier Project Papers.* London: Heinemann.

KAHN, H. (1969). The impact of the friendly computer. *The 'Times' Newspaper,* October 9th.

KAPLAN, M. (1968). Leisure as an issue for the future. *Futures,* 1, 91-99.

KLAPP, O.E. (1969). *Collective Search for Identity,* New York: Holt, Rinehart and Winston.

KRASNER, L. (1971). Behaviour Therapy. *Ann.Rev.Psychol.,* 22, 483-532.

LANCASHIRE, R. (1971). Occupational choice theory and occupational guidance practice. In P.B. Warr (Ed.), *Psychology at Work*. Harmondsworth: Penguin.

MARTIN, A.R. (1960). Mental health and the rediscovery of leisure. Paper presented at the 13th Annual Meeting of the World Federation for Mental Health, Edinburgh.

MASLOW, A.H. (1959). Psychological data and value theory. In A.H. Maslow (Ed.) *New Knowledge in Human Values*. New York: Harper.

MASLOW, A.H. (1968). *Toward a Psychology of Being*. New York: Van Nostrand.

MEADOWS, D.H. MEADOWS, D.L. RANDERS, J. & BEHRENS, W.W. (1972). *Limits to Growth*. London: Earth Island Press.

NEULOH, O. (1967). Automation and leisure. *Science J.*, 4, 79-83.

PARKER, S.R. (1972). *The Future of Work and Leisure*. London: Paladin.

PLOWDEN, B. (1967). *Children and their Primary Schools: a Report of the Central Advisory Council*. London: H.M.S.O.

POLAK, F.L. (1973). The industrialised society, origin of ever-shortening working-hours and of increasing leisure time. Paper presented at the International Congress: Leisure Activities in the Industrial Society. Van Cle Foundation, Brussels.

ROGERS, B. (1967). *Pilot National Recreation Survey, Report No.1*. British Travel Association—University of Keele.

SHAW, J.W. (1972). The personal imperative: a study of the evidence for self-actualisation. In R. Ruddock (Ed.) *Six Approaches to the Person*. London: Routledge, & Kegan Paul.

SHIMMIN, S. (1966). Concepts of work. *Occup. Psychol.*, 40, 195-201.

SILVERMAN, D. (1970). *The Theory of Organisations*. London: Heinemann.

SKEFFINGTON, A. (1969) *People and Planning: report of the Committee on Public Participation in Planning*. London: H.M.S.O.

SMITH, M.A. (1969). Process technology and powerlessness. *Brit. J. Sociol.*, 20, 76-88.

SMITH, M.A. (1973). Work and leisure: problems of culture and identity. Paper presented at the British Psychological Society. Conference. Lancaster.

SZALAI, A. (1973). Intervener's reply to paper presented by F.L. Polak, at International Congress on Leisure Activities in the Industrial Society, Van Cle Foundation, Brussels.

TORRANCE, P.E. (1964). Education and creativity. In C.W. Taylor (Ed.) *Creativity: Progress and Potential*. New York: McGraw-Hill.

WARD, B. & DUBOS, R. (1972). *Only one Earth*. Harmondsworth: Pelican.

WILENSKY, H.L. (1962). Labor and leisure: intellectual traditions. *Industrial Relations*, 1, 1-30.

WILLIAMS, R. & BLACKLER F. (1971). Motives and behaviour at work. In P.B. Warr (Ed.) *Psychology at Work*. Harmondsworth: Penguin.

ZWIEG, F. (1952). *The British Worker*. Harmondsworth: Pelican.

THEORY

MASSES AND MASTERS. A BRIEF COMPARISON OF APPROACHES TO THE STUDY OF WORK AND LEISURE

by I. EMMETT Sociologist.

On the face of it, the study of people at work and the study of people at leisure, when made by a sociologist, at least should involve similar problems and similar approaches: both are the study of people interacting with people in a normal, everyday setting. But the questions asked and answered and the research reports written in the two fields differ in important ways. Since I have been involved in both fields and have met similar problems and committed similar idiocies to those met and committed by others working in them, I shall in this chapter look at those differences and at the contributions made to them by the methods used in the research, thinking that informs the research, the relationship between the researchers and the commissioners of research, and the intrinsic differences between the two fields.[1]

In the early sixties I made a study of managers in one factory, using the method of going to that factory and its subsidiaries every day for long periods and in that time, talking and listening to managers, attending meetings held between them and generally observing, questioning and trying to understand events in that factory.

In the late sixties I enquired into the leisure pursuits of school leavers in the conurbation of South East Lancashire and into factors affecting the degree to which they actively participated in sport during their leisure. One of the methods I used to do this was to question school leavers from a sample of

---

[1] The world of industry and commerce and the world of work are not the same. Although the work of Everett Hughes and his students has been with us for some time, such a confusion does exist in some of the literature. However, most of the studies of men at work, in Britain at least, including my own, have been made in the field of industry and commerce and I have these in mind when I contrast studies of work and studies of leisure. The caricature of leisure studies below is based on work being done when I started my research in South East Lancashire. That work was done primarily in response to the demands of planners, educationalists and governmental decision-makers for hard data on which to base policies. More recently, serious theoretical approaches have been made to the subject, but there is certainly room for more, and for more probing empirical research.

schools in the conurbation whilst they were in their last year at school and to question the same children two or three years later, in their home.

The first research was financed by a body then called the department of Scientific and Industrial Research, which administered government funds for research, mainly through Universities, and the factory was chosen by dint of asking a number of firms for permission, the only firm to reply favourably being 'chosen'. Three research workers went into the factory: two[2] on the shop floor, doing manual work for part of the time and one amongst management, so that we could see the factory as a whole, and also, separately, see particular aspects of it. The origin of the study was that Professor George Homans, who had been associated with the Hawthorne studies in America, visited Manchester University and suggested to the then combined sociology and social anthropology department, that industrial research be made, and ours was one of several studies undertaken from that department.

In the 1920s, the Hawthorne experiment had begun as engineers' attempts to solve practical problems, such as how to make workers work harder, but their report Roethlisberger & Dickson (1939) was, amongst other things, a record of those engineers discovering sociology and the complexity of human affairs and abandoning hope of early and simple solutions such as 'more light will lead to more output.' Commentators and academics since then had built on that early work and by the 1960s, when we entered the field, quite other questions were in our minds. Thus I wanted to show events in the factory as stemming from decisions made by the managing director since for most of the managers and engineers, that is how it seemed; at the same time not losing sight of the fact that, seen from outside, some of the actions of the managing director were constrained, and others determined, by market conditions and by his position in a larger organisation. I also wanted to try to explain apparent irrationality in the behaviour of managers. Quite a lot had been written about the apparent irrationality of workers' behaviour: I wanted to look at how accountants, salesmen, development engineers and production managers spent almost as much time and used almost as dirty methods, fighting each other as fighting competitors. As a team we all wanted to refine the simple class struggle model of the factory with which we set out, to ask who confronted whom across the workbench and what were the elements of and the weapons used in the daily struggle over supervision, money, effort and control; and to build on insights of Marx, Durkheim and Baldamus into the struggle between employers and employees.

My leisure research was financed by the Leverhulme Trust Fund and originated in the desire of the Physical Education Department of Manchester University to understand more about the sports young people were interested in,

---

[2]Dr. David Morgan and Dr. Michael Walker.

and what factors contributed to a post-school drop in active participation in sport which was thought to occur. For practical and theoretical reasons I believed that I could only look usefully at young people's participation in sport in the light of their wider leisure patterns and on this understanding I accepted the job.

Thus in one case the research was inspired, financed and carried out by people whose interest in people at work was theoretical. In the other case the research was commissioned, financed and carried out under the auspices of people whose interest in people at leisure was practical. They wanted to know what sports should be taught at school and how; how physical education teachers should be trained; and what facilities should be built to meet demands for physical recreation in the future. In these respects the research was similar to several enquiries set up at that time. Research stemming from urgent practical problems does not have to be based on shallow thinking, but much leisure research has been.

Historically, the study of people at work has been a central concern of sociology for a longer time than has the study of people at leisure; and because of this, certain naiveties have been more or less worked through in the former field. I do not think any sociologist doing research or teaching in the field of industry would ignore the power factor:[3] the fact that workers and employers have different and often opposing interests: the fact that employers have greater resources than have workers; the fact that one of the things happening when people go to work is struggle over what is being done, by whom for how long and how energetically and carefully, and what is to be done with the product. It is not the only thing that is happening but it is an important one. Not many researchers in industry would set out to ask the workers what they wanted on the assumption that they would then get it. True, early industrial research began on the assumption that you could ask employers what they wanted and then work out how to get it, but the enquiries have grown up and widened out since then.

Many studies in the field of leisure and sport fail to take account of the fact that some parties to the game have more power than others: some own, build, plan, design, restrict use, make rules, allocate resources to train for this but not that, here but not there; whilst others have little or no say in such matters and use, or are persuaded to use or not to use, facilities, to spend their leisure time, in these and not those ways.

In exercising their powers, the suppliers of leisure facilities are not only pursuing their own interests, although they are doing this. Williams (1961) suggests that British public schools taught the British middle classes the idea of public service. They serve us, in serving law and order, or national security, or

---

[3] Such a fault, however, is present in some studies of service occupations.

the public good, and look to us in return, to accept the status quo which puts them above us, as higher servants. This idea helps to explain much that happens in leisure and sport as elsewhere. Some of our rulers are genuinely deluded into thinking that they are in some high and special sense of the word, merely serving our needs. And, on this understanding they do their best for us. In industrial sociology there is much argument about which groups of the working class have a "Them versus Us" model of the world. I suggest that the suppliers of leisure facilities who work for local and national governments, in voluntary organis- ations and in education, have a "We versus Them" model of the world so basic to their thinking that they are unaware of having it. They are thus unaware of their paternalism and do not see their preservation of their own exclusive leisure playgrounds as part of the 'leisure problem', and so can see themselves as simply serving our needs. 'Go out, find what the people want, and we shall build it,' they say, but in fact they know what we 'need'; they know what is best for us; and so they cannot 'give us what we want'.

In the field of industry, there is not much disagreement that money, status, lack of close supervision and short working hours are desirable and fought over. Some want more of one than another; some strive for some or all of these goods more energetically than others; but lots of the struggle and agreement is about getting these goods. Managements, boards of directors and shareholders want to maximise profits, keep firms going as money-making concerns, maintain their position. Employees want to improve their income and the amount of say they have in their working lives.

In the field of leisure, too, conflicting ends are pursued but it is frequently assumed that this is not the case. 'Everybody knows' what is wanted generally in the leisure field; it is only the details which need enquiring into.[4] In 1964-66 the Department of Social and Economic Research of the University of Glasgow conducted a Scottish study of leisure sub-titled "How those in the 15-19 age group spend their time." Item J on the interview schedule began 'Taking into account the boy's personal and home background does he appear to be using his leisure: unusually satisfactorily; quite satisfactorily; satisfactorily on the whole; rather unsatisfactorily; not enough information;" and a diverse collection of untrained volunteers were expected to have no problem in coding that; and I am sure they had none. Jeremy Bentham demonstrated that you cannot prove poetry to be better than pinball. We know better.

When towns had empty running tracks, money was made available to make them more attractive by providing changing rooms and like amenities, and efforts made to coax people onto them without charging entrance fees. When towns have empty cinemas there is no rush to make them more attractive and to

---

[4] The Glasgow research is only one of several I have seen carrying the same bland assumptions of unanimity.

coax people to go out with friends, make themselves warm, comfortable and entertained, without an entrance fee. If in reply to all the questionnaires we said we wanted bingo, old films on television, to get drunk, smoke pot or watch soccer rather than play it, our 'servants' would not contentedly provide more pot parlours, gin palaces, comedy programmes and seats in football grounds. The certain knowledge that such things are not good for us would intervene.

As well as conflicting notions of what it is reasonable to want, there are also conflicting interests. Our interests in leisure conflict. We want to take a risk, take a rest, get fat, get fit, be quiet, make noise, kill birds, save birds, be in caravans by the sea, ban caravans by the sea, build our characters by rifle shooting, join peace-loving peoples of the world in peaceful demonstrations, get into a horizontal position with someone we like, knock someone else into a horizontal position in the name of sport, watch television, supplant television by good books, have fun, educate ourselves, relax, exert ourselves, save Israel by shooting soldiers, rescue children from destructive boredom, stop children from polluting telephone kiosks, fly aeroplanes and drive cars which pollute the air, be alone, find where the action is, fish, water-ski.

Without any complications of an unequal distribution of power, influence and wealth, there would be problems of conflicting interests. My desires conflict with each other and conflict with your desires. Some of my desires would be deemed 'satisfactory' by the Glaswegian researchers and some of them, I promise you, would not, In addition, power, influence and wealth are distributed unequally and this matters in leisure as in every other field.

Many leisure facilities are supplied by commercial enterprises and the aim here is relatively simple: to make money. Paradoxically, commercial suppliers are more likely to act democratically and provide what we want than are our 'servants', because to provide us with what we want is often profitable. Nonetheless, if what we want is not a money-making proposition for them, the commercial providers are prone to persuade us that what we really want, though we may now know it, is to indulge in rather more expensive pursuits.

Since our servants have leisure too, not much public provision is made which might encroach on their playgrounds. University physical educationists say that local education authorities should build school swimming pools which can be used by the public. But few University swimming pools are open to the public. If in answer to all the questionnaires we said we wanted to look at golden eagles, walk on open moorland, shoot pheasants, or play golf at St. David's or St. Andrew's, I think our simple wishes would not be met, not only because it is not physically possible for us all to have peace and quiet on these islands, but also because the ladies and gentlemen who have traditionally had the peace and quiet, understandably want to continue their privileged situation. I live in Snowdonia and I do not want you to come and spoil it.

Suppliers of leisure facilities are not neutral, gift-giving Gods but much research in the leisure field is based on a presumption that they are.

Another naivety still existing in leisure studies is an expectation that practical results will ensue from such studies quickly. Mayo (1945) thought he could draw some quick practical lessons from industrial research done in the Hawthorne Work and felt that the world could be saved from the crises, wars and revolutions if only people would listen to him and follow industrial leaders trained in 'human relations skills.' In doing so he ignored many of the findings of the studies themselves. But that was quite a while ago and it is widely realised that things are not as simple as that. In the field of leisure the gap between planners' 'demands, and researchers' findings, is slow in being understood. Planners and policy decision-makers say: "Go and find what the people want and what they will want in 25 years' time so that we know what to build." We are not telling them loud enough that their problems cannot be solved like that. There are many reasons why they cannot be solved like that. The first is that if people knew what they would want in 25 years' time, the powers-that-be would not give it to them, even if they could, as I have argued above. A second reason is that our different wants conflict. A third reason is that people do not know what it is possible to do now, never mind what will be possible in 25 years' time. A fourth reason is that there are more factors in the situation than most of us take into account: not just the wishes of the leisure spenders, but also their time, their money, their mobility, their differential knowledge of existing and possible facilities; the values and the power of the suppliers of facilities; the influences of Europe and America; and the subtle ways in which all these interact.

Another reason why we cannot predict with any precision is that demand is dynamic; it is changing all the time and we do not understand the routes of fashion change.

Fashion changes affect the world of work; constant technical innovation is a distinctive feature of a large part of industry today. Though some sociologists study the effects of that innovation, few, if any, study the innovation and certainly none try to predict it. Businessmen do not ask us to predict changes in fashion and changes in demand: and I doubt if the Social Science Research Council would finance such study in the field of industry. The SSRC and the businessmen know that if we could make such predictions with any degree of accuracy we would be rich enough not to need any grants. Yet without a qualm, serious and important institutions plan and finance just such enquiries in the field of leisure, and are reluctant to believe that we shall be lucky if we achieve much more modest aims. This needs accounting for. Notions of morality have something to do with it. Even if we could predict demand changes for industrialists, many of us would have moral qualms about serving the mere money-making process in this way. Perhaps one of the reasons why research workers have not been quick enough and firm enough to tell planners they cannot predict for them, and planners so slow to listen, when they do, is that it seems a harmless, indeed a progressive enterprise to give the people the leisure facilities they want. It would be nice to make democracy work like that. Some progress in that direction will be made, but only when we cease to operate with over-simplified models of humanity which suggest that we can count the number of people in a sample with 'a desire for baseball', 'a dislike for hockey' and 'a propensity to canoe', do a sum and thus discover the Demand for Canoeing in the population at large; look at the population trends and discover The Future Demand for Canoeing in the population at large.

Another reason for the dynamism of the situation being underestimated is that the social nature of the human world is ignored. Insofar as change is taken into account it has been seen as an almost mechanical if sometimes unanticipated consequence of intentional action by planners. It is seen that sometimes increased supply creates increased demand. This is true. Sometimes, however, increased supply does not create demand. The key to why it sometimes does and sometimes does not, lies in social values, and the ways in which particular leisure activities become popular with different social groups.

The reason for the popularity of particular leisure activities can have very little indeed to do with the intrinsic nature of those activities. The range is so wide, the choice almost limitless. A bird watcher I know frequently sits for eight hours at a stretch on top of a high tree watching buzzards in the New Forest. Some young men and women lounge on settees chewing chocolates and toffees till their teeth rot. Squash players break their jawbones, soccer players their knee caps, not infrequently. Bernard Levin, and indeed quite a few of us, pay large sums of money to listen to large German ladies sing Wagner. Rugby players roll in mud; boxers get knocked down; rock-climbers cling in the rain to narrow ridges of rock; some of my best friends have been known to drink beer until they vomit; and I have heard of those who pass their time making models of Windsor castle out of human hair. Since all these activities appeal to some people it follows that, potentially, we are all capable of finding pleasure in doing them. I suggest that when we do find pleasure in doing them, the intrinsic rewards are less responsible—there are so many quicker ways than these of getting wet, cold, sick or hospitalised—than are social factors.

Another difference between studies of work and of leisure then is the recognition of the part played by social factors. When we try to define work and leisure, the notion of relative freedom to decide enters into our definition of leisure. Leisure is our free time; there are fewer obvious constraints on us. When we study men at work we cannot help but see the constraints and arguments about them: the time-clock, the supervision, the punishments, the dismissals, the absences, the chains of command, and the daily niggling battle over noise, open windows, bonus, overtime, tight jobs and gravy jobs. Social influences take effect within the limits of these more obvious, sometimes physical influences. When we study people at leisure, the constraints, the influences, the 'factors that effect' are less apparent. It can only be for this reason that so much research in the field has been written as though there were hardly any constraints, influences or social factors that affect our leisure. We do what we wish in our spare time. Ask us what we wish and all is understood. The influence of economics on leisure pursuits is obvious, although it has its effect in ways not always obvious, as the Keele, British Travel Association study (1967) showed when it reported that the cheapest pursuits are often followed by the well-to-do. The influence of the power structure, I have suggested above is widely ignored. And the social influences, immensely important in the field of leisure, are insufficiently studied partly because of the stress on 'freedom' in leisure; and partly because of the method generally used in the study of leisure: we ask people what they like, and since they are largely unaware of social influences, we do not hear about social influences.

Fashions move through networks of people; leisure activities are attractive to particular groups not so much because of their intrinsic rewards as because of the social meaning those activities have for those groups. The central concern of sociology has two sides: what divides and what unites people. They are the same concern in different guises because what unites people—a certain group of people, is just precisely their difference from others: they are divided from some by the same factors that unite them to others. In our leisure pursuits we want to be accepted by, and we therefore conform to the expectations of, some people who matter to us; and we want ourselves and our group to be distinguishable from other groups. Smoking may be a physical addiction, but also it is a powerful symbol of group membership, and not only of adulthood for schoolboys. The non-smoker in my stereotype, a long time ago, was one who knew best, was given to the clean life, to early rising, brisk walking and milk drinking, and we smokers haunted by such a spectre, feared to join his ranks. When I fail to fasten my seat-belt, what fussy, obedient, always careful seatbelt snapper lurks in my anti-puritan, anti-authority, soul, notwithstanding, or perhaps precisely because of a disc-jockey who is trying to break that association down. When teenagers see something they like the look of on television, it often occurs that they do not try it because the idea of doing it is unthinkable given the social group to which they belong. Some young men cannot say to their mates: 'Let's go pony trekking tomorrow'; just as in other circles it would not be acceptable to go to a horror film or on a big dipper. But explanations are not given in these terms. I smoke because if it was good enough for Bogart it is good enough for me, but if you ask me I'll say I smoke 'because I like it, it's a relaxing habit.' You do not go to horror films 'because you like the theatre better.' He does not go pony trekking 'because he has a date.' We are ignorant of the fact that we are influenced so much by our reference groups and/or we grossly underestimate the degree to which we are so influenced. This makes it impossible to get at 'Why?' by asking.

Because we do the kind of things in our leisure which 'our kind of people' do, we erect a fine social filter around each facility: park, club, stretch of water or street-corner which lets some people in and keeps out others. In diverse and sometimes subtle ways we make the outsider aware of who is 'in' and who is 'out', and these social skills are exercised not only in exclusive men's clubs but also in the motor-bike gang, the discotheque and the Women's Institute. Such a social filter tends to inhibit change; to keep us doing the kinds of things 'our kind of people' do and going to the kind of place we are used to. A similar inhibitor of change is the formal, suppliers' filter, a grosser mesh around each facility than the finer, informal mesh placed by the consumers or habitues. The golf club committee rejects some applications to join and accepts others. The groundsman patrols the course. The cafe or discotheque has a notice on the door saying 'No denims' or 'minimum age 16' or a bouncer who says 'we are full' to undesirable entrants.

That there are social dimensions to every physical facility results in each of us having a unique mental map of the leisure universe. For a man who wants to play squash and moves in a network of people to whom playing squash is permissible or admirable, his mental image of his physical environment will stretch out to include a squash court, or, if he does not know of a squash court, will contain gaps with question marks in it so that from time to time he will mention to people that he would like to play squash, until he discovers some places where he can play it. And he will use a vehicle if he has one, but get there anyway if he has not. In my leisure research, more of the children who took part in sports than non-sporty children said they lived near to open country, to parks and to swimming-pools. But what their answers meant was not that the nearer you get to facilities the more you like sport, but that the two groups perceived the world differently and those who used facilities knew where those facilities were: the facilities were part of their universe. To those for whom sport is a square activity: what the adults want them to do; sporting facilities are not perceived as a meaningful part of their universe: it is the cinemas, dance-halls, pubs and other haunts of their set which are their landmarks. Thus supply does not always create demand. It is possible to provide facilities and lay them open totally free and find that no-one uses them.

The values currently held by particular groups inhibit change but they themselves also change. Some changes are due to economic changes: people can afford cars so they stop cycling; they can afford Majorca, so they no longer camp in Devon; they can look at beautiful people on television so they do not go for a walk to look at the moon. Some changes are due to the fact that it pays manufacturers if we keep changing our pleasures. But changes are also due to the fact that groups wish to distinguish themselves from other groups. The other side of the coin of conformity to our group is distinction from other groups.[5] If the

---

[5] Elsewhere I have begun to look at some of the routes that fashion changes take in young people's leisure and tried to see the relationship between changes moving through social classes on the one hand and changes moving through various groups more or less committed to distinctive adolescent values, on the other hand. See: Griffiths, I. "Gentlemen Suppliers and With it Consumers" in International Review of Sport Sociology, 5, 1970.

teeny boppers go on to the Slade, we go on to the Incredible String Band. If the middle classes go on to golf, we go on to polo. Changes in leisure pursuits are mediated through social groupings but the methods we use on the whole ignore social groupings, and approach individuals.

I have discussed some differences between studies of work and studies of leisure. There is a difference between the two fields, rather than between the studies in those fields, which may contribute to the kinds of study we get in each field: the specificity of place. Work, for most people, takes place so that there are walls around the social interaction one wishes to study. The extent to which this is the case is exaggerated. One of the main weaknesses of factory studies is failure to recognise that whilst for most *manual* workers, apart from delivery men and wandering service engineers, the factory walls matter and do delimit the social interaction, for most *managers* the walls do not matter and do not delimit the social interaction at work. Their world is physically situated over a very scattered area—in the offices of suppliers, rivals, customers and other branches of the same firm. It has been shown, in a study of middle class kinship, (Firth et al. 1969) how the telephone enables middle class families to keep contact with wide ranges of kindred and in a similar fashion the telephone, together with Telex, conferences and inter-city trains, allows the working world of the businessman and manager to exist over a large physical space. Nevertheless, for very many people, work and the social interaction which is part of it, takes place in a specific and confined place; whereas leisure can be spent anywhere.

I have picked out some differences between the study of leisure and the study of work. Naiveties exist in the field of leisure studies, stemming from an underestimation of the effect and complexity of the economic and political realities of the world. The power factor is ignored, practical results are expected too quickly, it is assumed that values and interests do not clash in the field of leisure in the same way that they do in the field of work, and the dynamism of the situation is underestimated. The methods commonly used in leisure studies are partly a result of these differences. One of the reasons that sample surveys are used is because the people commissioning the studies assume that all there is to do is to find out in detail what consumers of leisure want. It is assumed that there is only one population, the entire leisure-consuming population of Britain, speaking one language, to enquire of. But the use of the survey method in itself may lead to or facilitate the holding of an unstratified, simplistic view of the world. Practical results are expected quickly by those commissioning the studies, and so representativeness, reliability, numbers and precision are aimed at from the start. A questionnaire technique may encourage the researcher to ignore that there are several populations with attitudes and values which may not co-incide. Government Surveys should always include a study of the relevant Government officials, parliamentary committee members and House of Lords select committee members, but I do not think they do. The masses have attitudes: the masters *know.*

A further difference was the part played by social factors: the influence of values held by those people who are important to us. It is not adequate to ask for the consumers' version of why he does not do things, since he is largely unaware of social influences. I do not think that the effect on leisure patterns of differences in wealth, time, fitness and knowledge, and the ways in which they interact with each other, are properly understood, but the first three at least are given some recognition. Social constraints are neither understood nor recognised.

A further difference was the specificity of place. The fact that people work in a specific place and that most people are brought together with numbers of other people in the same place to work, encourages the use of intensive observation in the study of work. It is not very practical to administer questionnaires in the work-place. It would be fairly difficult to persuade management to stop all work so that the questionnaire is administered simultaneously to all; but if it is administered to all workers one by one, so much consultation and collusion about what to answer and what attitude to take to the questions will have taken place before the enquiry is halfway through, that the questions would mean something quite different for the first recipient than for the last. There are other reasons why intensive observation is common in the study of people at work, and questionnaires have been administered in workplaces, but specificity of place does facilitate *observation*. Leisure takes place all over the place: in fields, front rooms, bingo halls and beds. The intensive observation method seems naturally inappropriate. We cannot observe all this action, so we ask questions.

Are the two fields as disparate as the kinds of work produced in each make it appear?

For most people constraints on their behaviour are more powerful and more recognisable at work than at leisure. For many people the walls of the workplace act as boundaries to social interactions at work. Except in total institutions such as the armed forces, prisons, boarding schools and the like, this is not the case for people at leisure. These are real differences between work and leisure. The other differences are naiveties: they come from differences in the kind of thinking that has gone into research design and the kinds of questions that have been asked as a result of that thinking, as well as having been caused partly by the method used. Research into leisure has less of a history than has research into work. Those who have been commissioning the research into leisure have been anxious for practical and numerical results, quickly. It is possible that research workers have been less willing to question the demands being made on them in this than in other fields because those demands seem to serve purposes they could subscribe to without bad consciences. Thus different kinds of questions have been asked, different kinds of thinking have designed research plans and different methods have been used and these methods in turn have helped to keep the enquiries wide and shallow, rather than narrow and deep.

The real differences in the fields are not adequate or of the kind to result in the differences in the studies. The fact that constraints and influence on leisure patterns are less sharp and less visible than those on work behaviour should not lead to their being ignored or underestimated. It is true that because leisure activity happens all over the place and is extremely diverse, we cannot see all the action, and certainly not at once, but each workplace is unique and in each workplace so much is happening that we cannot observe all the action. In both fields it is worth having a proper look at some of the action; both involve similar approaches and problems, and will benefit from a recognition of this fact.

For the purposes of this chapter I have spoken as though there were only two methods of enquiry used in sociology and I have assumed that the method of observation of a single case is the one most commonly used in work studies, and the method of sample survey and questionnaire is the one most commonly used in leisure studies.

If the two methodological approaches have an ideal sequence in time the obvious one would be that first intensive observation be used, in order to explore the area, to learn the languages commonly used in it, and to derive hypotheses which may be tested later by wider and shallower enquiries amongst all the parties discovered by the first technique to be important. But in the field of leisure the opposite sequence has been followed. Apparently only after the expenditure of much time and money on large-scale sample surveys, can we hope to persuade the powers-that-be that the time has come for small-scale but intensive studies, for learning the languages, uncovering the power factors, articulating the structures, and above all thinking about the matter.

Historically, much research in workplaces in Britain has been done by people trained in social anthropology and historically the central technique of social anthropologists has been the intensive observation of one case. Where the subjects of study were Pacific islanders or African tribesmen, the necessity to learn the language, in modern jargon to learn how the actors perceive their world, before an analysis could be made, was obvious. But acting as though the workshop, factory or hospital were a strange and foreign island has yielded dividends. There is a special jargon in every workplace. Each geographical floor, bench, desk, corridor, brewing-up point has social connotations, so that when a man asks "Are you going upstairs?" more often than not he is referring to more than a physical journey. The man called works manager in one concern may have totally different powers and responsibilities from the man with the same title in another concern. In a like manner, in the 1940s and 50s, a schoolchild who said he belonged to a club was commonly placed by researchers into one category— the attached— and the child who said he did not was placed into another category—the unattached, and. several inferences were made about the two categories; in particular, the inference that the attached were more like each other than they were like the unattached. This was a reasonable thing to do at that time: virtually the only clubs then open to young people were youth clubs run by churches, Scouts, Boys Brigade, or local authorities in which activity was organised and supervised, and from which children classified as rebellious, off-beat or otherwise undesirable were excluded. In the 1960s many commercial clubs had opened to offer young people places where they could meet each other, listen to music and sometimes dance or buy drinks, without being organised or supervised. The meaning of the word club and implications of a "yes" to a question about membership of clubs had completely changed. A researcher who did not know the language of teenagers in the 1960s could make some mistakes. There is therefore, a case for intensive studies to be made into leisure.

It would be fruitful for someone to look at the degree to which, and the circumstances in which, commercial provision is more successful and popular than other provision. One way to do this would be by spending some time in a commercial establishment: coffee bar, bingo hall or amusement arcade; and also some time in a club run by a local authority, or charitable institution. It would be fruitful for some research to be done by spending time with a few young people with the intention of observing how changes take place in leisure pursuits: how suggestions for new activities are made and met by different members of the group, and what then happens.

It would be fruitful to look at one sport and try to discover the changes in participants over a period of time. There must be some sports clubs which keep records showing over the past fifty years the age, occupation, address and perhaps other characteristics of members.

It would be fruitful for someone to look at how the social filters I have referred to operate differently in the case of different facilities.

It would be fruitful for study to be made of a youth centre or community centre. By spending a good deal of time in such a place, looking at records and minutes kept, and systematically recording what happens there: how decisions are made; how people are recruited in and kept out; on what lines people group and divide; how much organisational effort is put into the running of each activity; how much publicity is received from outside and inside for each activity and how such publicity is used and received by the membership; and by watching over a period of time the formation of leading cliques and the waxing and waning of these and of the influence of opinion leaders, it might be possible to understand better the ways in which groups of people interact in leisure time, and in relation to leisure facilities.

References

FIRTH, R. HUBERT, J. & FORGE, A. (1969). *Families and their Relatives* London: Routledge and Kegan Paul.

MAYO, E. (1945). *The Social Problems of an Industrial Civilisation.* Cambridge (Mass): Harvard University Press.

Pilot National Recreation Survey. (1967). Report No. 1. British Travel Association and University of Keele.

ROETHLISBERGER, F.J. & DICKSON, W.J. (1939). *Management and the Worker.* Cambridge (Mass): Harvard University Press.

WILLIAMS, R. (1961). *Culture and Society* 1970-1950. Harmondsworth: Penguin Books.

2

EDUCATION

RAY IS
IMPOSSIBLE.

EDUCATION

EDUCATION FOR WORK OR FOR LEISURE?

by A. D. C. PETERSON Director General,
International Baccalaureate Office, London.

The traditional distinction between work and leisure is that work is undertaken for the sake of an end product, whether in the form of wages or in that of a changed environment, while leisure activities are undertaken for their own sake. This latter objective may be related either to the enjoyment which the individual derives from the activity itself or to the self-improvement which he derives or believes himself to derive from it. In neither case is there any external, measurable end product.

Education is, by tradition and in theory, a leisure activity. The word school is etymologically associated with leisure and the belief that 'study' and 'scholarship' and 'learning' should be undertaken for their own sake and arise from the individual pupil's interest is a cliché of the educational theorist and of the prize-giving address. Yet the activity is commonly referred to as 'school work'. The purpose of this essay is to examine some of the implications of this contradiction.

It may be that the contradiction derives from the fact that 'education' as distinguished from 'training' in certain necessary skills, such as ploughing or writing, was for many centuries the privilege of a leisured class. This was certainly the basis for the Aristotelian distinction between 'liberal' and 'vocational' education which now seems so dangerously anachronistic. Yet if this is historically correct the historical influences are very rapidly losing their force. One of the most insistent trends in contemporary education is the demand that secondary education should be 'professionalised'.

Whether it be in the U.S.A., Brazil or Europe we see a determined effort to unify secondary and technical education and to provide courses which not only 'educate' the adolescent but provide him with a marketable skill on leaving the secondary school. All this is, of course, related to the demand for 'relevance' in their studies made by secondary school pupils themselves. The final accolade to this movement was given by the choice of the relationship between secondary school education and 'work opportunities' as the theme for UNESCO's 1973 conference.

An examination of practice rather than of theory, of what actually happened and is happening in our schools rather than of pedagogical exhortations, suggests that the concept of education as leisure has dominated the choice of content in class room activities, while that of work has dominated the choice of method. This distinction is now clearest in the secondary school.

If we examine the curriculum followed by a child in school today we find in the primary school a much decreased role allotted to the three Rs, reading, writing and arithmetical calculation, which were once important, as directly work-oriented skills, to children who entered employment immediately from the elementary stage. In their place activities which are associated with leisure or with self-improvement, such as creative art, music, dance, a foreign language, social studies, mathematics and scientific principles have been greatly expanded. This is, of course, not surprising when we remember that the primary phase is no longer for anyone the end of education and the initiation into work. The first two Rs at least remain important, but as skills essential to the next phase in education, not as work skills. It is also significant of the change that the typically work-oriented attempt to measure an end product by means of 'standards' or an examination within or at the end of the primary phase is passing into history.

When we come to look at the content of secondary education it is just as difficult to see it as being related very significantly to the world of work. The tradition of the liberal arts, historically transmitted through the grammar school, is still the dominating factor. The concept of education within the liberal arts tradition led Lord Eldon to condemn the teaching of mathematics or French as training clerks for the manufacturers of Leeds rather than giving a true grammar school education, and Guizot to condemn the introduction of science and geography as 'an education for grocers'. These attitudes have had a long and continuing influence. So long as secondary education was reserved either for the sons, and less often daughters, of gentlemen, who were not expected to use their education as a direct preparation for work, or for those exceptionally gifted, children of the working class who could expect to become gentlemen through their education, this kind of educational content seemed perfectly acceptable. Its purpose was to form the mind and to impart a general culture, not to equip the individual immediately to earn a living. It was an education for leisure, for self-improvement, for citizenship perhaps, but not for the transmission of marketable skills or knowledge directly applicable to working life. When, after the second world war, secondary education for all was introduced, there were many who thought that the new secondary modern schools, whose pupils, unlike those of the grammar school, were all expecting to go straight into active working life on leaving school at fifteen, would develop more work-oriented curricula. They proved mistaken. The Newsom Report (1963) found that the content of education in the secondary modern school was mainly a watered down version of that of the grammar school. The same subjects, English, Maths,

History, Geography, perhaps a foreign language, some Science, together with Art and Music and Physical and Religious Education formed the basis of the curriculum.

Apart from the classically accepted truth that it is harder to change a curriculum than to move a graveyard, there were two perfectly sound reasons for this development. One was the very persuasive argument that an education designed to develop the full spiritual, intellectual and aesthetic powers of the grammar school pupil, as a person, rather than to equip him to do a commercially rewarding job, should not be denied to the secondary modern pupil. We did not want two nations, one of educated men and women and the other of hewers of wood and drawers of water. It must be noted that this argument depends on the assumption that the traditional subjects of the liberal arts curriculum have some particular virtue as media through which spiritual, intellectual and aesthetic powers can be developed; and that work oriented subjects have not. It may be that geometry and mechanics and geography develop powers of the mind in a way that accountancy and photography and marketing theory do not, but on an unbiased assessment of the mental processes involved it does not appear to be self evident. The second reason was simply that teachers were available to teach the traditional liberal arts subjects, but not to teach newer work-oriented subjects, had it been desired to introduce them. Lecturers in Teacher Training Colleges and subsequently in Colleges of Education, apart from those specialising in educational theory, were drawn from successful teachers of the traditional subjects in grammar schools. Entrants to the colleges came with a strong sixth form preparation in those subjects. They were, by and large, the subjects taught in the universities and therefore acceptable, when it was introduced, for the B.Ed. It would have been strange indeed if the Colleges had taught any significantly different range of subjects or if the students had gone out to their first school appointments prepared or eager to teach anything else. Only a very strong and very determined government with full control over the content of education and working on something like a ten year plan could bring about a major change in the content of what is taught in the secondary school. What is proving possible in Brazil or Rumania is not so easy in Britain or the U.S.A.

This very leisure-oriented and even idealistic approach to the content of education is prolonged into the tertiary phase. There are, of course, technological and vocationally oriented courses in universities and polytechnics, but prestige (and recruitment) goes to the pure rather than to the applied studies. For a small, and perhaps already over inflated, proportion of those who carry the pure studies further this may relate to work rather than leisure, in the sense of full-time paid research or teaching. But for the great majority the pure studies are simply a means for developing the powers of the mind and acquiring a general culture. The argument usually put forward for degree courses is that they primarily teach people to think. The corollary to this is that the subject matter is secondary. This is a wasteful process. By all means teach people to think—educate them in the broadest sense—but at the same time use subject matter which is of practical use. The two requirements are not necessarily in conflict.

When one turns from examining the actual current content of secondary education to examining the actual current method, the picture is very different. In method a work-oriented approach is predominant if not exclusive. Everyone has their traumatic memory of school. Mine is of my first term at a public school and a reverend cleric who was in charge of us saying: "Peterson, if you don't work harder than that you'll never get your certificate." *NOT* "it will be displeasing to God", *NOT* "you will never know the delight of appreciating Virgil" *NOT* "you will never develop the power to understand better yourself, your environment and your fellow men": but "you will never get your certificate." The school certificate was an end product which I understood. So I started to work to order so as to obtain it.

Ever since formal education beyond the elementary stage became general even for a limited class it has sought, through its method, to initiate young people into the pattern of working life.

School pupils, like young people in employment, are expected to clock in at their work place at or before nine o'clock in the morning and to perform specified tasks at times determined by their masters. For a great many, almost certainly the majority of secondary school pupils, most of the 'work' they do is not intrinsically interesting or rewarding. When idealistic educators deplore this situation, reverting to the leisure-oriented theory of education, they are met with the argument that since a great deal of the necessary work of the world is in fact boring and repetitive, the best preparation for it is to accustom children in school to boring and repetitive work. The more sophisticated version of this argument, which tries to combine the idealistic leisure-oriented view of content with the realistic work-oriented view of method, by arguing that a willingness to face drudgery is a necessary part of commitment to pure scholarship, as a leisure-oriented activity undertaken for its own sake, is manifestly inapplicable in a context where not one pupil in a thousand is likely to engage in pure scholarship. Initiation into the work pattern demands that there should be some measurable output of the process and this is provided by an examination system. Examinations, particularly external examinations with their widely recognised rewards in the form of certificates—the equivalent of wages for the industrial worker—provide the main motivation for continued work at the 'drudgery'. This was made very clear by the reaction of the teachers when it was proposed to bring forward the date of the 'A' levels into May in order to allow university admissions officers to make use of the results. How could pupils be expected to work, they said, when they had nothing left to work for? It would have been as unrealistic as expecting workers on the line to demand no wages for the last two weeks before the holidays and go on producing motor cars for fun.

It may well be that this contradiction between the theory of education as a leisure-oriented activity undertaken for its own sake and education as a work-oriented activity undertaken to earn examination results accounts for the ambivalence about examinations which is so widespread among English teachers and which is often commented upon. On the one hand they will inveigh against the 'tyranny' of external examinations and apparently long to be free of the shackles which inhibit teaching and learning for its own sake. On the other, they appear to love their chains, vehemently oppose any proposals to reduce the amount of time given to examinations and are now proposing that, whether or not a pupil has reached the school leaving age, he should at least be allowed to leave school in his sixteenth year as soon as he has completed his last examination.

It is worth considering whether this ambivalence about examinations, if it arises from the fundamental contradiction between education as a work-oriented and a leisure-oriented activity, may not be the underlying reason for our own peculiar degree of commitment to *external* examinations. Ever since the Norwood report (1943), theorists have been urging that examinations at the sixteen year old level should become 'internal', designed and assessed within each school and related to the curriculum as it has been taught, rather than external, based on a curriculum and syllabus imposed from outside and assessed by external examiners with the maximum possible degree of impartiality, fine distinctions of grading and reliability. No other industrialised country maintains a battery of external examinations at this stage (the French BEPC has written papers in French and Mathematics only and is all over in two days), but we, not content with G.C.E. 'O' level and C.S.E., are now engaged not only in a mammoth experimental programme to combine these two, but to introduce a Certificate of Extended Education as well. All experience of the C.S.E. indicates that the new extended examination system will also be predominantly examined externally. The operational need for externality at this stage seems as much diminished in England as elsewhere in Europe, now that such examinations no longer determine by selection the chances of further or higher education. Yet we have hardly even begun to consider the possibility of abandoning it. Could this be because teachers as leisure-oriented idealists long to engage in 'real education', based upon the interests of their pupils, while as work-oriented practitioners they see little or no hope of interesting the majority in the content of what is taught and believe in any case that preparation for the working world involves learning to endure drudgery for a reward? Perhaps for people in this dilemma an external examination system, imposed from outside, which can be treated by pupils and teachers alike as a common enemy, is the ideal solution.

It might be, also, that the conflict between the two concepts of education accounts for another of the contradictions found only in the English secondary school system. This is the curious case of 'general studies'. In all European countries it seems generally recognised that the objective of 'sixth form' education is to provide a final phase of general education, with varying degrees of opportunity for specialisation or orientation in one direction or another. In the rest of Europe this is structured through a pattern of subjects ranging from as many as twelve in conservative Switzerland to five or six elsewhere. All are within the range of prescription and enter at some point into assessment. In England and Wales there is no prescribed pattern, but what is described as normal is three subjects taken to 'A' level, heavily specialised in one direction or another, balanced by a substantial programme of 'general studies'. The 'A' level subjects are assessed and on them depends university entrance: the general studies are not.

The rationale of this system has never been easy to see and it produces anomalies and contradictions in practice which have been constantly pointed out in the fifteen years since the publication of the Crowther Report (1959). Perhaps the most startling was the evidence produced by the Schools Council Sixth Form Survey (1970), the only full scale investigation of the sixth form curriculum ever carried out by a body outside the educational profession. This found that in theory 92% of teachers 'considered General Studies a valuable part of the Sixth Form curriculum', while in practice 47% of all sixth formers "were taking little in the way of General Studies except physical training (including games) and religious instruction! The only rational explanation of this apparent contradiction, in what is ostensibly a system where the curriculum is not imposed by any central authority, is that the idealist leisure-oriented approach governs the theory, but the work oriented, university-place earning approach the practice.

That education should be both work-oriented and leisure-oriented would be the only rational ground for dividing it into 'examination work', undertaken to earn a reward, and 'non-examination activities' undertaken for their own sake. But for this to be practicable we should have to accept the continental European practice of prescribing the amount of school time to be allotted to non-examination work. Otherwise that which 'counts' towards examination success will always squeeze that which does not out of the time-table. To do this, and so to make a reality of what is at present largely the myth of general studies would be technically very simple. If we do not do it, it is because we do not really want to. More difficult would be to decide which sort of studies should be leisure-oriented. We are accustomed to not assessing (and therefore not bringing within the work-oriented sector) religious and physical education. Perhaps we could add aesthetic and moral education? While this contradiction between leisure-oriented theory and work-oriented practice runs right through secondary education, it is far less evident in higher education. Here the distinction seems to be much more based on the subject which the student is studying. In the scientific, technological and professional faculties education becomes work-oriented both in content and method. This is not surprising since most students in these faculties expect to work in these fields. In the Arts and Social Sciences however content remains and method becomes leisure-oriented. The Arts student who has regularly clocked in at his work-place at nine o'clock since he entered his primary school and will do so again if he enters the 'working world' finds that for three years he need not, if he does not wish, get up in the morning at all. In some courses in some universities he is free from all serious threats of external examinations for two years or more. He is not learning material which he intends to use professionally. He is treated as if he were, what some indeed are, a genuine scholar in a community of scholars and masters, motivated entirely by his genuine interest in the subject he is studying. In fact he is either a dedicated scholar, a comparatively rare phenomenon, or a gentleman of leisure albeit an impoverished one. It can be a blissful interlude between school work and gainful employment, but as a preparation for entry into a work-oriented society it can be disorienting. Even starting to get up at a fixed time in the morning again can be quite traumatic. It would not therefore be surprising if, as higher education expanded, a significant proportion of young people, having become acclimatised over three years to a life-style which brought as its reward existence on the poverty line but with no obligations beyond following one's own interests and inclinations, preferred to continue it and opted out of the working world and 'regular jobs' altogether. Since in many of the arts and social science subjects there has also been a diminishing emphasis on the 'scholarship' of the subject and an increasing respect for creativity, originality, non-conformism and social action, the old belief that the 'discipline' of academic work at least prepared students for the 'discipline' of administrative work no longer holds good.

It would be easy to see this as a disastrous result of a strange pattern of conflicts between leisure and work-oriented education. People as widely different as I. Illich (1972) and Rhodes Boyson (1974) seem to be in agreement that a great deal of the education that goes on at present does more harm than good. The production of a significant number of potentially able young people who neither want to work regular hours at a humdrum job nor are fitted by their education to do so could be an example of this. Or it could be a reaction of the young and of the educational system to changes in the prevailing culture. It is always dangerous to assume that education does more to influence social change than the other way round. What changes in the prevailing culture might be responsible for this wavering uncertainty about relationships of education to leisure and to work?

It is of course fairly easy to see the possibility of a post-industrial society in which leisure, if people could become acclimatised to what is now so often the frightening prospect, occupied a much larger proportion of the average working man's time (and I mean workers by hand and brain). The usual response to this prospect, one which I have used before and to which I still adhere, is that education should now be turning much more to preparing people to enjoy this additional leisure in an educated way. We should bring our syllabuses up to date and teach the modern techniques of D.I.Y. rather than nineteenth century woodwork, scuba diving instead of breast stroke, golf instead of hockey. We should teach people to paint and enjoy good painting, to play instruments and enjoy good music. But all this is very old-fashioned. It assumes that there are such things as 'good' music or painting, that playing golf or building a kitchen cabinet from a kit are somehow 'better' employments of leisure than either leaning against a wall or doing a second job in order to buy a fur-lined refrigerator like the Joneses have. But this judgement runs counter to the prevailing materialistic culture. Getting and spending we lay waste our time and that is life.

This materialism, however, seems to be one which denies the validity of anything except immediate experience. The one characteristic which most of the activities which I have suggested as education for leisure have in common, is that they take time and some effort extended over time. It is this, I suspect, which makes them unacceptable to the prevailing culture. The idea that it was worth developing a taste for Beethoven as well as a taste for the Beatles was largely based on the belief that a taste for Beethoven would last and develop throughout life, while a taste for the Beatles, though possibly more immediate was likely to have done all it could for you within a year to two. To earlier generations a work of art was 'a possession for ever' and if one did not appreciate it immediately, it was assumed to be worth spending some time trying to see what earlier generations or other people had seen. The hope was that if you spent some time and trouble on it then, for you too, it might become a possession for ever. One of the features of the prevailing culture in its purest form seems to be a rejection of linear time. A work of art is an event. Five years hence it will be better forgotten. Psychedelic experience is experience of trips, not of continuing states and not of anything that the temporary illumination, if there has been illumination, will leave as a residue. The individual's search for an identity is interpreted not as the search for a continuing identity, associated with continuing, if gradually changing and developing roles within the family and society but, apparently, as a search for 'fun identities', though how the concept of identity can be freed from continuity in linear time is hard for one bred in an earlier tradition to understand.

One might answer, as Riesman (1950) once did in another context, that if those are the fashions of the age (and the age itself would not claim any higher status for its views than fashion) then the role of education should be to act as a countervailing force. And so, I believe, it should. But in trying to do so it lays itself open to a further charge from the avant garde, that in valuing more highly experience which has a longer time span of influence than a year or two it is not really concerned with the interests of men and women who may have seventy years more to live, but with preserving a bourgeois and rejecting a proletarian culture. Cox (1973) quotes an illuminating example from a university admissions interview:

Candidate: "The school forces middle class values on the working classes."

Interviewer (with intended irony): "You mean Beethoven and Shakespeare?"
Candidate: "Yes."

There is an element of truth on both sides here which bedevils the approach to leisure-oriented education. Of course it is true that some attempts to initiate the young into a 'high' culture have been insincere and no more than intellectual snobbery. Similarly some reactions of school headmasters to 'pop' culture have been no more than social snobbery. I remember one telling me he would allow the establishment of a 'skiffle group' in the school only over his dead body: I doubt if he would now remember what this presumably immoral form of music was. The truth is surely that both 'pop' and 'high' culture have their devotees in both proletariat and bourgeoisie; both also may involve an extended time span, for the 'high' the novels of Henry James, for the pop the Victorian Music Hall and Old Tyme Dancing.

The political ideology from which the cult of immediacy derives this part of its intellectual justification is not that of the nineteenth century reformers or revolutionaries, whether Liberal or Marxist, but that of the 'permanent' revolution'. It comes neither from the proletariat nor the bourgeoisie, but from the nihilist intelligentsia. As such it is, for all its romantic appeal, a destructive force. That those concerned with education should go on complacently unaware of its power or oblivious of the legitimate elements in its appeal to the young would go some way to justify those who bring this charge of upholding bourgeoise culture against us. But it is not a charge which should deter us from putting our own house in order and educating, as all good teachers have, for the future and not merely for the present, for life-long leisure as well as life-long work.

References

BOYSON, R. (1974). Public Speeches.

COX, C.B. (1973). *Examinations.* Papers in educational reform. vol. III. Illinois: Open Court Publishing Co.

CROWTHER, Sir G. (1959). *Fifteen to Eighteen.* London: Central Advisory Council.

ILLICH, I. (1972). *Deschooling Society.* London: Calder & Boyers.

NEWSOM, J.H. (1963). *Half our Future.* London: Central Advisory Council.

NORWOOD, Sir C. (1943). Report of the Secondary Schools Examination Council. London: Schools Council.

RIESMAN, D. (1950). *The Lonely Crowd.* New Haven: Yale University Press.

SCHOOLS COUNCIL SIXTH FORM SURVEY (1970). London: Schools Council.

EDUCATION

EDUCATION FOR LEISURE:
A SOCIOLOGICAL CRITIQUE

by A. BASINI Lecturer,
Whitelands College of Education, London.

Introduction

There has been an upsurge of interest in leisure. The number of publications in
the area has greatly increased in the last decade, stimulated by recreationalists,
town planners, some educationalists and others who have assumed that:–

1 we are in or entering a leisure age;
2 which creates a problem of leisure;
3 which is best remedied by education for leisure.

The argument I want to develop is that the "leisure age" is an unproven
assumption; that concern with leisure has been stimulated by those with a vested
interest, which, therefore, makes problematic whether we have a problem of
leisure, and that if there is such a problem, its solution in terms of education for
leisure may not be reflected amongst most of the teachers in the secondary
section of the educational system. This paper therefore attempts a critique of
the assumption that there is an age of leisure and its relevance for education.

The problem of leisure?

There has been little research examining the stages in the development of
social problems. However some steps can be identified in the process whereby
social problems become defined as such; when individuals or groups perceive
conditions as problematic, difficult or dangerous; when this concern becomes
widespread and expressed through organisations or institutions; when such
organisations and institutions define their existence and measure their success in
terms of the now emerged social problem. As Becker (1967) cogently argues "to
understand a social problem fully we must know how it came to be defined as a
social problem". Implicit is the claim that social problems are the result of a

102

political process. That such a process consists in the advancement of opposing views, in which people are motivated to persuade others so that public action will be taken to further the ends they consider desirable. The overall objective is to have the problem officially recognised so that the authority and power of the state can be engaged. This process is seen in many areas, deviance, race relations, education, housing, and now applies to leisure with the emergence of government sponsored and voluntary bodies, professional courses in leisure and recreation training and a growing volume of research and research workers.

The reasons why leisure has achieved the status of a social problem inspire conjecture. Hollander (1966) states that "leisure has come to be seen both as an ultimate value and a social problem, indeed a potential threat to social stability. . ." It is apparent that much of the concern directed towards leisure may be related to the breakdown of social stability, that leisure itself may perform a stabilising function in society. This point is stressed by Kraus (1967) when he advocates "constructive recreation" programmes to divert people from rioting and as an outlet for their aggressive instincts. This view that leisure is a potential threat to political stability or can be used as a social control mechanism is not new. As long ago as 1926 Cutten wrote that:—

> . . . the coming of the machine before man was ready for it has forced leisure upon us, and turned us, whether we wish it or not, from a people for whom toil was our breath to a nation of idlers little knowing what to do with our surplus time: every hour of leisure adds in a geometrical progression to the danger.

The potential threat of free time not usefully filled appears the most basic assumption made by those who define leisure as a social problem. What never seems to be doubted is that free time is increasing, that there is a quantitative basis to the new leisure society. This assumption is too important to go unchallenged.

The leisure age is upon us. The central element is the ever increasing amount of time created by declining hours of work. The argument is simple and profound. One hundred years ago men worked seventy hours a week, now the average working week is forty hours, soon it will be thirty and by the year two thousand it may only be fifteen. To state the case more graphically, the workless society if not actually about to dawn, is already pink in the Western Skies! More time + more income = leisure. Everyman is freed. What Crutchley (1971) calls "the vulgar myth" has even become an element in educational policy, for example the Newsom Report (1963) stated that:—

> In Western Industrialised countries the hours which necessarily must be spent in earning a living are likely to be markedly reduced during the working life of children now at school.

How well founded is such optimism? Are we moving towards a society of more free time as a consequence of the decline in hours of work? Historically there is some reason to doubt that industrialisation has created a time utopia. As Burns (1932) notes the working week prior to the industrial revolution was forty to forty six hours a week, with the addition of numerous saints days and festivals. Compared with the pre-industrial situation we may well be working more hours not less. There is also contemporary evidence which bears on this possibility. Linder (1970) commenting on the professional classes claims that they are compelled to:—

> . . . read for profit, lunch for contracts, bowl for unity, gamble for charity, go out in the evening for the greater glory of the municipality, and stay at home for the weekend to rebuild the house.

They are the harried leisure class. Gretton (1971) shows that in relation to Britain the average working week is 46.1 hours which is only marginally less than in 1946. Some evidence is also available about second jobs, or moonlighting. In America, Life Magazine found that 20% of those working a four day week were moonlighting because they wanted more money. There is no reliable data for the U.K. but there are some hints from the popular press. The Sun newspaper (30.6.1972) reported that "more than four million people in Britain are moonlighting when more than one million people are on the dole". The Guardian (30.6.72) reported on the Department of Education finding that 21% of men and 7% of women teachers had a second job. Keynes (1936) may well have been right when he suggested that in general people prefer increased income to increased leisure time. Not only may higher income be preferred, but what may also have been misunderstood is that whatever time people may have free from paid work, does not mean such time is itself unobligated. Time spent in family activities, household repairs, attending social functions, these directly limit 'free' time. So too does the distance people live from their work i.e., commuting adds considerably to the tally of obligated but not strictly work time. All these factors lead DeGrazia (1962) to claim that there has been no real reduction in work time and if anything people are more time constrained than ever before.

So what of the alleged 'leisure boom'? Perhaps as Crutchley (1971) suggested, we are faced not so much with a revolution in consumption patterns but a change in tastes and life styles. Commonsense euphoria regarding an imminent society of leisure is premature. The obligations of work and family, and ancillary roles, still tightly circumscribe men's lives.

Education and leisure

Education processes not only people but knowledge itself. What knowledge should be transmitted, and what models should be used to explain the way education and society are related, is open to debate. Some models tend to assume that, because society itself is a total social *system*, the knowledge processing function is about the creation of consensus in terms of societal values and goals. The need for the system to function effectively creates the assumption that knowledge at the societal level is about establishing consensus. But the obvious danger is that under a gain of consensus an absolutist model of knowledge is fostered by a centralised intellectual elite with close links to those holding economic and political power. Mills (1939) argues the case for such a linkage. Young (1971) more specifically relates the stratification of knowledge to the way in which it may be expressed by educators, and states that understanding this relation explains the way in which dominant categories of knowledge are legitimised. Understanding some of the problems of education for leisure requires some discussion of the liberal and vocational models in terms of which the purposes and consequences of education have been viewed. This discussion may illuminate the general point already made, namely, that educational aims may be elite oriented and reflect the norms and values of those holding economic and political power within a society.

Robinson (1968) traces many of the current ideas about liberal and vocational education to the need amongst workers for increased skills consequent to industralisation. The education of the poor was supported by the bourgeois of the victorian period because they realised it was in their interests, in terms of greater efficiency and profits, to have a better educated work force. On the other hand it was felt by many owners and managers that education of their own sons should not provide specific vocational skills but rather a general education as a basis of decision making. The growth of public schools in the 19th century, with a stress upon non-technical and non-scientific curriculum, encouraged "the gentlemanly pretence of English businessmen and industrialists that they were gifted amateurs, not intellectuals or technocrats" (Robinson 1968). Education of the poor, in contrast, was "a limited and even limiting process—the poor were not to be encouraged to think but to learn to comprehend and carry out instructions completely" (Simon 1960). State provision of education emerged with a specific vocational and social control emphasis. Vocational education was for the working-classes, liberal education was for the ruling classes. The distinction was embodied in the policy thinking for educational provision. For example the 1867 Taunton Commission envisaged three grades of secondary school; those for the upper and upper middle-classes, keeping their boys until eighteen and giving a 'liberal education' in preparation for the universities and older professions; those for the middle-classes, keeping their boys until sixteen and preparing them for the Army, the more recent professions and the Civil Service; and those for the lower middle-classes, keeping their boys until fourteen and preparing them for life as small tenant farmers, tradesmen and artisans. As the Commission noted:—

it is obvious that these distinctions correspond roughly, but by no means exactly, to the gradations of society.

Two factors towards the end of the 19th century tended to change the situation. Changes in the economy, especially the growth of industrial scale and complexity; and changes in the nature of representative democracy, especially the growth of an organised working-class. Education in terms of conception and purpose was affected by these changes. Williams (1965) detects two areas where these effects were linked to education; firstly in terms of the demand for education for all, and secondly in the questioning of the exact nature of 'liberal' education. Those who advocated liberal education opposed education for all since the former would be "vulgarised by extension to the masses", and be transformed into a "system of specialised and technical training". Williams states that the argument between the two viewpoints was:—

> ... clearly muddled by the liberal's claim of a fundamental distinction between their traditional learning and that of the new disciplines, and it was from this kind of thinking that there developed the absurd defensive reaction that all real learning was undertaken without thought of practical advantage.

In effect, however, a liberal education for the ruling class could be conceived of as a vocational education which gave access to a career in public office or some high status job. As Wilkinson (1963) suggests there was a link between access, the idea of a gentleman ideal and the maintenance of a political elite. A gentleman was something quite special; he had "chivalrous instincts, fine feelings and good breeding, (he was) a man of social position, a man of wealth and leisure". It was not a status that could be earned by hard work or acquired knowledge. As Oscar Wilde remarked:—

> If you are a gentleman, then you know enough. If you are not a gentleman, then it is hopeless to know anything at all.

Veblen (1925) was undoubtedly correct in his theory of the leisure class, claiming that the debasement of manual work was so that the ruling class could gain esteem and parade their leisure. The liberal view of education was closely tied to the gentleman ideal of the cultured life; leisure and culture were properties of the elite. As Marx observed:—

> the construction of a corpus of knowledge is inextricably linked to the interests of those who produce it, (who generate)

their own self-justifying standards of evaluation (Young 1971).

The 19th century heritage of different kinds of education for different groups, has a link with 20th century debates, especially the issue of education for leisure.

The Crowther Report (1959) sees the task of education in a modern industrial society as two fold: One is a:—

> ... duty to train children for vocational purposes; whilst a second aim is to remember those other objectives of any education, which have little or nothing to do with vocation, but are concerned with the development of human personality and with teaching the individual to see himself in due proportion to the world in which he has been set.

The Report does not try to resolve the paradox but comes down firmly on the side of the development of human personality. It expresses the view that:—

> children are not the 'supply' that meets any 'demands' however urgent. They are individual human beings, and the primary concern should not be with the living they will earn but with the life they will lead.

This sounds most laudable, however, in terms of educational practice and the curricula, the Report sees two avenues, one for the able and one for the less able child. Perhaps the Report would have made a more critical appraisal if it had adopted the kind of question asked by Young, namely, what are the social assumptions implicit in the criteria used to delineate a less able group who "should be taught a sensible practicality, moral standards and a wise use of leisure time"? As Young asks, how does the education which working-class children fail at, come to be provided? An obvious answer, of course, is the 19th century one, that education of the poor is still seen as a social control process, an inculcation of appropriate standards and values. There is enough overlap between the poor and the less academically able as a social group to justify such an assertion. Perhaps the answer in 20th century terms is given by Robinson (1968):—

> ... the elite can expect to live through their work but the majority must try to live in spite of their work. Liberal education for the workers is conceived as education for leisure.

Failure is part of the inegalitarian society and education itself is geared to predisposing some people to accept failure and lack of self-fulfilment in work. There seems to be within education an acceptance of the idea that because we exist in a segmentalised society, unrewarding work experiences should, and can, be offset by creative and challenging leisure. It is in this assumption that the danger of education for leisure exists.

Educational aims and curriculum content

The concept of education for leisure raises serious difficulties. What is meant by this aim and how is it to be achieved? How as a subject is leisure to be evaluated and how does it relate to the rest of the curriculum? These issues are posed by Leigh (1971) who states that education for leisure attempts:—

> . . . to increase both the true range of choices available and the ability of the individual to make effective and significant choices.

This aim, Leigh suggests, is not achieved and in some cases the ideas about leisure and leisure education in schools are unhelpful. The 1944 Education Act itself accelerated interest in non-academic secondary education, whilst the Newsom Report (1963) implies that leisure can be used as a compensation for dull boring work; the report asks "can their time at school help them to find more nourishment for the rest of their personal lives than loony-coloured phantasies"? Leigh argues the values of work and leisure are inter-related because education in leisure activities will make dull work not more bearable but less. As Dumazedier (1967) correctly asserts therefore:—

> It is impossible to deal with the problems of leisure and work separately. Indeed, the humanisation of work through the values of leisure is inseparable from the humanisation of leisure through the values of work.

At present the activities which educators see in terms of the future leisure lives of pupils are sports, games and practical subjects, such as woodwork, metalwork and technical drawing, which even though they may have a vocational bias in a narrow sense, are useful for 'do it yourself'. Leigh also identifies such activities as the 'Duke of Edinburgh' award scheme as stimulating interest in leisure activities although as one headmaster observed this scheme itself is now the province of Army and Police cadets and boys from good homes. There is, in fact, little evidence about what contribution schools are making to leisure education and thus some empirical research in this area would be useful. What is clear however, is that very many schools are short of facilities and teach pupils in fairly hostile educational environments. As Bernstein (1970) has suggested perhaps less worry should be about 'compensatory education' and more concern directed towards the whole issue of what constitutes an adequate educational environment.

Robinson's idea that leisure activities are a kind of liberal education, and the stress by Newsom on education *through* leisure rather than education for leisure, both assume that leisure activity skills and interests are taught and therefore that education through leisure is promoted. However, this is not sufficient if education for leisure is what is required; it involves many social, verbal and physical skills, such as the very basic one of how to join and participate in existing organisations. Leigh feels that the omission of such skills from a leisure education curriculum is disastrous. As he suggests in relation to social and organisational skills, "some by chance learn a great deal, some learn enough to manage, but the majority pack up and go home". And the burden of responsibility for the development of such skills rests on the teacher. Perhaps, apart from the acquisition of various kinds of skills, a second aim in leisure education has been seen to be that of 'widening the horizons' of interest and enjoyment so that leisure time will be enriched. This too has been inadequately pursued and realised. As Longland (1969) points out, the many hours spent on arts and crafts and on physical and cultural development, is not reflected in the activities of young people after school. If this is so then school based leisure education has little interest or relevance for pupils in later life. Instead of trying to promote opera, ballet and the theatre as recommended by the Council of Europe (1969) would it not be more realistic to deal with the popular arts in a critical way? We live in a world of television, cinema and modern popular music, therefore young people would be better equipped to be discerning about such media if they were given opportunities to try and decide what is well executed cinema and what is not. Times change and consequently the curriculum must change too. This is a more optimistic approach than the bemoaning of the effects of mass society. As Simpson (1969) points out, mass culture is not automatically inferior even though it may be exploitative. What seems important is to make the general point that leisure education curricula are often irrelevant and middle class in their assumptions. That, as Halsey et al (1963) suggest:—

> . . . from the point of view of schools in a class society, class is culture; and education is a process of cultural assimilation. . .

Curriculum reform is urgent but it needs to be accompanied by flexibility and discernment in terms of the assumptions being made about what constitutes desirable leisure. 'Trivial', 'escapist', 'stultifying', 'unconstructive', are easily used perjoratives for prejudice. What is least needed perhaps is the kind of approach by McFarren (1965) where the:—

> . . . worthy use of leisure time (is) one of the seven cardinal principles of secondary education.

High culture versus mass culture

There is no doubt that a central issue in the leisure education debate, as in education generally, is how far it is desirable that any one kind of culture ought to be upheld or promoted. We live, not in a small homogeneous society, but in a huge heterogeneous one, characterised by disagreement over life styles and values (Gans 1966). The high culture proponents fear that traditional values may be eroded by the masses of the culture market. Two groups defend the high culture position, the intellectuals and the liberals. The intellectuals are pessimistic about rising popular taste, and see the social stratification of culture as inevitable. The liberals are more concerned with the way in which mass culture exists because of the exploitation of low taste for the end of profit. The gratification of a paying audience is the prescription for cultural debasement. Both groups view mass culture as harmful to the individual and society and would uphold the principle of self realisation and self-expression through the fine arts.

Popular culture is lumped in with mass culture and viewed as part of the same disease. Popular culture borrows from high culture, thereby debasing it and luring away many potential creators of high culture thus depleting the reservoir of talent. The consumption of popular culture at best produces spurious gratifications, and at worst is emotionally harmful to the audience. The wide distribution of popular culture not only reduces the level of cultural quality—or civilisation—of society, but also encourages totalitarianism by creating a passive audience peculiarly responsive to the techniques of mass persuasion.

Gans seeks to answer these charges. He suggests that the conditions in which culture is created and within which creators work in the two cultures, differ in degree mainly with audience size. As long as the audience for high culture is smaller than for popular culture, the high culture creator finds it easier to work as an individual; he is freer to reject producer and audience demands than the popular culture creator. Even so, to think of the former as concerned with individual self expression and the creation of culture, and the latter as an opportunistic hack, giving the audience 'what it wants', is to surrender to stereotypes. In Gans' view the most serious charge against popular culture is the negative effect on its audience so that it can be emotionally destructive.

Other writers level a range of charges against mass culture and popular cultures. Wright Mills (1939) indicates mass leisure as one of the most ostensible and frenzied features of social life. Leisure activities:—

> ... astonish, excite, and distract but they do not enlarge reason or feeling, or allow spontaneous dispositions to unfold creatively; it is the "amusement of hollow people".

Greenburg (1957) describes the borrowing by mass culture as "using for raw material the debased and academicised simulacra of genuine culture". Van den Haag (1957) asserts that "corruption of past high culture by the popular culture takes numerous forms starting with direct adulteration. Bach candied by Stokowski, Bizet coarsened by Rogers and Hammerstein, Freud vulgarised into columns of newspaper correspondence advice".

Critics have been bemoaning the undesirableness of commercialised leisure for at least forty years, before the advent of television, popular motoring, bingo, bowls, sports stadia etc., Mills' suggestion that people are like sheep, as unthinking pleasure seekers, is prescriptive, patronising, and starts from the assumption that high culture is more desirable than mass culture. Often critics make inferences about popular culture because they come to it with aesthetic standards of high culture and are shocked aesthetically by its content. Such people are frequently in positions of power and influence in education and elsewhere and assume that all should share their standard. Maybe as Rosenberg and White (1957) state:—

> ... at its worst, mass culture threatens not merely to cretinise our taste but brutalises our senses while paving the way to totalitarianism. And the interlocking media aspire to that end.

Maybe however, as Gans (1966) argues, the effects logically inferred from the content of mass culture do not take place. There is little evidence that either popular or mass culture lowers the level of taste of society as a whole, or that people are more susceptible to mass persuasion.

In education many teachers and theorists feel that mass culture represents a threat to traditional values; the school and the home are often seen as oases constantly threatened by the surrounding desert. The N.U.T. and the Crowther Report imply this distinction between the culture of the mass media and the traditional culture of the sophisticated arts. Crowther sees young people, exposed to the full force of the mass media, as threatened and menaced. The N.U.T. calls for a counter balancing assistance which is defined in terms of traditional culture, "art, literature, music or drama". Popular culture is implicitly seen as the enemy of 'good' culture. Of course the view one takes of the argument depends largely on what view is held about the function of education. If the aim is, as Simpson argues, to put people in a position of "forging out their own values" then a critical evaluation of the cultural context of leisure is a necessary consequence. Leisure education is seen as central rather than peripheral. The important aim is to develop critical faculties in relation to young peoples' culture, a culture to which by choice and experience they will devote a great deal of their free time. And such an aim may not best be served by adopting traditional culture which is outside of the experience and interests of most young people.

There are other dangers and problems. The teacher is often in a dilemma.

There are social pressures to produce 'good citizens' or 'skilled workers' but the teacher himself may not be committed to such aims. Also it is clear that the 'culture of the school' may no longer represent the coherent body of knowledge it once did! Teachers have had little preparation in their training for such conflicts and often feel inadequate to cope or encourage the necessary critical appraisal. There is too the more general problem that is faced when a programme for leisure is initiated. It is easy to design it so that its effect will be to give young people a false consciousness to be satisifed with their situation. Entwhistle (1970) sees this danger of unreflective environmental studies aiming at social adjustment and argues that these:—

> . . . will become an educational device not essentially different in their social implications from the 19th century conception of popular education as something designed to confirm the learner in his divinely ordered, but modest, station in life.

White (1968) makes an equally critical view and asks whether it is right to switch less able children from traditional subjects to low level studies of the environment. He suggests that the Schools Council humanities programme aims at creating acceptance and obedience, although the methods employed are more subtle than those used in the last century. One begins with the child's interests and leads him towards his 'needs'. The emphasis is on guided discovery, so that groups come to accept certain attitudes, such as that "control is an essential attribute of freedom". White also points to the danger of the humanities programmes only being offered to the less able children; "no one expects the high fliers of Manchester Grammar School to drop their geography and history and their English in favour of community studies". It is generally true to say that high status academic subjects lead to high status well paid jobs and vice versa; examinations and subjects are therefore important in the way they affect life chances and opportunities. It is interesting that the humanities programme is envisaged for the comprehensive school; the danger is that it may be implemented with an emphasis upon the less able child. Elite education and a different education for the rest will then be under one roof. Given such a situation of overt inequality, and the fact that examinations and subjects differ in status, it would seem irrelevant for Howell to say, in promotion of his Early Retirement and Holiday Extension Bill (1972), that:—

> . . . the education system is geared to education for examinations when its true purpose should be to educate people for life and its rich possibilities, and most important of all, for showing young people how to use their leisure time (Hansard 1972).

The debate about the nature of high culture and mass culture, and their relation to the kind of educational opportunities and curricula available, is very relevant to education for leisure. It is significant that the humanities programme is thought most suitable for the less able. The able are not seen as having a leisure problem. They will be involved in long and arduous studies leading to a well rewarded and satisfying profession. It is the rest, in fact the majority with only 3% of children of manual workers going on to higher education, who must be given courses, attitudes and skills that will make them accept their position which is the dismal one of unsatisfying, poorly paid and insecure employment. The fallacy in the leisure education argument is the idea that somehow leisure can be used to compensate or socialise young people for inadequate work opportunities and experiences and more generally to accept the inequality inherent in the structure of society.

Conclusion: opportunities and choices

There are clearly optimists and pessimists, radicals and conservatives, pragmatists and idealists involved in the leisure education debate. One strand running through the discussion by proponents of different views is the concern that leisure should be properly used. Bockler (1967) states:—

> ... the only real problem is the use of leisure. It is to be feared that man, left to his own resources, will become the victim of his own laziness or commercial entertainment.

A similar attitude is shown by Lord Arran's (1971) comments:—

> There is a prospect of tens of millions of leisure persons with few responsibilities and incomplete education. What are they going to do with their spare time? Judging by present social habits one envisages a great sea of blank gaping faces stretching out before innumerable television screens from midday to midnight with short pauses for the absorption of tinned foods recommended by the advertising programmes.

The pessimists fear that leisure, newly created as a mass phenomenon, will be 'misused'. Decadence and decline are viewed as impending, to quote Kinser (1968):—

> History indicates that the downfall of great civilisations has been the result of a definite misuse of leisure time,

therefore people

must be educated to use leisure time wisely in addition to learning vocational and professional skills.

However it is not that simple to train people to use their leisure 'wisely'. As Aron (1962) cogently points out:—

> It would be vain to decree dogmatically what should be the leisure activities of men in industrial society. Men fill their leisure time in relationship to what they are and what they do.

It is paternalistic and elitist to presume, as does for example the Council of Europe Manifesto "Leisure in our Lives", that it is necessary to guide and cajole those unable to help themselves, into using their time wisely. It is well worth remembering Tawney's comment made in the 1920's:—

> . . . before a man offers advice to a miner on how to spend his evenings, he had better have seen the inside of a pit, and the best preparation for an attempt to improve the taste of shop assistants is to stand for a day or two selling expensive rubbish to rich fools.

It is quite disturbing to see just how paternalistic contemporary thinking is about leisure and how much it combines pessimism and conservatism. The sort of attitude adopted by the professional recreation movement illustrates the point; Sutherland (1957) writes:—

> . . . since the average citizen is unable to invent new uses for his leisure, a professional elite shares a heavy responsibility for discovering criteria for ways of employing leisure and creating enthusiasms for common ends within the moral aims of the community.

In general then there is a fear that leisure will not be used properly, that therefore there should be mechanisms of training and constraint, helping people to choose 'wisely', that people, especially working-class people, unless helped will fail to adopt a protestant ethic view of their leisure and 'degenerate', preferring beer and T.V. to ballet and creative self-expression.

It is from such assumptions that much of the education for leisure impetus has derived. Leisure education is seen as a compensatory process, helping the less able child to adjust to poor work opportunities and satisfactions. Schooling is primarily concerned with the transmission of middle-class culture, the maintenance of certain values and norms rooted in high culture and the prestige and status of traditional academic subject areas. The able, middle-class child does not 'need' the leisure education programme. Such programmes, and the social theory which legitimises them, support and maintain the status quo in society. Pupils become labelled which itself changes the teacher's expectations of academic performance and reflects through to educational success or failure. The Newsom curriculum will only stratify society more rigidly, for it effectively restricts access to high status knowledge and occupations. Such an education is closely linked to the economic and social structure. Education for leisure is closely tied to the kind of society one wishes to live in or aspire towards. As Miller suggests, (1966) it is fanciful to think that it is possible to give "non-academic children a richer leisure life" by altering the curriculum. Adolescents "who feel rejected, in their turn reject the values of the people or social organisations perceived as letting them down".

It has been the contention throughout this paper that leisure for the majority of people is either a non-problem, or at least a very over-stated one. As Durant observed before the last world war, for the working-classes the problems of life were not leisure, but, "low wages, unemployment, insecurity, long hours of work, in many cases monotonous and fatiguing jobs, bad housing and poor health". We have seen few improvements and this situation still applies. It is my view that we need to concentrate more on the grosser inequalities of our society before being concerned too much with leisure. It also seems important to view work and leisure together, not as separate aspects of life. A great deal of factory work is dull and boring. As Parker (1970) suggests, man has a fundamental need to participate in the work he does. Work therefore should be organised towards that end rather than the maximisation of profits. It is difficult to be too concerned with leisure and its provision when, after forty years of working in a motor components factory, a man is invalided out on a £2 a week pension. Or where a man knows that after the age of forty-five his earnings will fall because he is unable to keep up with piece work rates. The 'problem' of leisure leads directly to a fundamental appraisal of the meaning and nature of work in contemporary capitalist society. Perhaps because of the radical implications of such a view, there is some resistance to seeing the problems of leisure as the problems of work. As Durant (1938) suggests:—

> . . . because the dominating values arise from people who need not toil, and because a substitute for integration by labour must be given to the millions who know work only as an evil necessity, leisure is offered as the supreme goal. Leisure, therefore, attempts to supplant work. Only when this division ceases, when leisure is complementary and not opposed to work, can its problems be solved.

What needs consideration is both the leisure and work aspects of people's lives, and maybe it is even more important to be concerned about the vocational aspects of education which will provide people with more satisfying jobs. Leisure then, perhaps, will look after itself. Mills' claim seems still valid in terms of the on-going debate about leisure education, namely that "the deeper problems of leisure, and the culture content of leisure time, can be solved only when leisure and work are easy companions rather than tense opposites".

References

ARON, R. (1962). On leisure in industrial societies. In J. Brooks (Ed.) *The One and the Many in the Modern World.* New York: Harper & Row.

ARRAN, Lord (1971). Quoted in H. Blenkinsop, Some problems of leisure. *J. Royal Soc. Arts.* June.

BECKER, H. (Ed.) (1966). *Social Problems: a Modern Approach.* New York: Wiley.

BERNSTEIN, B. (1970). Education cannot compensate for society. *New Society,* Feb. 26th.

BOCKLER, W. (1967). *Leisure–an International Problem in Sport.* West Germany.

BURNS, D. (1932). *Leisure in the Modern World.* London: Unwin.

COUNCIL OF EUROPE (1969). *Leisure in our Life.* London: H.M.S.O.

CROWTHER, Sir G. (1959). *Fifteen to Eighteen.* London: Central Advisory Council.

CRUTCHLEY, J.B. (1971). Play power–the politics of leisure. Unpublished paper, The Middlesex Polytechnic.

CUTTEN, G. (1926). *The Threat of Leisure.* New Haven: Yale University Press.

DE. GRAZIA, S. (1962). *Of Time, Work and Leisure.* New York: Twentieth Century Fund.

DUMAZEDIER, J. (1967). *Towards a Society of Leisure.* London: Collier-Macmillan.

DURANT, H. (1938). *The Problem of Leisure.* London: Routledge.

ENTWHISTLE, H. (1970). *Education, Work and Leisure.* London: Routledge & Kegan Paul.

GANS, H.J. (1966). Popular culture in America. In H.S. Becker (Ed.) *Social Problems: a Modern Approach.* New York: Wiley.

GREENBERG, G. (1957). Avant garde a Kitsch. In B. Rosenberg & D. White (Eds.) *Mass Culture: the Popular Arts in America.* New York: Free Press.

GRETTON, J. (1971). The hours we work. *New Society,* January 7th.

HALSEY, A.H., FLOOD, J.E. & ANDERSON, C.A. (Eds.) (1963). *Education, Economy and Society.* New York: Collier-Macmillan.

HOLLANDER, P. (1966). Leisure as an American and Soviet value. *Social Problems*, Fall, 179-188.

HOWELL, D. (1972). Reply to questions asked by Ian Hamilton a student at the Polytechnic of North London on my behalf to whom I am most grateful. House of Commons, March.

KEYNES, M. (1936). *The general Theory of Employment, Interest and Money*. London: Macmillan.

KINSER, J. (1968). Leisure time, a challenge for physical education. *Physical Education*, May.

KRAUS, R. (1967). Riots and recreation. *J. Health, Phys. Ed. & Rec.*, March.

LEIGH, J. (1971). *Leisure and the Adolescent*. London: Routledge and Kegan Paul.

LINDER, S. (1970). *The Harried Leisured Class*. New York: Columbia University Press.

LONGLAND, J. (1969). In Simpson, J. Education for Leisure. *Trends No. 7,* London: Dept. of Education & Science.

MCFARREN, B. (1965). At our leisure. *Physical Educator*, 22, 109.

MILLER, D. (1966). Leisure and the adolescent. *New Society*, June 9th.

MILLS, C. Wright (1939). Language, logic and culture. *Am. Soc. Rev.*, 4.

MILLS, C. Wright (1953). *White Collar American Middle-classes*. New York: Oxford University Press.

MINISTRY OF EDUCATION. 15 to 18. Report of the Central Advisory Council for Education.

MINISTRY OF EDUCATION (1963). Half our future. Report of the Central Advisory Council of Education. London: H.M.S.O.

NEWSOM, J.H. (1963). *Half our Future*. London: Central Advisory Council.

PARKER, S. (1970). *The Future of Work and Leisure*. London: MacGibbon.

ROBINSON, E. (1968). *The New Polytechnics*. Harmondsworth: Penguin.

ROSENBURG, B. & WHITE, D. (1957). *Mass Culture: the Popular Arts in America*. New York: Free Press.

SIMON, B. (1960). *Studies in the History of Education 1780-1980*. London: Lawrence & Wishart.

SIMPSON, J. (1969). Education for leisure. *Trends, No. 7*. London: Dept. of Education & Science.

SUTHERLAND, W. (1957). A philosophy of leisure. *Annals of the American Academy of Sciences*. Sept.

TAWNEY, R. Quoted in Groomsbridge, P. (1966). Leisure for all. *J. Physical Educ. Assoc.*, 58, 57-69.

VAN de HAAG, P. (1957). Of happiness and despair we have no measure. In D. Rosenburg & J. White *Mass culture: the Popular Arts in America*. New York: Free Press.

VEBLEN, T. (1925). *Theory of the Leisure Class*. London: Allen & Unwin.

WHITE, J. (1968). Instruction in obedience. *New Society*, May 2nd.

WHITE, J. (1968). Curriculum mongers. *New Society,* March 6th.
WHITE, J. (1968). Learn as you will. *New Society,* Dec. 4th.
WILKINSON, R. (1963). The gentleman ideal and the maintenance of a political elite. *Sociology of Educ.,* **37,** 9-26.
WILLIAMS, R. (1965). *The Long Revolution.* Harmondsworth: Penguin.
YOUNG, M. (Ed.) (1971). *Introduction, Knowledge and Control.* London: Collier-Macmillan.

EDUCATION

EDUCATION, CULTURE AND THE
MYTH OF CLASSLESSNESS

by G. MURDOCK Reader in Sociology,
Centre for Mass Communication, University of Leicester.

Introduction

Much of the discussion about the relationship between education and leisure over the last fifteen years or so has revolved around the notion of 'youth culture'. Consequently any attempt to describe or explain the ways in which contemporary adolescents relate their life in schools to their life outside, must necessarily begin by re-examining this concept, and the general assumptions about social stratification and social change in which it is embedded.

The first part of the chapter examines the three key propositions linking the notion of 'youth culture' to the idea of increasing classlessness: (1) the argument that the Second World War marked a crucial watershed in British social experience, and that since 1945 the gap between the pre- and post-war generations has been accentuated by the development of age-segregated educational institutions; (2) the idea that generations are replacing classes as the decisive determinant of life styles and social consciousness; and (3) the idea that the generational consciousness of youth is expressed and sustained primarily through their participation in the symbols, styles and meanings provided by the adolescent-oriented leisure industries in general, and the pop music industry in particular.

The second part of the chapter discusses the results of recent research showing marked class differentials in adolescent leisure patterns, and more particularly in their involvement in pop, and suggests that taken together these results require the decisive rejection of the 'youth culture' notion and the reinstitution of a class analysis.

The third and final part of the chapter briefly sketched the outlines of such an analysis and argues that the involvement of particular groups of adolescents in patterns and styles of leisure can be explained in terms of their continuing attempt to negotiate and resolve the contradictions in their class situation as mediated firstly through their work situation (which for adolescents under sixteen is their school situation), and secondly through their non-work situation in the family and local neighbourhood.

The myth of classlessness: variations on a theme

The idea that the traditional British class structure has been steadily dissolved during the post-war period, is one of the most pervasive and powerful of our contemporary myths (Westergaard, 1972). The central proposition underlying this myth is that full employment and rising real wages have decisively shifted the pivot of social relations and social consciousness from production to consumption, and that universal access to the emerging patterns of consumption and leisure attendant upon the newly arrived affluence has steadily eroded traditional class differentials in values and life style. There are two main variants of this myth of increasing classlessness. The first, and the one that has received the lion's share of sociological attention, is the idea that the acquisition of consumer durables such as cars and washing machines by the working-class has been accompanied by an increasing adoption of middle-class values and styles of life. The essence of this thesis of working-class 'embourgeoisement' was succinctly stated by Abrams, one of its most vigorous proponents:

> In the post-war world . . . class barriers have tended to lose their clarity and become confused. Some working-class families have incomes as high as some white-collar families and there is little to choose between their styles of living and the goods and services they consume (Abrams, 1964).

The central figure in this mythical landscape of affluence is the 'new' working man: a man preoccupied with home and family, seeing his work 'instrumentally' as a means of acquiring the income necessary to support his leisure time life-style, and pragmatically voting for whichever political party can guarantee him increased opportunities for consumption.

Over the last five years or so, however, the key propositions of the 'embourgeoisement' thesis have been increasingly challenged both by the results of sociological research, and by the general course of events. Sociologically, the decisive watershed was reached in 1969 with the publication of the third volume of the 'Affluent Worker' study, containing the authors' conclusion that although the workers studied enjoyed a high level of consumption:—

> . . . specifically middle-class social norms are not widely followed nor middle-class life-styles consciously emulated; and . . . assimilation into middle-class society is neither in process nor, in the main, a desired objective.

> . . . prophets of 'embourgeoisement', need to be reminded that 'a washing

machine is a washing machine is a washing machine' (Goldthorpe et al 1969).

The 'embourgeoisement' thesis attained its greatest credibility during the peak years of post-war affluence in the early 'sixties. The period since then has been characterised by a steady worsening of the general economic situation and concomitant resurgence of working-class industrial action. (In 1964, 2.2 million working days were lost in strikes. By 1973, the figure had risen to 17.2 million.) The strike-proneness of affluent and advanced industrial sectors, most notably the car industry, has prompted a sociological re-examination of contradictions in the work situation and a renewed recognition that the 'instrumentality' of the archetypal affluent worker co-exists alongside a latent potential for militancy (Westergaard 1970, Mann 1973). By far the most damaging counter to the 'embourgeoisement' thesis has come from the overwhelming evidence of the persistence of marked inequalities in the distribution of wealth, and the rediscovery of family poverty. Despite these challenges the 'embourgeoisement' thesis still retains a certain residual sociological currency. It is clearly discernible as the implicit framework underlying Young and Willmott's recent study of London families for example (Pahl, 1973). On balance, however, there is little doubt that the 'embourgeoisement' thesis has suffered a serious loss of credibility. This has undoubtedly dented the myth of classlessness, but it has not in itself been sufficient to dissolve it completely. For the myth has another variant, a second line of defence; the idea of a classless teenage culture.

The widely publicised landscape of coffee bars, Italian suits, rock and roll, and the rest, which emerged during the mid 'fifties, immediately provided the most glamorous and widely publicised manifestation of the affluence theme announced by Harold Macmillan in his famous 'Never Had It So Good' speech of 1957. Subsequent developments have amplified and embellished this connection but they have not dissolved it, and the imagery of teenage leisure remains the most potent symbol of the coming classlessness of a society of consumption. Consequently, a sufficient challenge to the myth of classlessness must necessarily involve a critique, not only of the 'embourgeoisement' thesis but also of the idea of youth culture. This present chapter therefore attempts to do three things; to trace the key propositions linking the idea of youth culture to the myth of classlessness; to point to recent empirical findings which undermine these propositions; and finally to suggest a more adequate framework of analysis.

The making of the myth: the death of class and the rise of youth

The idea of youth culture is linked to the myth of classlessness by three interconnected propositions. They are: that there is an unprecedented gap between the social experience of those who grew up before or during the Second

World War and those growing up in the post-war period; that generational membership has displaced social class as the key determinant of social consciousness; and that the generational consciousness of adolescents is sustained and expressed through the mass entertainments aimed primarily at the youth market, and more particularly through pop music.

The argument that the Second World War marked a decisive rupture in social experience and social consciousness and precipitated an increasing gap between the pre- and post-war generations comes in several versions. In the simplest variant the break is identified with the war itself, symbolised by the first atomic bombs.

> . . . right at the point . . . of the dropping of the bombs on Hiroshima and Nagasaki, the generations became divided in a very crucial way. The people who had passed puberty at the time of the bomb found they were incapable of conceiving of life without a future. . . The people who had not reached puberty . . . were incapable of conceiving a life with a future. . . The so-called 'generation gap' started then and has been increasing ever since (Nuttall 1968).

In more sophisticated versions, such as the one proposed by Margaret Mead, the rupture in social experience is attributed not to war itself but to the rapidity of technological change in the post-war period.

> The generation gap is between all the people born and brought up after World War II and the people who were born before it (Mead 1971).

> Within the two decades, 1940-60, events have occurred that have irrevocably altered men's relationships to other men. . . The invention of the computer . . . the linking up of all parts of the world by means of jet flights and television . . . the first steps into space . . . the transformation of man's age-old problems of production into problems of distribution and consumption—all these have brought about a drastic, irreversible division between the generations (Mead 1972).

Other commentators have been more specific and have singled out particular social changes as playing a decisive role in creating and sustaining the gap between generations. The change most frequently stressed in this connection is the prolongation of schooling in age-specific educational institutions. The strongest statement of this point is Coleman's argument that an American high school pupil:—

> . . . is 'cut off' from the rest of society, forced inwards towards his own age group. With his fellows, he comes to constitute a small society, one

that has its most important interactions *within* itself, and maintains only a few threads of connection with the outside adult society (Coleman 1971).

In England, the 1944 Butler Act also drew attention to age grades by instituting the primary/secondary division, which for the first time separated *all* children into age-specific institutions at age eleven. This marked a distinct break with the pre-war situation, where even as late as the outbreak of the war, almost half the post eleven year olds receiving elementary education were still in all-age schools (Seaman 1966). The salience of age in the post-war period was further reinforced by the assumption that the new system of universal 'secondary' education would substantially reduce the hitherto marked inequalities in educational opportunity. By emphasising the break between the pre- and post-war social orders and by ignoring or devaluing the continuities, most crucially the persistence of class inequalities and class-based meaning systems, the 'generation gap' theorists prepare the way for the second central proposition; that generations are now more important than classes as dimensions of social stratification and determinants of social consciousness.

Again there are several variations on this central theme. The first is that generations are *replacing* classes at the centre of social life. This attractively simple argument enjoyed a very considerable currency among both journalists and more sociologically-minded commentators. Here are two representative examples. The first is Colin MacInnes, writing in 1958 at the height of the 'rock and roll' boom which marked the first flush of adolescent consumer spending.

> The 'two nations' of our society may perhaps no longer be those of the 'rich' and 'poor' (or, to use old-fashioned terms, the 'upper' and 'working' classes), but those of the teenagers on the one hand and, on the other, all those who have assumed the burdens of adult responsibility (MacInnes 1966).

Notice how 'class' is presented as an 'old-fashioned term', a relic of more austere times, which is increasingly out of place in a society emerging into affluence. Six years later the tone was even more affirmative. The note of tentativeness detectable in MacInnes 'may perhaps' had disappeared, and Abrams could confidently proclaim that:—

> Under conditions of increasing general prosperity the social study of society in class terms is less and less illuminating. And its place is taken by differences related to age. . . For example, the middle-class teenager has more in common with a working-class teenager than he has with middle-aged, middle-class people (Abrams 1964).

Other commentators have proposed a second variation on this same basic theme by arguing not that generations have superseded classes but that they have themselves *become* classes. Lenski (1968) for example, has argued that the conflicts between:—

> . . . 'age-classes' especially those between youth and adults should be seen as a 'distinctive class struggle in its own right' and should not 'be confused with economic class struggles'.

Similarly, Musgrove (1969) has contended that youth should be seen "in effect as a 'social class' (and as a class relatively independent of the social stratification system of adults)". A further twist to this version of the argument has been added by the Rowntrees. Writing in 1968 against a background of increasing campus militancy and growing opposition to the Vietnam War, they argue that in their role as students and soldiers they have developed a genuine class consciousness and have become "the potentially revolutionary core in the United States today" (Rowntree and Rowntree 1968). This argument that a newly 'proletarianised' youth is filling the vacuum left by the 'new working-class', adds a further interesting embellishment to the 'embourgeoisement' theme. This version of the argument remains comparatively rare, however, and the dominant variant remains the idea that generations have replaced classes as the major dimension of stratification.

The move from this assertion that generations are now the most salient dimension of stratification to the proposition that generations have become a key focus of social consciousness is, however, problematic. As Mannheim (1952) pointed out in his seminal essay 'The Problem of Generations', the fact that a particular age group share certain experiences in common by virtue of having been born at the same historical moment, is no guarantee in itself that they will share a common set of meanings and understandings. Nor is it a guarantee that generation-based meanings, once established, will necessarily supersede the meanings deriving from class situation, or from other dimensions of stratification such as sex roles and ethnicity. The minimum prior condition for this transition is that all generational members should at least have access to a set of meanings and modes of expression, a culture which is largely generational specific.

In their search for an agency capable of transmitting and sustaining a universally available but age-specific meaning system, commentators very soon alighted upon the mass media in general, and the pop music industry in particular. Coleman (1971) for example, commenting on the Presley era, assigned pop music a key role in reinforcing the 'generation gap', lamenting that:—

> As if it were not enough that . . . today's high school exists segregated from the rest of society, there are other things that reinforce this separateness. For example, adolescents have become an important market,

and special kinds of entertainment cater almost exclusively to them. Popular music is the most important. . .

English commentators were more cautious and tended to regard the 'rock and roll' era of the mid 'fifties as a point of transition between old class-based cultures of the past and the new generation-based cultures of the future. Even Abrams, whose much quoted pamphlet on 'The Teenage Consumer' put the 'affluent teenager' on the sociological map, was ambivalent. On the one hand he argued that the emerging patterns of adolescent consumption represented:—

. . . distinctive teenage spending for distinctive teenage ends in a distinctive teenage world,

while adding at the same time that:—

. . . the teenage market is almost entirely working-class,

and that consequently:—

. . . the aesthetic of the teenage market is essentially a working-class aesthetic (Abrams 1959).

Summarising the situation a little later, Mays felt that the transition from class cultures to youth culture had progressed a little further, and maintained that although:—

. . . it is still valid . . . to characterise the teenage culture and market as predominantly proletarian in style . . . there are indications that children of higher income families are coming under the same influences (Mays 1961).

Then in 1964, with the emergence of the British groups led by the Beatles, Britain experienced a pop explosion as annual record production reached an unprecedented peak of 101.2 millions (the previous peak being 85.4 millions in 1963). And from this point on commentators have tended to assume that the transition from class cultures to generational cultures has been accomplished, and that pop music has become the cornerstone of a new classless culture of youth. This proposition enjoys a considerable contemporary currency among sociologists as well as among 'cultural critics'. Here are two representative examples from recent writings; the first from Jarvie (1972) and the second from Steiner (1971):—

One of the things which links those at work with those who have stayed on at school is precisely the shared pop culture. There seems to me to be a growing homogeneity in teenage mores, which seems now to begin taking hold around the age of eleven and to end only with marriage in the twenties (Jarvie 1972)

... the vocabularies, the contextural behaviour-patterns of pop and rock, constitute a genuine lingua franca, a 'universal dialect' of youth (Steiner 1971).

At first sight this proposition seems plausible enough. Certainly there is evidence that the great majority of pop record buyers are aged between twelve and twenty. The estimate prepared by the Economist Intelligence Unit for example, puts the proportion at 80% (E.I.U. 1971). However, it is one thing to assert that adolescents dominate the pop market; it is quite another to argue that pop provides them with an age-specific pattern of meanings, symbols and modes of expression—a pop culture—which has superseded the meaning-systems derived from their class situation. However, if the myth of increasing classlessness is to be sustained, this assertion is indispensable.

The unmaking of the myth: the rediscovery of class

The proposition that pop provides the basis for a culture of youth is based on the assumption that audience members regard the various pop styles as part of a unitary and more or less homogeneous system of symbols and meanings, which they share in common with everyone else in their particular age group. Recent research among secondary school pupils in an English Midlands town (Murdock and McCron 1973) casts doubt on this assumption, however, and indicates that they construe contemporary pop as being divided into a series of distinct and separate sub-styles. Two of the most frequently mentioned of these sub-styles were the American Soul and Jamaican Reggae featured in discotheques, and 'Progressive' pop. The term 'progressive' was applied to a wide range of attempts to break with the standard pop formulas through extended instrumentation, personalised lyrics, and individual improvisation. These classifications had a social as well as a musical content, however, and together with clothes, and milieu, they were seen as important elements in signifying and confirming the divisions between different youth groups. In particular, the reggae-soul/'progressive' distinction was understood as one element in the complex of symbols and styles which defined the opposition between the two main sub-groups in the locality. The first group were variously labelled as 'skins', 'smooths' and 'townies', and the second group as 'hairies', 'freaks', 'hippies' and 'scoobies' (the local term for students). Further, these divisions were themselves seen as corresponding to the demarcation between those who had been classified as educational 'failures' and who consequently wanted to leave at or near the minimum age, and those who had been labelled as educationally 'successful' and who wanted to continue on into higher education and become students. Although preliminary and therefore tentative, this evidence suggests that instead of forming the basis of a common culture of youth, contemporary pop music provides one of the key symbolic resources through which adolescents articulate the contrasts in their educational experiences, contrasts which are themselves principally derived from the operation of structured class inequalities.

These results are part of a growing body of research findings, both from Britain and America, which directly contradict the notion of a homogeneous culture of youth and redirect attention back towards the centrality of class inequalities in structuring both social experiences and social consciousness. Summarising the results of recent American survey research, for example, Tyler (1972) has concluded that:—

> The non college, lower income, blue-collar youth is far more like his parent than like his rich intellectual counterpart on the campus. The kultur-kampf is less one of age against age than class against class.

In addition, observational studies of specific settings have increasingly revealed the importance of class-based meaning systems in structuring life styles. Davis and Muroz (1970), for example, have argued that the differential patterns of drug usage which they discovered among the 'Hippie' community of Haight-Ashbury reflected:—

> ... the basic contrast in expressive styles extant in the American class structure; put crudely, LSD equals self-exploration/self improvement equals middle-class, while Methadrine equals body stimulation/release of aggressive impulses equals working-class.

Even commercial researchers and marketing specialists are now beginning to deny the existence of a distinct 'youth market' for consumer and leisure goods. As one marketing consultant recently put it:—

> There isn't—there never was—a youth market. There are still different markets for different kinds of products, and some products appeal to different social groups, but age has surprisingly little to do with it (Murphy 1973).

In order to adequately map or explain the configuration of contemporary adolescent subcultures therefore, it is necessary to decisively reject the notions of 'youth culture' and to restore social class to the centre of the analysis. The final section therefore attempts to briefly sketch a provisional framework for such a reconstituted analysis.

Class situations: structural contradictions and subcultural solutions

Class situation permeates the everyday life of adolescents through the mediations of the work situation on the one hand, and the non-work situation of the family and local neighbourhood. Up until their sixteenth birthday, the work situation of adolescents is synonymous with their educational situation. For the sake of convenience, therefore, I shall illustrate my remarks with reference to the situation obtaining in secondary schools, and more specifically the situation of the two 'ideal typical' pupils groups: the working-class adolescents who are defined as educational 'failures', and the middle-class pupils classified as educational 'successes'.

The structure of secondary education is characterised by contradictions; that is to say, elements in the situation are simultaneously affirmed and negated (Esterton 1972). Most frequently these contradictions take the form of disjunctions and gaps between what is supposed to be happening and what is in fact going on, between what has been promised and what is actually being practised. In principle for example, by abolishing divisive selection procedures comprehensive schools are intended to substantially reduce the operation of class differentials on educational opportunity. In practice however a number of comprehensives operate their own internal sorting procedures, which effectively reconstitute the selective system within the same administrative unit. The resulting gap between promise and practice is often recognised by pupils on the receiving end. As one working-class boy in the low stream of an East London comprehensive put it:—

> Because they put on the board 'Robert Montifiore Comprehensive' it doesn't mean it is a comprehensive, does it? That's the theory, isn't it, while in practice it ain't (Daniel and MaGuire 1972).

Once they have recognised the contradictions in their situation, pupils experience them as personally problematic and search for ways of coming to terms with them. The nature of the contradictions experienced varies with a pupil's position within the secondary school system. Educational 'success' as well as educational 'failure' poses its own distinctive problems.

There is a good deal of evidence to indicate that English secondary schools are in large part reproductions in miniature of the social and ideological universe of the professional and managerial middle-class, and that the underlying assumptions are those which underpin the middle-class career—individual achievement, rational calculation, forward planning and deferment of immediate gratification in favour of long-term gains. Yet the majority of secondary school pupils are from working-class homes and are destined for manual employment. They are thus placed in the contradictory situation of being socialised into assumptions and responses appropriate to a middle-class career while at the same time being excluded from the rewards of this system. Faced with this definition of themselves, and with the prospect of a lifetime of dull, repetitive work on the factory floor or behind the shop counter therefore, they are presented with the problem of constructing a distinctive identity and retrieving their self-esteem.

The situation facing the middle-class 'successes' is somewhat different. They are being offered a career but at the price of a certain lopsidedness in their personal development. As they progress successfully through the secondary system they are expected to consistently improve their level of intellectual performance, while at the same time sublimating their emotional capacities and channelling their creativity into channels approved by the school. The contradiction in their situation, therefore, is that the school persistently encourages them to achieve, to 'develop' as individuals, and to 'make the best of themselves', while simultaneously limiting the means through which these ends can be legitimately fulfilled. They are therefore faced with the problem of retrieving these expressive areas of experience. Due to the very low level of control which pupils possess over the structure of their school situation, these contradictions must necessarily be resolved within the sphere of leisure.

The attempt to resolve the contradictions contained in the work situation through the creation of meaningful styles of leisure frequently takes place within the context provided by a subculture. Subcultures are the patterns of ideas, values, symbols and ritualised activities through which groups respond to their shared situation. They offer ways of coming to terms with the problems posed, the contradictions in the situation, and provide a social and symbolic context for the development and reinforcement of collective identity and individual self-esteem (Cohen 1972; Brake 1973). Since subcultures develop primarily to provide solutions to the problems presented by specific work situations, and because these contradictions are in turn mediations of the contradictions inherent in specific segments of the class structure, it is scarcely surprising that support for particular subcultures is concentrated among particular class factions. However, while this goes some way towards explaining why subcultural support should be strongly differentiated along class lines, it does not account for the specific content of particular subcultures. For this we need to turn to the mediations of class in the non-work situation.

Class position, as mediated through the non-work situation, operates to limit the range of subcultural solutions available to adolescents in particular localities, both structurally and subjectively. The structural limitation stems from the simple fact of differential access to the social groups and milieux which provide the foci for subcultural activities. The second limitation is more subtle, however, and arises from the continuing strength of class-based meaning systems.

The notion of 'youth culture' rests on a grossly oversimplified account of post war social change, which ignores persistence of class inequalities and the resilience of the 'situational' meaning systems rooted in the cumulative social experience of particular class factions. The symbols, styles and leisure activities sponsored by the adolescent oriented sectors of the mass entertainment industry have not obliterated or replaced these class-based meaning systems. Rather they have been laid over the top, setting in motion an increasingly complex series of relationships between 'situational' and media-relayed cultural systems (Murdock and Phelps 1972). But it is the class-based meaning systems into which they have been socialised since birth which continue to provide the basic framework of beliefs and values through which adolescents respond to their situation. The basic values of group solidarity and physical competence which underpin the skinhead subculture, for example, are derived from and supported by the parent culture as mediated through the family and local neighbourhood. Consequently, media-relayed elements such as particular styles of dress and music are incorporated into the subculture to the extent that they resonate with these class-based values. Similarly, the middle-class pupils' preference for 'progressive' pop performers who 'do their own thing' can be seen as a 'stretched' version of the middle-class values of individual achievement and self exploration. It would, however, be a mistake to see youth subcultures as entirely determined by the class situations in which they are embedded. Once formed, they assume a certain degree of autonomy and self-sufficiency, and the relations between them become an important additional factor in their development. Monod (1967) for example, has shown how working-class Parisian youth groups typically define themselves twice over; as belonging to a specific locality (and hence a particular class faction), and as not being members of surrounding youth subcultures. The demarcations and oppositions between different youth subcultures may therefore be seen as versions of the divisions and conflicts within the wider class structure, *transposed* into the specific context of youth.

Conclusion

This brief chapter has been based on the premise that the relationship between education and leisure is a specific instance of the more general relationship between production and consumption, work and non-work, and as such can only be meaningfully studied within the context of an overall analysis of social stratification and social change. While it provides such a general frame-work, the notion of 'youth culture' which has underpinned much of the discussion to date fails because the analysis of post war social change on which it rests is fundamentally mistaken. More particularly, because the idea of 'youth culture' by-passes the continuing and decisive importance of class inequalities, it cannot account for the diversity of contemporary adolescent leisure styles. Consequently, I have argued that it must be discarded and replaced by a conceptualisation which starts from the proposition that "the class system continues to constitute the fundamental axis of the social structure" (Giddens 1973).

References

ABRAMS, M. (1959). *The Teenage Consumer.* London: The London Press Exchange Limited.

ABRAMS, M. (1964). *The Newspaper Reading Public of Tomorrow.* London: Odhams Press.

BRAKE, M. (1973). Cultural revolution or alternative delinquency. In R.V. Bailey and J. Young (Eds.). *Contemporary Social Problems in Britain.* Farnborough: Saxon House.

COHEN, P. (1972). Subcultural conflict and working-class community. *Working Papers in Cultural Studies,* 2, 5-51.

COLEMAN, J.S. (1971). *The Adolescent Society.* New York: The Free Press.

DANIEL, S. & MCGUIRE, P. (1972). *The Paint House: Words from an East End Gang.* Harmondsworth: Penguin Books.

DAVIS, F. & MUROZ, L. (1970). Heads and freaks: patterns and meanings of drug use among hippies. In J.D. Douglas (Ed.) *Observations of Deviance.* New York: Random House.

THE ECONOMIST INTELLIGENCE UNIT, (1971). Special report number 1: gramophone records. *Retail Business,* **159**, 18-34.

ESTERTON, A. (1972). *The Leaves of Spring: Schizophrenia, Family and Sacrifice.* Harmondsworth: Penguin Books.

GIDDENS, A. (1973). *The Class Structure of The Advanced Societies.* London: Hutchinson.

GOLDTHORPE, J.H. et al. (1969). *The Affluent Worker in the Class Structure.* Cambridge: The University Press.

JARVIE, I.C. (1972). *Concepts and Society.* London: Routledge and Kegan Paul.

LENSKI, G. (1968). *Power and Privilege: A Theory of Stratification.* New York: McGraw-Hill.

MACINNES, C. (1958). Pop songs and teenagers. In C. MacInnes (1966). *England, Half English.* Harmondsworth: Penguin.

MANN, M. (1973). *Consciousness and Action Among the Western Working-Class.* London: Macmillan.

MANNHEIM, K. (1952). The problem of generations. In K. Mannheim. *Essays in The Sociology of Knowledge.* London: Routledge and Kegan Paul.

MAYS, J.B. (1961). Teen-age culture in contemporary Britain and Europe. *Annals of the American Academy of Political and Social Sciences,* **338**, 22-32.

MEAD, M. (1971). Future family. *Transaction,* 8, 87-89.

MEAD, M. (1972). *Culture and Commitment: A Study of the Generation Gap.* London: Panther Books.

MONOD, J. (1967). Juvenile gangs in Paris: toward a structural analysis. *Jrnl. Res. Crime & Delinq.,* 4, 142-165.

MURDOCK, G. & PHELPS, G. (1972). Youth culture and the school revisited. *Brit. Jrnl. Sociol.*, **23**, 478-482.

MURDOCK, G. & MCCRON, R. (1973). Scoobies, skins and contemporary pop. *New Society*, **23**, 690-692.

MURPHY, P. (1973). The great youth myth. *Campaign*, February 16th, 1973. 22-27.

MUSGROVE, F. (1969). The problems of youth and the structure of society in England. *Youth and Society*, **1**, 38-58.

NUTTAL, J. (1968). *Bomb Culture.* London: MacGibbon and Kee.

PAHL, R. (1973). Four jobs for two. (Review of M. Young and P. Willmott. The Symmetrical Family). *New Society*, **25**, 653-654.

ROWNTREE, J. & ROWNTREE, M. (1968). Youth as class: the political economy of youth. *Our Generation*, **6**, 155-186.

SEAMAN, L.C.B. (1966). *Post Victorian Britain* 1902-1951. London: Methuen.

STEINER, G. (1971). Tomorrow. *The Listener*, **85**, 472-474.

TYLER, G. (1972). Generation gap or gap within a generation? In I. Howe and M. Harrington (Eds.). *The Seventies: Problems and Proposals.* New York: Harper Row.

WESTERGAARD, J.H. (1970). The rediscovery of the cash nexus. In R. Miliband and J. Saville (Eds.). *The Socialist Register 1970.* London: The Merlin Press.

WESTERGAARD, J.H. (1972). The myth of classlessness. In R. Blackburn (Ed.). *Ideology in Social Science.* London: Fontana Books.

EDUCATION

COMMUNITY EDUCATION

by J. RENNIE Community Education Adviser,
City of Coventry.

Attempting to give an appraisal of community education in 1974 is rather like being asked to describe a football match when one has had to leave after the first ten minutes. In this country, it is, as they say, in its infancy. This, despite the plethora of jobs advertised in education nowadays prefaced by the word 'community', the ambiguity of which often makes the title meaningless. Despite also, the increasing use of the word 'community' as an adjective to describe Schools, Colleges, and Centres, which has led to a situation where it is hardly surprising that Professor Cox, on a television programme, could reasonably ask, "What *is* a community school?"! This state of affairs is predictable enough, of course. In our media-orientated society, almost any emergent concept is immediately analysed under the microscope, often with the full glare of publicity, and instant opinions passed as to its efficacy or otherwise. 'Progressives' and 'trads' alike feel the urge to categorise at once, and we are left with two sets of entrenched and polarised attitudes, unhelpful philosophically or practically.

What is possible at this stage, then, is of necessity fairly unambitious. It may be possible, and it would certainly be helpful, to clarify some of the confusion caused by the multitude of names used to describe places where community education may take place. A definition of a community school, which is the main agency for community education with some discussion of the rationale, may also be helpful. A discussion of the modus operandi of the community school, what it can attempt to do, its structures, attitudes, curriculum, relationships with the community it serves, seems essential. Finally, an attempt will be made to look at the implication of adopting the concept in terms of social values, and, re-distribution of resources.

Whenever teachers are presented with a new development, the doubters amongst them tend to have two standard responses,—"It can't be done" and "We've been doing it for years". Sometimes, these responses even come from people who work together in the same school. Paradoxically there is an element of truth in both, and they may not be as mutually contradictory as they at first seem. Very little in education *is* new, most developments coming from a long line of antecedents which sometimes crystallise into a "new" theory. Community education is no different. Its antecedents include Henry Morris's village colleges, the old 'night-schools' and the latter-day evening centres. When teachers say, "It can't be done", they usually mean they cannot visualise the end-product. Many teachers, like the "convergent thinkers", of Liam Hudson (1968) feel the necessity to visualise such an end-product before casting aside some of their own well-tried notions. Simply *because* community schools are so new, because they are still feeling their way towards an agreed philosophy, even their supporters find difficulty in describing their ultimate values and goals. When the validity of the concept of community education is considered, therefore, there may be, as Eric Midwinter has said of the Halsey Report, "uncertainty about whether or not it is accepted: there is not much uncertainty about the consequences of not accepting it".

First of all, it is worth examining the way in which the confusion about community education has arisen. 'Dual-use' of buildings is nowadays advocated largely on economic grounds. The 'optimum use of plant' is a phrase frequently heard in local authority offices. Yet for many years, these same local authorities have used school buildings in the evenings for 'night schools', still referred to as such by most people but now known officially as evening centres. In the late nineteen sixties, schools began to appear which had additional "community provision"—youth wings, dual-purpose sports halls and swimming pools, and even community centres. Some began to call themselves community colleges, or community schools—one went so far as to call itself an 'educational and recreational centre'. Led by places such as Cumberland, Nottinghamshire and Shropshire, more and more were built with increasing sophistication. In Coventry, the Sidney Stringer School has a community restaurant and lounge, squash courts, dual-use sports hall and drama-studio. There will shortly be a branch of the social services department in the building alongside an information and opinion centre run by local residents. There will be a bar, so that we will have a headmaster who is also a licensee! Manchester, as ever seeking to lead the field, has produced the enormous Abraham Moss Centre, serving an even wider variety of needs in the Cheetham/Crumpsall area of the city. All these developments owe something in concept to the village colleges of Cambridgeshire devised by Henry Morris so many years before. Serving groups of villages in rural areas, these colleges aim to do more than provide resources for schools and communities jointly. They represent the first real attempt to make the school a focus for the interest and activities of people in the locality. In this, if in nothing else, they share aims with the community school concept of the national Educational Priority Areas experiment described in the Halsey Report.

For the layman, perhaps the single most confusing argument in the community school debate has been the opposing views expressed about the idea of neighbourhood schools—schools attended by all the children from one neighbourhood and by no children from outside it. Supporters of the old tripartite system have argued against them on the grounds that they rarely give the right social 'mix'. One wonders whether they feel secondary school children need to mix more than younger children who have always attended neighbourhood schools—the primary school. They argue also about the need for 'variety of provision' as if any two comprehensive schools were alike. Many argue against the loss of parental choice, forgetting that 80% of parents have never had a choice and have had their children sent to secondary moderns—nearly always a neighbourhood school.

Towards a definition of community schools

Two of the basic principles upon which the community school must be made may have become obvious in the last paragraph. By nature, they are neighbourhood schools, and they are comprehensive. Primary schools, simply because they usually serve a smaller, more compact and therefore more obvious natural catchment area, can more readily be seen as neighbourhood schools. A larger comprehensive school may serve two or even three adjoining neighbourhoods. Although there would be a variety of sizes, of socio/economic groupings and of housing in various neighbourhoods, their schools would have the one unifying value of being neighbourhood schools.

It would be unthinkable for community schools to be anything other than comprehensive schools. Not the least powerful reason for the acceptability of most primary schools for parents may be their comprehensiveness. Children in them have not been separated from their next-door neighbours on the grounds of either the wealth of their parents or their ability to perform well on certain so-called objective tests. The difficulty appears to arise, somewhat mysteriously, when the child reaches the age of eleven or twelve. It is almost as if some immutable law of nature changed the child at that age and made it possible for him to be categorised as either bright or dull. No one questions the comprehensive idea up to that age. These arguments for comprehensivation are well-known. Increasingly they are being accepted on a national scale. Less acceptable to some are the arguments in favour of making schools co-educational and inter-denominational. Single sex schools, though decreasing in number, are still defended on the grounds that some parents prefer them, and that we must therefore maintain that element of choice for those parents. What happens, in practice, of course, is that in some areas, the large majority of parents who prefer co-educational schools are given no choice other than to send their children on long and expensive daily bus journeys. One wonders if we have some national sexual hang-up that persuades us to separate boys and girls between the ages of eleven and sixteen, when they seem to get on so well together in primary schools before, and at work and play after, this unnatural hiatus.

With due respect to those religious pioneers who did so much to get schooling started in this country, must we not be asking ourselves now, more than a hundred years later, whether the time has come for our schools to be integrated. One could argue forcibly that the problems in Northern Ireland are the bitter fruits of an unjust society. But it could also be argued that the separation of children into sectarian schools underlines, for them, the differences between them from a very early age. Integration at this time might prove painful. In the long term, though, some benefits could accrue, as long as there was a concomitant change in other political and social policies there. Perhaps the greatest benefit might go to the teachers. A devout Catholic teacher told me recently that she had been to a Catholic school, spent much of her leisure time in a Catholic church, trained in a Catholic College of Education, and found herself teaching in a Catholic School. She now finds herself doubting whether she is able to bring to her charges the breadth of experience which might have been possible had her own life followed a less narrow path.

Inside the community school

What will go on inside this comprehensive, co-educational, interdenominational neighbourhood school? If it is truly to serve the community, it will be concerned with many more things than the needs of the school-age children within its catchment area, of course. Nevertheless, these form a sizeable and important sector of any community (in whom we invest our future).

Before making decisions about how to meet the needs of this group, we need to reflect upon the failure of the present school system, for few can doubt that it has failed. And it has failed, what's more, by its own criteria. The emphasis in the traditional school system has been on academic achievement. Yet we now see that the proportion of working-class children gaining places at our universities has scarcely risen since well before the last war. Are we to assume that the working-class child is intellectually inferior? It seems unlikely when we know of the wide discrepancies between local authorities of children gaining grammar school places, and of qualitative differences in educational provision. One result has been that we are now desperately short of doctors, engineers and scientists whose value traditional educationists are so fond of extolling when they are defending the status quo in education. But community schools do not concentrate solely on this narrow concern for academic excellence. Halsey has described them as equipping children to be "eager apprentices for community life". It sets out to equip youngsters for life as it *is* in a multi-cultural, multi-racial society with the many roles they are called upon and will be called upon to fill. This does *not* mean preparing children *for* life. One is reminded of the girl in the book by Edward Blishen (1969) who said she was sick of being prepared for life,–she said "I'm alive now". Nor does it mean that community schools are to prepare children to fit into society as it is. On the contrary, they are to enable children to develop the skills to change society for the better,— rationally and peacefully, with full knowledge of all the alternatives open to them, and with full knowledge of what has happened to people who have tried to do just that in other places and at other times—from Socrates to Allende.

Appropriate structures

All the arguments used earlier in favour of comprehensives can be used equally powerfully in favour of unstreamed schools. Too many unfortunate examples are available for overnight de-streaming to be advocated. Barker-Lunn (1970) has shown the dangers of having teachers operate a system they do not believe in. But the hair-raising experiences I have had in streamed secondary schools convince me of the need to advance in the direction of de-streaming even if the advance is slow. A group of fourteen year olds in a 'D' stream who referred cynically but realistically to their class as the 'dustbin' was only one of many such experiences in schools where streaming was carried out with varied degrees of subtlety, sophistication, flexibility and rigidity. It is not only streaming we need to look at critically. So many of the old, familiar structures and strategies of schools—house systems, prefect systems, assemblies and, not least, the way teachers speak to pupils—carry their own implicit social messages across to the children. Frequently these messages have the opposite effect to that which the teacher desires. This is not to say that by abandoning all such structures we also lose these social messages. Needless to say, whatever they are replaced with will also carry their own equally potent social messages. Hopefully, though, they could be more appropriate and consistent with the aims of the school.

Perhaps most essential is the need for teachers to change their role from mere information-givers and disciplinarians to that of senior colleague working with junior colleagues. An 'open' classroom is thus produced where communal decisions are taken, real choices made. This, more than any other strategy will produce a change in the ethos of the school to combat the dangers of the "hidden curriculum" highlighted so startlingly by Henry (1966), Kohl (1970) and Holt (1964) amongst others.

A relevant curriculum for the community school

So much of the rationale for community education has come from Halsey and Midwinter through their work on the national E.P.A. project and its subsequent reports. For the practice in curriculum terms, a debt is owed to Midwinter (1972) for his descriptions of the work of the Liverpool project in his Penguin special. The theme for so much of the Midwinter argument, and one which seems to be shared by so many curriculum developers, especially those who have been connected with Schools Council projects, has been that of relevance. In brief, the argument runs, the community school must have a community curriculum. Midwinter (1972) says:—

> . . . the primary duty of the school would be so to familiarise its pupils with their type of community and its likely future that, as citizens, they would be better equipped to cope with the social issues presented to them.

Since the best preparation for a participating democracy is a participating democracy, then such a curriculum will need all the more to be set against a background of the kind of structures described earlier in this paper. But how will this curriculum differ from the traditional one. Will all the old values be cast aside and replaced by studies of streets, shops, football, bingo and sewage systems? This seems to be how it is visualised by its opponents,—and once more, there is a grain of truth in it. Nobody who has taught children could fail to recognise the child's need for fantasy, adventure and many things outside his own experience. The community educator sees no reason to deny him. So the community curriculum need not be inward looking nor inhibiting. Instead of a concentration upon the teaching of the mechanical skills of mathematics and English, it would, without denying the necessity for learning such skills, shift the emphasis to a recognition that children are already brothers and sisters, classmates, schoolmates, neighbours, boy-friends, girl-friends, leisure pursuers, and yes, consumers. It would, concomitantly, recognise that they are to become parents, neighbours, husbands, and wives, lovers, and workmates. It would recognise, also, that every child has the capacity for leadership—even if only for leading himself. Such a shift of emphasis would be an explicit recognition of the social role of the school in enabling children to live fully rather than conditioning them to be conforming acceptors of what is provided for them.

To quote Midwinter (1973) yet again, this would:—

> . . . most wisely be accomplished by teaching (often team-teaching) by social themes, centres of interest or projects. These need not be exclusively local in nature; for instance television and space are significant aspects of the child's social environment today.

It would include, therefore, projects on the social environment, leisure pursuits, and creativity. In Coventry, the Community Education Project is awaiting publication of a housing and redevelopment kit prepared jointly with "Shelter". This was tested in twelve Coventry schools and includes sections about decision-taking, priorities, community housing needs, historical interest as well as the more technical issues of planning and design. The kit seeks to use the neighbourhood a child lives in as a resource for learning. It demands that he studies his area in terms of the land usage, planning, the physical state of the housing, and social provision. Further, by teaching through small groups, each of whom are identified with a particular fictitious family in the area, for which they are provided with a full profile, they also examine social issues. Thus they 'live through' many of the crisis situations being faced by families, who live right outside the school gates—families, what is more, which bear close resemblances to their own. Other kits are planned on the transition from school to work, vandalism (not forgetting that committed by local authorities), and an urban survival kit. This last one may seem rather pretentious and even, to some, unnecessary. Yet a third of the children in one class, selected at random, had spent fairly long spells in hospital—all of them as a result of accidents rather than illness. The urban child is always at risk from traffic, derelict houses, faulty old wiring, fire in overcrowded or unsafe housing, and a host of other dangers. His leisure is limited by the lack of playing space in the home and in the community and his de facto playgrounds are clearance sites, empty houses, car parks and busy side roads.

One needs to study the family, the peer-groups, the neighbourhood, to understand the dynamics of these groups; to recognise how the child relates to them. A family study would not simply look at the child's own family. It would look at the family in China, in America, in Africa, in the Victorian era and in the 'thirties. A neighbourhood study might look at an African kraal, a kibbutz, a new town as well as a downtown 'twilight' area or an English rural village.

At the secondary level, the community school curriculum would need to develop the skills of community participation more explicitly, not through community service which so often seems to concentrate on whitewashing old ladies' back-yards, and is fine for helping the teacher salve his own social conscience vicariously through the efforts of his pupils. It would look at those groups which are most important to a student in school,—his class, his school, his peer-groups, his community. Once again it would not be inward-looking but would have the same spatial and temporal dimensions of the primary school curriculum. It would seek to enable the pupil to understand these groups, to find a sense of identification with them—the only process which will lead him to participate in them as a result of a decision taken by himself and not imposed upon him by a concerned adult, be he teacher, community worker, vicar, or union official.

When people are told that the main leisure provision in one working-class community school is three squash-courts, they are usually, with some justification, amazed. They see immediately the incongruity of such provision. Yet a suggestion that the curriculum itself, the sacred cow of our educational system, should recognise the culture of the area it serves, is frequently met with protestations about 'erosion of standards' and 'too much permisiveness''. Far from eroding standards those schools which have had the courage of their convictions have found that the revitalised interest of pupils has enhanced standards and that the learning process has been more effective as a result.

Home and school links

The Advisory Centre for Education recently ran education shops at two Butlin's holiday camps. The holiday-makers there are overwhelmingly working-class,—the same people so frequently regarded by schools as feckless and disinterested in their offspring's education. Teams of three or four experienced educationists at both the camps met with enormous interest and were inundated with requests for information, for help and simply for opportunities to discuss what education is all about. It seems that middle-class dinner-parties are not the only places where little Johnny's education is a prime topic of conversation.

This latent interest of the working-class parents needs to be tapped imaginatively. Unfortunately, over the years schools have alienated successive generations of working-class parents who have come to recognise schools as places for 'them' and not for 'us'. Schools have formed an important part of the cycle of deprivation. In the last few years, however, perhaps as a consequence of the work of Douglas, Halsey, the Plowden report, and not least, by the Liverpool E.P.A. project, a substantial minority of schools have begun to take down the signs forbidding parents entry to the schools, and to erect new ones inviting them in. Using some of the ideas of the Liverpool project and not a few of their own, the schools working with the Community Education Project in Coventry have gone further than most in this direction.

Their first step was to attempt to change the lines of communication between home and school. Commonly, these consist of requests for money, reports, requests for parents to visit school to discuss a behaviour problem or, at best, the stereotyped invitation to the annual parents' evening, or open-afternoon. All too often, the cry comes from the teachers, "We never see the parents, we most need to see". Coventry's answer, or at least that of the schools in the Hillfields district, was to produce a termly newsletter whose style is unrepentantly more reminiscent of the 'Daily Mirror' than of a traditional school magazine, which sets out to inform parents of what is going on in schools, and invites them to join in. Another strategy was the "Education Happening" where the schools took over a local park for a day and a half at weekend to put on a live exhibition of children's work. Large marquees accommodated standing displays, an education shop, closed circuit television, and refreshment bars. An arena was created for displays of Indian, Irish and English folk-dancing, improvised drama, play-ground singing games, physical education displays and the like. A paint-in for parents and children was held continuously in one corner, a West Indian steel band played, and the Belgrade Theatre in Education team took part. A procession of 500 children in fancy-dress wound its way through the community to be met by Eartha Kitt, who opened the event, at the park itself. Over three thousand parents came to it. This year, at a second 'Happening', opened by Joe Mercer, over five thousand came. A carnival atmosphere was achieved by having Hillfields rock on sale, 'Happening' tee-shirts and ball-point pens, and a monster balloon-release. For many of the parents and teachers who took part, it was their first contact with the 'other side'.

Such initiatives, consciously and unapologetically 'gimmicky', need to be backed by a network of ongoing grass-roots contacts if the impetus of the initial contact is not be be lost. Hillfields schools have done this by holding weekly coffee-mornings, parent-run tuck-shops, after-school play-centres, and the like. Some schools have parents' rooms where parents bring their toddlers and meet for a cup of tea and a chat with teachers. This spills over into the classroom where parents can mix with the children freely during lessons. Special skills which some parents have, are used to support the teachers' work and to add further dimensions to the curriculum. One school has a 'community day' each week for every class, where the curriculum is geared to the community and where parents are encouraged to participate actively in the children's work. Thus the first steps towards a happy marriage between community development and adult education on the one side, and relevant curricula and community schooling on the other, are slowly being taken.

What becomes increasingly clear, of course, is that the needs of the parents can now be identified, and to some extent, met, in such an approach. These may range from the need for language classes for immigrants to co-operative sewing groups for disadvantaged mothers, and in these days of high-rise flats and expensive leisure provision, simply a meeting place where parent can meet parent.

Community participation and the provision of leisure facilities

Such extensions of home/school links, are probably essential phases for the alleviation of the in-built barriers between school and community discussed earlier. The Director of Education for Coventry has recently received a disproportionate amount of publicity for an article in which he described his vision for the community college—a concept to which his local authority is committed, financially and philosophically. He facetiously talked of their providing 'beer, bingo and belly-dancing'. The beer is on the way, the bingo is soon to start and some of us wait, expectantly, to see if belly-dancing was anything more than an alliterative convenience!

Unfortunately, much of the more serious contribution to be made was lost in the welter of publicity which seems inevitably to follow any authority figure who dares to stray from the path of orthodox thinking. In a city where working-men's clubs are enormously successful in providing each of these ingredients, usually in quite luxurious surroundings, community colleges which set out to provide no more than the traditional fare of evening centres are unlikely to meet with an enraptured welcome from local residents. There may be an important lesson to be learned from the working-men's clubs in another important respect, too. All these clubs are run by their members. A professional steward is employed who is nevertheless the servant of the members' elected Management Committee. Most schools are managed by governing bodies of local worthies, mainly councillors and representatives of the ruling political party. It seems as if the lip-service paid by one or two local authorities who have the occasional resident on the governing body may not be enough. Can we look forward to the headmaster being in the same position as the steward of the local social club—a true servant of the community who will be responsible to a governing body containing a majority of local residents?

Such an arrangement would probably be less likely to arrive at a mis-match of community and provision as exemplified by the squash-court facilities mentioned earlier. By all means let us have dual use of sporting facilities such as swimming pools, courts, pitches and sports-halls. These cannot be matched by local social clubs, and therefore constitute a valuable additon to community provision. But can we not think also of allowing people to *give* to the community school? Some way must be found of involving residents in the classroom situation—in the art and craft rooms, in the domestic science rooms most easily—which will not fall foul of local union branches as has happened in some quarters. These are practical problems of overlap between work and leisure which, increasingly, will arise with the expansion of community schools.

Adult education

In common with most working-class areas, the take-up of adult education in the Hillfields area of Coventry is negligible. The W.E.A., so effective in the past and so effective still in some areas, is failing to attract people from the city-centre neighbourhoods. It is not unfortunately, simply a question of providing more appropriate courses. In soccer-mad Merseyside, a course offered on football appreciation had hardly any takers! It seems that the general disillusionment with the education system is almost total. The Russell report, apart from suggesting an increase in expenditure equivalent to the cost of building one mile of the London motorway box, has suggested no innovatory modes of coping with this problem. The Coventry Community Education Project's response has been to appoint an unattached adult education tutor to work in pubs and clubs in the area. His task is to become a 'local', to know people in the area and to become known. He is not going out to sell this course or that, informally or otherwise, but to identify what people themselves are interested in. Then, by the establishment of informal groups in the uniquely uninhibited atmosphere which the British pub provides, he hopes to enable them to reach their own conclusions.

It may be that the tutor will channel his clients into some of the formal education channels, be they open-university courses or classes for teaching reading and writing to adults. It would be fatal, however, to use such cases as criteria for 'assessing' his effectiveness. His concern will be with the personal and social growth of his clients. Such growth will be manifested in many ways. It might be seen in a man who is prepared to talk about an interest he has, say in science fiction, without feeling that, in some way, he is odd. Or it could mean others becoming involved in a community group concerned with some specific local problem. Certainly, the community school itself could be a vital link in such a chain of events. By being open to various methods of accepting interested people into its varied activities, it offers the adult education tutor an obvious ready-made organisation in which to interest his clients.

Community development—implications

This paper is not offered as a panacea for the social and educational ills of our urban society. The whole realm of education, as we have so depressingly seen in the hundred years since state education began, cannot hope to do that. A more realistic aim is for community education to become a significant factor in the field of community development. It can have a complementary role alongside community planning, community politics, community law and order and the rest. Perhaps, community education should be seen as the first among equals, providing an underpinning kind of support without which community development is unlikely to be effective.

The implications are, of course, enormous. Schools represent the largest single community capital investment. Are local authorities likely to agree to sharing responsibility for their management with local residents? Are examination boards and universities ready to accept a radical change in the nature of the qualifications for entry into higher education which this paper implies? Is the teaching profession ready to abandon its long-held belief that it is responsible solely for the teaching of a class of children, or is it prepared to begin thinking about the 'educative community' which the Halsey report talks about?

The community educator has some enormously powerful allies to support his case—vandalism, violence, drugs, delinquency and all the other manifestations of alienation so starkly apparent in our society. The intelligent sixth-former who rejects higher education or the young student seeking more 'sophisticated' release from a system he frequently regards as corrupt are just as much failures of our education system as the football hooligan who kicks other youngsters and smashes shop-windows.

It seems that, educationally speaking, we are at the cross-roads. On the one hand lies the retreat to formal, unimaginative curricula and traditional structures which so clearly have failed. On the other hand is virtually unknown territory. It would mean an attempt to make the school become a beacon in the community not only for five-a-side football, bridge or even beer and bingo, but for fraternity, fellowship, co-operation and community action. School needs to be a place where the teacher ceases to be a joke to the community (as we so often see on T.V., in films, and on the stage) and to become a catalyst—no longer a social pathologist but an activist. He will be seen not as someone to be left behind at the earliest opportunity, but as someone to be sought out after compulsory schooling has ended, as a colleague and as a friend. This may seem rather dewy-eyed, pie-in-the-sky idealism. Fortunately, in a number of places up and down the country, the first tentative steps are being taken and its practioners are optimistic. If I may return to my original footballing metaphor, there is no score yet but the attack has been mounted!

References

BARKER-LUNN, J. (1970). *Streaming in the Primary Schools.* Slaugh: National Federation for Educational Research.

BLISHEN, E. (1969). *The School that I'd Like.* Harmondsworth: Penguin.

HENRY, J. (1966). *Culture against Man.* London: Tavistock.

HOLT, J. (1964). *How Children Fail.* London: Pitman.

HUDSON, L. (1968). *Frames of Mind.* London: Methuen.

KOHL, H. (1970). *The Open Classroom.* London: Methuen.

MIDWINTER, E. (1972). *Primary Education.* Harmondsworth: Penguin.

MIDWINTER, E. (1973). *Patterns of Community Education.* London: Ward-Lock Educational.

3

PLANNING

PLANNING

PLANNING AND LEISURE

by B. MELVILLE Planner,
Directorate of Planning, Engineering and
Transportation, West Yorkshire, Metropolitan County.

Recently, the town planning profession has been charged, as a body of men of undoubted goodwill who have developed a set of techniques of undoubted political impartiality, with misunderstanding every urban problem they encountered (Rex 1973). Therefore, it must be with some diffidence that I, a planner, approach the subject of leisure and the question of whether or not it raises problems for the planner, the *a priori* probabilities of my misunderstanding the complex which occurs when we try to relate 'leisure' and 'planning' being so high. The charge by Rex is a serious one, and I would not, as a number of my fellow professionals might, dismiss it as characteristic animadversion by a social scientist when faced with a particular piece of bureaucratic vandalism. Naturally I do not feel the charge is entirely just; but I am sufficiently alarmed by what my profession is involved in when attempting to 'plan for leisure', that I am inclined to ignore my normal claim for justice, and attempt to set down some doubts and queries as a notional public agenda for discussion.

I had better say right away that there is nothing impartial in my own attitude towards these doubts. Judgements must be personal or they are nothing, and I would, therefore, not lay any strong claim to objectivity or the role of a professional spokesman. These doubts, of which I am aware, I have discovered empirically (so to speak) by consulting myself. Also I use the word 'doubt' quite deliberately, to avoid any impression that I have discovered the right way to see how 'planning' and 'leisure' can be appropriately related. So these notes cannot pretend to be offered as a strong coherent argument, which could clinch the ongoing debate about public policy and leisure (Smith, Parker & Smith 1973). What I want to do here has the more limited objectives of raising doubts regarding the trends towards leisure pursuits which rely on the extensive use of the motor car, the way in which our bureaucracies accommodate these trends, and whether the arrangements for public participation in the planning process are adequate to affect these trends. The lack of adequate public participation becomes more important, the greater one's conviction of the folly of public policy.

I had thought, that one step in such an attempt to stir up doubts would be to define exactly what 'leisure' was, and that this definition would play a leading role in the rehearsal of these suspicions; but I find that this is not something I can easily do. I have a sense that the word 'leisure' can evoke larger questions of the significance of our own lives and the condition of our society. Any meaning that 'leisure' has for us cries out for some philosophical or sociological elucidation of some model of social relations, which in turn can raise deeper moral problems of what our relations with others should be, and the directions in which society should be persuaded to make these relations possible.

My sense of this difficulty of definition is brought out beautifully by Dickens in *Little Dorrit,* who at least makes it clear that 'leisure' is not some sort of inverse of 'work':—

> 'Yes I have always some of 'em to look
> after. But I like business, said Pancks,
> getting on a little faster.
> 'What's a man made for?'
>
> 'For nothing else?' said Clennam.
> Pancks put the counter question, 'What
> else?'
> It packed up, in the smallest compass, a
> weight that had rested on Clennam's life;
> and he made no answer.
> 'That's what I ask our weekly tenants',
> said Pancks.
> 'Some of 'em will pull long faces to me,
> and say, Poor as you see us, Master we're
> always grinding, drudging, toiling, every minute
> we're awake. I say to them, what else are you
> made for? It shuts them up. They haven't
> a word to answer. What else are you
> made for? That clinches it'.
> 'Ah dear, dear, dear! sighed Clennam.

Here Dickens locates in Panck's sardonic fierceness the desperation felt by the inhabitants of the Bleeding Heart Yard in their daily lives, their work and leisure, their poverty, and their relations with their landlord. Their leisure (such as it is) is highly constrained by their unfortunate circumstances, the desperation often giving way to a quiet celebration of life in the face of adversity. This aspect of their lives is underlined by the portrait of Cavalletto, the easy going Italian who has fallen into their company and exhibits what I can only describe as a stoic cheerfulness as he whittles his sticks of wood, his only leisure.

In contrast, the Dorrits are free spirits. On release from the debtors' prison at Marshalsea, they use their inheritance to live a life of ease, comfort, luxury, and continental travel. It is not inappropriate to pencil marginal comments such as 'conspicuous consumption', 'the leisure class', and 'yesterdays getaway people'. The total meaninglessness of this form of life is registered in the temporary failure in human relations of Amy Dorrit, who cannot escape the concealed reality of the Marshalsea prison—dark, a menacing fact of her society, always present and bringing apprehension. Clearly Dickens is engaged on *social enquiry*. The nature and significance of human relations is being located *delicately* in their relation to social and economic conditions—the whole novel forming a potent picture against which we can see ourselves and are brought face to face with our historical existence in its unhappiest aspects.

I rather hope the delicacy, insisted on above, is sufficient to carry my sense of difficulty with definitions which would leave me free to find an account of leisure located surely in social and economic conditions with due attention to 'production', 'distribution' and 'income', and yet at the same time free me from any identification of 'income' with 'life'. For I find it important not only to raise questions regarding the distribution of the wealth of society, but to raise questions of the worth of that product itself. If public agencies make available public goods, which were previously available to minorities (not *necessarily* with dominant values), in the belief that such goods are increasing the area of choice for those who were formerly denied access, then we may be in danger of neglecting important truths. After a certain level the provision of such goods may actually defeat the objectives which made such provision a cogent force in public policy. The philosophy of more jam tomorrow needs critical re-examination (Leavis 1972). The model of social relations which treats us as consumers, always demanding more, and envious of those who consume more than us, needs replacing with a profounder model which places us as responsible in a body politic where questions of meaning and significance are admissible and treated seriously. The Lawrentian question of 'what for, what ultimately for?' arises directly out of the concern with industrial society (Leavis 1972), the poverty of human relations, and the feelings of anomie and dissatisfaction with work, which no amount of meaningless leisure can balance.

At this point it would seem useful to develop a severe cultural critique of industrial society and modern capitalism. The development of such a critique is essential if an intelligible role for 'planning' is to be found in our society. A useful step towards such a critique lies in examining the contemporary practice of planners when faced with the problem of leisure.

Typically a planning agency would regard itself as setting out to meet the 'needs' of the public. For example, one of the main issues for Structure Planning in the Greater Manchester Area is described as 'what are the present and likely future needs (of leisure and recreation) and to what extent can these be met?' (Joint Working 1972). In pursuit of this objective, the agency would conduct household surveys of the intensity of use of recreational facilities, and attempt to estimate in some statistical manner the relationships between household and occupational structure and the intensity of use of facilities. Particular attention would be paid to relationships with the level of car availability, and the spatial separation of household and recreational facilities. The agency would then attempt to forecast household and occupational structure, and again particular attention would be paid to future levels of car-ownership. The relationships previously calibrated in the survey year would be assumed to hold in the future. The forecasts would then be substituted into the relationships, and so an estimate of the 'demand' for recreational facilities could be derived.

Our typical agency would also conduct surveys of existing recreational facilities, and ponder the problem of land management in the peri-urban areas. The uncertain future of agriculture in some of these peri-urban areas would certainly bear on any strategic consideration of the suitability of land development as a recreational facility. Little by little a picture of the 'supply' side would emerge. The 'supply' side would be *matched* with 'demand'; and no-one will be surprised to find that '. . . demands for leisure . . . have outstripped the facilities available to them. We are caught short in our countryside—space designed and managed for modern leisure' (Dower 1973). Can we cope? The question will go unanswered. It will automatically be assumed that we must cope, and it will be argued by most agencies that we can cope—provided we are imaginative, adaptive, prepared to integrate leisure in our countryside, use skilful management, develop partnership between public and private bodies, and above all use our common-sense (Dower 1973).

To achieve this matching, dialogue will take place with National Parks and surrounding rural counties to provide facilities. Soon the development process will be under way. Roads will be improved at considerable cost because:—

> . . . in many areas, the inadequacy of roads is becoming a serious impediment to the growth of recreation and tourism (Dower 1973).

The government will disgorge grants and subsidies for hotel construction. Remote areas will be persuaded to believe that development as a tourist area will bring employment and economic benefits (but to whom?). The development of our already overcrowded coasts may be intensified. Public open space on any large scale will be provided for metropolitan areas in the peri-urban areas and not where it is needed, because this solution simultaneously solves the land-management problem and avoids the difficulties and costs of land acquisition within the built-up area. Also the growth rate will increase for the new breed of planners expert in leisure and the countryside, academic experts in the economics of recreation, countryside officers and National Park police.

Now it may be objected that planning agencies are not using the best set of impartial techniques. There may be something in this. Cross elasticities of demand could, in principle, be calculated, and this may well lead to a modification of the demand schedules generated by the relatively naive methods outlined above. This would involve the estimation of supply and demand curves, those abstractions of the neo-classical and general equilibrium school of economists (Robinson 1971). Cost-benefit analysis could be applied to compare strictly comparable recreation projects, if one is prepared to waive objections to unacceptable assumptions (Hunt & Schwartz 1972; Adams 1973). Econometric techniques could be used (given reliable data!) to integrate the demand and supply sides in a more coherent fashion. Obviously if one thinks that this sort of extension to the existing set of techniques is worthwhile, then it is important that these extensions are carried out. My concern is to show what the average agency could hope to do in contemporary practice given the level of expertise it could muster now. The advantage of the existing set of techniques is that it makes visible what is involved in the attitude of mind towards 'planning for leisure', which more sophisticated techniques may only serve to obscure.

Perhaps the root of the trouble lies in our expectations that planners should look beyond the end of *our* noses, and predict the patterns of social relations, which may arise in our community. However, patterns of social relations are inherently unpredictable, not only because such patterns are subject to rapid change and there are no known laws to predict such change, but also because such patterns are, to a certain extent, a question of choice and not determined. In these exercises we see that although the question of 'need' is raised, the criteria of what human beings require for leisure are naive, and are based on the notion of the human being as an individual consumer 'with no relationships with his fellows, and whose needs can be measured in isolation from his fellows'. This attitude has been trenchantly parodied by Rex (1973):—

> . . . if there are at the moment X per cent of the population in the income group earning above £2000 per year, and a high proportion of these have country cottages and go ski-ing, then we must calculate what the percentage of this income group will be in the future, and provide the appropriate number of country cottages, ski-slopes, and ski-cupboards under the stairs.

Sophisticated techniques could modify the simplicity of these calculations, but would obscure the fact that planners tend to centre their thinking around the category of admissible trends. The success (if that is the right word) of British town planning is due to keeping more or less in step with the major trends operating in society (Donnison 1972). Thinking about trends may be valuable in helping to identify constraints and paint broad scenarios, but the significance and meaning of these new pictures is barely discussed, and any sense of choice forgotten under the overwhelming evidence of the trend. One could have a fine time here, blaming the planner for his involvement in this utter blankness. It is well to remember, though, that planners do not go through this sort of exercise on their own simple accord. To implement this sort of project, a planning agency will usually collaborate extensively with organisations such as the Recreation and Sports Councils. The statistical work may well be handled by recreational research workers in some university department or private research organisation. Those interested in justice could spread the blame a little further. I prefer to ask, what it is we expect of planning agencies in the development of these pseudo-sciences of unexperienced futures. Perhaps the expectation stems from powerful psychological demands not to be overtaken by events—the developments of technology and the trends in social forces. Whatever the reason, the expectation fails to grapple with the problem of what sort of community we want, which would provide us with the relevant criteria for controlling technological development, and free us from our worship of trends.

In some ways our attitude to the provision of recreation facilities is in the same state as transportation planning several years ago. Trends were the main factor, trends in population and employment growth and above all trends in car ownership. An abstract concept known as the 'value of travel-time' became the principal justification for an expensive programme of motor way construction to meet the demand for car usage. Since car ownership is distributed unequally, the main recipients of the benefits of this expensive programme were affluent 'middle-class' surburbia. Public transport patronage declined, and the *radical monopoly* (Illich 1974) of car useage increased the travel times of public transport facilities, leading to further declines of patronage and so on. The destruction of the inner areas by badly considered comprehensive clearance schemes to serve the urban highway programme, and high density housing schemes, led to a political reaction against the programme. No-one in transportation planning circles now accepts that our cities must be torn apart to satisfy the trends in car ownership—at least for the journey to work. (Expenditure Committee 1972). Access to leisure is quite another matter.

Transportation planners concentrate their efforts on the journey to work, and now concern themselves with the pseudo-issue of public versus private transport. Needless to say the new public transport programmes are expensive, relevant only to a radial journey to work; movement from the suburbs to the centre, and by and large continue to benefit suburban residents. Movements from inner area locations to the new industrial trading estates are still difficult, as these estates are located near motorways to benefit firms and their proximity to good public transport seems largely accidental. All this serves to point to the importance of transport for access to facilities, and few would deny the importance of car ownership for modern leisure pursuits such as mountaineering, sailing, ski-ing and water based sports (Hillman et al 1973). The use of the car is integrated into the pursuit itself. Without the car the pursuit would be impossible. In providing large scale recreation facilities which rely heavily on car useage, planners are encouraging the use of the car, distributing the supposed benefits of such provision to car owners leading to further inequalities, destroying the countryside, wrecking rural economies, and generally helping us to avoid the problem of creating the conditions for an authentic civilised life.

It is by falling in with these particular trends, that planners betray their allegiance to modern industrial society—a society which makes the car the key product of its technological output, reduces us to consumers, and fosters the illusion of 'escape' by fast travel, from its imprisoning structures. As O'Neill (1968) puts it:—

> The automobile becomes the true symbol of the North America flight into privacy. It has hollowed the cities and drained the countryside, melting each into the atomised living space of suburbia, it is the instrument of urban congestion and rural uglification. At the same time, the automobile is perfectly geared to the values of technical rationality, private ownership, individual mobility, sex equality, and social rivalry—pre-eminently the values of the liberal ideology and the stock-in trade of the corporate economy. The automobile is eminently the equilibrator of the tensions in the corporate culture: it is a family headache and a family joy, an air-pollutant indispensible for trips into the fresh air of the countryside, an escape mechanism from all the problems with which it is structurally integrated.

And of course it is impossible to escape, when everyone else (it seems) is attempting to escape at the same time. Windermere is covered with water-skiers. There are queues for golf and rock climbs. Scafell is littered with orange peel and cans. International airports are built to ferry tourists round the world. The Mediterranean coast presents a cliff of nauseating hotel architecture and extensive pollution. Hippies turn Nepal into a colony of the West Coast of the U.S.A. An imperial monoculture conquers the world leaving pockets of dirt, squalor, and the forgotten remnants of those who are victims of its process (Adams 1971).

This almost brings me back to my *donnée*—that not only are we being pushed into meaningless pursuits of Dorrit-like pleasures, and that there are still countless Bleeding Heart Yards throughout the world—but that offering these pleasures to those formerly denied access not only increases the meaninglessness (if that is possible) of the life-style of the Dorrits of this world, but also offers a false promise of hope and a dull waste of the efforts of society. It is simply not good enough to focus attention on inequality, and then redistribute 'income', if that 'income' actually decreases the possibility of radical and hopeful alternatives, and in effect 'rolls up the carpet of opportunities available to us' (Mishan 1967). Naturally, one would need to keep a sharp eye open for reactionary developments in this area of discourse. It seems to me to be fairly pointless to blame planners for the sort of world we live in. Planners can only deal with what society can admit to fall within their sphere. The 'planning machine' exists to serve society and reflects, in its purpose and its subject matter, the distribution of power and the ethos of that society. Only a limited amount can be done from inside the machine, and thus the organisation of 'pressure' from outside the machine is all important in 'determining' the output of our bureaucracies.

Our example from transportation planning ought to make this clear. The political planning machinery produced transportation plans. Inside the covers of these plans all is sweetness and light, technical, and rational, appearing to brook no argument. It has taken several years of practical inner area politics, the organising of conservation lobbies and finally problems of increasing costs, to 'politicise' transportation planning, and make the output of these studies oriented towards public transport. A key question is whether we can 'politicise' the field of recreative planning. Any answer to this question would require more clarity and self-perception than went into politicising transportation planning. Focussing on inequality resulted in a simplistic slogan of public versus private transport, and these results affect inequality only marginally. A slight environmental improvement in the fabric of urban areas may ensue, but the problems associated with high energy transformation necessary to movement in the city will still be present (Illich 1974). Focussing attention on unequal access to leisure will only help if we are not tempted to provide such unequal access, and if we create genuine meaningful alternatives that redistributed 'income' could buy. In practical terms this must surely imply a reduction in dependence on the motor car in particular, and all transport in general, for access to urban goods, and the recreation of civilised urban areas. (Illich 1974). A simplistic solution along the above lines remains in the hearts of a previous generation of planners (Foley 1960), and is now almost forgotten under the broadsides of spokesmen for the corporate state (Webber 1963). It must seem quixotic to suggest that we reread the early generation of planners, patiently disentangling what is sound from the liberal ideology, and recast the material in a revised framework associated with a critical re-examination of the formation of wealth and the distribution of income. In this sort of context argument about 'access to leisure' can play the part of a political resource, the real problems and solutions will lie much deeper.

If one reads the early generation of planners, one is struck by their concern for social relations, their attempts to build garden cities and villages, and the guiding light of some concept of a community. It is all too easy to point to the ludicrous paternalism and middle-class naivity of much of their thinking (Eversley 1973a). The contrast between this attempt at thought and today's slick, mindless, rational planning documents, is often overlooked. Any attempt to return discussion in planning documents to some concept of people living lives in particular communities, with relations with other human beings, must be welcomed—and this is something that planners may actually be able to do something about. Such planning documents would prove a more useful political resource than the dull prose of most bureaucratic output, and would help those interested in the political-planning process to focus on the genuine difficulties in the allocation of urban resources. The desirability of town parks may be apparent, the reality of land-values all too obvious.

If we began to treat the planning process as a dialogue (McDonald & Boyce 1971) between various social groups whose interests conflict, instead of artificially contrived pitched battles between local authorities, regarding the disposition of crumbs from the developers' table, we might begin to get somewhere. However the signs are not conducive to such treatment. The planning function (as currently conceived) is 'divided' between two tiers of local authorities, (Buxton 1973) who certainly insist on 'division of responsibilities'. In metropolitan areas, the metropolitan county council is responsible for 'structure planning', and district councils are responsible for 'local planning'. Structure planning is supposed to be concerned with what is rather loosely described as 'strategic' matters—transportation, population, employment, major shopping, recreational facilities and so on. A Structure Plan is required to show that it has taken account of national economic policies (assuming they exist), and social policies. Where these social policies come from remains a mystery. In the new system central government define priorities, budgets and allocations for education, housing, health, and social welfare. Some of this expenditure is directly implemented by central government, and the remainder by the district councils, leaving the county somewhat out in the cold on 'social policy'. The districts have extensive power to implement programmes in physical terms, the theory being that they can only implement schemes which are certified as being in accord with the County Structure Plan. However in the fields of education, housing, health, and social welfare the county has no real chance to lay down policy in concrete terms, as they are excluded from the policy-making machinery for all practical purposes, and are left with the rump of a research role (Eversley, 1973b). This obviously makes it difficult to certify proposals in the social policy field as being in accord with the county's policy. The county can hardly have a policy in such a field.

This leaves recreation planning and transportation planning as positive fields of practical planning available to the County. And yet our story has been that these are two evil geniuses in the dereliction of the modern metropolis. We are bound to suffer from their promotion as the key aspects of a county's function. For the next few years our professional talent will be devoted either to fighting absurd battles between local authorities on who does what, or effectively promoting those functions which contribute to the closure of radical alternatives in our cities. Is the planner to blame for this state of affairs?

What is really new in the reformed local government machinery is the possibility of public participation. The newness takes some time to take in, and early reactions have been to regard participation as a way of improving the 'input' and hence the performance of the 'planning machine'.

I am sure this is unhelpful. Although there is no definition of public participation in the legislation (surely a strange omission?), to my mind it summons up the need for those who hold power to listen to, and be seen to be ready to act on the advice of, the powerless. It implies the frequent publication by the local authority of policy statements, and a continuous programme of dialogue with local institutions and the general public, with revision, review of policy, and extensive discussion of the implications and wider ramifications of public policy. The structure plan is supposed to be the policy of the local authority, and yet it is only possible for the county to have policies in a few so-called strategic fields. In any event, a local authority is, by-and-large the agent of central government and can only offer alternative policies within the narrow spectrum of possibilities allowed by legislation or treasury discretion. This allows us to formulate a little criterion—any critical public participation worthy of the name must by critical of central government policy. But will such a critique develop and be heard?

The arrangements for our undefined participation are almost rudimentary. The specified minimum is that the authority publishes an Initial Announcement giving details of the planning programme, and specifies where one may submit comments. At the end of the programme, the draft policy proposals are to be published, and a minimum period of six weeks is allowed for comments to be submitted to the authority. The authority is then assumed to amend its policies in the light of any representations, before submitting the finalised policies to the Secretary of State for the Department of the Environment. This is the minimum provision and hardly offers genuine possibilities for dialogue. It will be interesting to see which authorities offer other programmes, which go far beyond such a minimum. The Secretary of State expects the authority to certify that it has carried out participation, to indicate the points of significant dispute, to relate what the authority has done to accommodate itself to dissenting views or to offer reasons why it has felt unable to do so. Once this has been done, the Secretary of State can hold an Examination in Public of the local planning authority's policies. Will such an Examination offer genuine possibilities of dialogue?

The Examination replaces the old Development Plan Public Inquiry procedure (D.o.E. 1973). Objectors are now replaced with 'participants'. These 'participants' are selected by the Chairman of a Panel appointed to assess the Structure Plan. The principles of selection are obscure, and seemed to be based on the chairman's judgement on whether the 'participant' can effectively contribute to a discussion restricted to the 'strategic' nature of the Structure Plan. Of course it would be useful to have a wide ranging dialogue on public policy as it is enshrined in the Structure Plan, and one can sympathise to a large extent with the bureaucrats' desire to streamline procedure, and to unclutter the debate between the selected participants by removing 'objectors' whose sole interest in attending the usual sort of Public Inquiry is to complain that their property is affected by the plan's proposals. These latter objectors are supposed to have a full chance to raise their objections at a Public Inquiry into the detailed local plan implementing a local aspect of the Structure Plan.

There are some grounds for unease. It is one thing to remove 'irrelevant' objectors on the grounds that they will not contribute to a wide ranging 'strategic' debate. It is quite another to leave the selection of 'participants' to a Senior Public Servant. I am quite sure that participants will be allowed to offer a fierce critique of the local planning authority. I am less sure that participants can submit a critique of central government policy, which by my little criterion, is what a public participation dialogue, worthy of the name, would be mainly about. The visibility of the whole process is, of course, new and interesting, and will provide fascinating insights into governmental processes. However, it is probable that radical criticism of public policy will be driven into other forms—channels of protest and all the frustration which such forms imply.

The new local government system outlined in the Local Government Act of 1972, and the new planning procedures can offer little hope that there will be no further misunderstanding of the problems that urban society poses for us all. A relevant 'planning', dealing with public policy, would deal with the inter-relationships between the various strands in our society. At its heart could be an urban sociology which emphasised the importance of social class-relationship to 'income' and 'production', in understanding the conflicts with which planners have to deal in preparing advice on public policy. It could emphasise the constraints which affect people's lives, and the manner in which these constraints arise. It could suggest that the notion that the bureaucracy can prepare long term policies which represent consensual values is probably misleading. It could highlight that urban society is made up of many sides and give the planner insights into society which would be of use, once he has decided which one of the many possible sides he is on (Rex 1973). The current reconstruction of political economy (Robinson 1971; Harcourt, 1972) could be used to undermine the utility maximising theories of consumer behaviour which under-pin economic aspects of our current planning exercises. The 'value of travel time' could become meaningless gabble, and be replaced with the possibility of debate on the value of a civilised life. Economics, as conceived by neo-classical authors (Hunt & Schwarts 1972), can only treat us as 'consumers'; political economy however makes us consider technological conditions, the distribution of output, and the criteria for choice—all of which are urgently needed in updating urban economics (Apps 1973).

In essence our Metropolitan Planning handbooks need re-writing (Eversley 1973a). It is unlikely that changes can be made in planning education curricula without causing considerable controversy. Recently the Royal Town Planning Institute have tended to opt (not without dissent) for its more familiar role of physical planning (RTPI, 1971, 1973). There can be little surprise if the leisure aspects of public policy continue to constitute little more than physical proposals for recreation facilities. The physical bias of the profession will fit in neatly with the major trends in our society. If Eversley (1973a) is right, that planning is concerned with the allocation of scarce resources, then even if we ignore how that scarcity arises, it would be important for us to question why particular goods are produced, who benefits, who pays, and who is excluded. If we had the right sort of planners, a real opportunity for dialogue, and a real perception of the difficulties in reordering the city, we might stop trifling with these questions and together make some sort of beginning.

References

ADAMS, J.G.U. (1971). London's third airport, *The Geog. J.*, **137**, 468-504.
ADAMS, J.G.U. (1973). . . . and how much for your grandmother? *The Haltwhistle Quart.*, **1**, 25-33.
APPS, P. (1973). A critique of urban planning: directions of research. *Royal Austral. Inst. J.*, **11**, 8-15.
BUXTON, R. (1973). Planning in the new local government world. *J. Planning Law,* February 1974.
D.o.E. (1973). *Structure Plans: the Examination in Public.* Department of the Environment. London: H.M.S.O.
DONNISON, D. (1972). Ideas for town planners. *Three Banks Rev.*, **96**, 3-27.
DOWER, M. (1973). Planning for leisure. In M.A. Smith, S.R. Parker & C.S. Smith (Eds.) *Leisure and Society in Britain.* London: Lane.
EVERSLEY, D. (1973a). *The Planner in Society.* London: Faber.
EVERSLEY, D. (1973b). Planning futures. *New Society,* 8th Nov. 339-340.
EXPENDITURE COMMITTEE (1972). *Second Report, Urban Transport Planning.* London: H.M.S.O.
FOLEY, D.L. (1960). British town planning: one ideology or three? *Brit. J. Sociol.*, **11**, 211-231.
HARCOURT, G.C. (1972). *Some Cambridge Controversies in the Theory of Capital.* Cambridge: University Press.
HILLMAN, M., I. HENDERSON & A. WHALLEY, (1973). *Personal Mobility and Transport Policy.* Political and Economic Planning Broadsheet 542.
HUNT, E.K., & J.G. SCHWARTZ, (1972). *A Critique of Economic Theory.* Harmondsworth: Penguin.
ILLICH, I. (1974). *Energy and Equity.* London: Calder and Boyers.

Joint Working on Structure Plans in the Greater Manchester Area (1972). *First Review of the Study Area,* Manchester Town Hall.

LEAVIS, F.R. (1972). *Nor Shall My Sword.* London: Chatto & Windus.

MCDONALD, C., & BOYCE, D.E. (1971). Prototypical terms of dialogue for metropolitan planning. Paper presented at the 40th national conference of the Operations Research Society of America, Anaheim, California.

MISHAN, E.J. (1967). *The Costs of Economic Growth.* London: Staples Press.

O'NEILL, J. (1968). Public and private space. In T. Lloyd and J.T. McLeod (Eds.) *Agenda 1970: Proposals for a Creative Politics.* Toronto: University Press.

REX, J. (1973). *Race, Colonialism and the City.* London: Routledge and Kegan Paul.

ROBINSON, J. (1971). *Economic Heresies.* New York: MacMillan.

RTPI (1971). *Town Planners and their Future.* London: Royal Town Planning Institute.

RTPI (1973). *Implications of Changes in Education and Membership Policy.* London: Royal Town Planning Institute.

SMITH, M.A.S., R. PARKER & C. SMITH, (1973). *Leisure and Society in Britain.* London: Lane.

WEBBER, M. (1963). Order in diversity: community without propinquity. In L. Wingo Jr. (Ed.). *Cities in Space.* Washington: Johns Hopkins University Press.

PLANNING

11

PUBLIC PARTICIPATION AND PLANNING

by N. BOADEN Lecturer,
Department of Sociology, University of Liverpool.

The present preoccupation with encouraging public participation in various public activities creates an impression of uniformity in terms of needs and problems. Common elements are of course present within the theme, but the field is extremely complex. The desire for participation and the willingness to participate varies with the programme concerned, with the sets of decision-makers and publics involved, with the purposes sought by participation and so on. None of these is a simple issue. The key problem seems to lie in the difficulty of reconciling the needs and goals of possible participants and those of the people making decisions. While these are never mutually exclusive they are seldom wholly reconcilable. The public may want to take over effective decision-making powers. Decision makers may want to hear their opinions but invariably wish to reserve the right to decide.

Attention here will be focussed on participation in the public sector but it may be worth dwelling initially on some of the differences between public and private sector activity. Most fields of activity display a combination of provision from both sectors, though the precise mixture varies widely. Both the subjects of this book, work and leisure, provide examples of mixed provision. In each field public activity interacts very closely with private, both directly and indirectly, and this has some bearing on participation. But the public elements have particular characteristics. While employment in the public sector raises similar issues to employment in the private sector, the nature of public services and their political elements add another dimension. Political control has clearly affected the treatment and participation of public sector employees during the recent periods of wage restraint and freeze. Similarly the social service aspect of much public work restricts worker opportunities as well as adding a different dimension to the decision rules and the criteria used in planning such services.

The problems of participation in such direct activities are matched by those in other public sector activities which have indirect effects on work situations and employment generally. Thus National economic planning and location policies and the development of major transport links are dealt with by central government. Physical land-use planning and key decisions about housing and schools are taken by local government. Each decision area affects employment widely and each creates particular problems so far as participation is concerned. Some issues involve broad questions, high levels of abstraction and a good deal of technical expertise. Others are narrower, more concrete and more obviously within the competence of the layman to make a contribution. Some issues contain all these elements, but each also tends to raise particular problems.

In the field of leisure the same combination of direct and indirect public activity is present. Public agencies offer a wide range of leisure facilities ranging from the hire of football pitches to the provision of galleries and museums. Besides having the service features and the political overtones (museum charges) already suggested, such provisions also compete with those of the private sector, though not always as direct substitutes. Such competition may affect the bases of decision and therefore the possibilities of participation. Equally leisure provision is affected indirectly by other government decisions which profoundly modify leisure opportunities and costs.

The point is that public and private sector decisions differ in their content and in the way they are taken. Private sector decisions are usually judged by economic criteria, and profitability offers a rough but acceptable guide to decision. Competitive markets are the arena of decision, though covert decision making is the accepted norm. The public sector rarely displays such characteristics. Indeed its operations often arise where the private sector could not or would not provide, at least not on a wide enough scale and at an acceptable cost. Thus in the leisure field, libraries would be difficult to market and would probably discourage readers if privately offered at economic rates, while public parks are difficult to market at all in individual terms. The result is that they are usually public services, though there are of course exceptions to this rule.

Given these features of the public sector one can begin to see some of the reasons for the pressure for greater public involvement in the planning of services. The private sector sees the market as an effective and acceptable form of consumer involvement, though the 'average man' may well not support such a view. Market research is used increasingly to predict market behaviour and so permit firms to plan more efficiently with consumer intentions in mind. Such market research often follows intensive advertising and public relations to try and influence the sovereign consumer. Also markets are often highly imperfect and reduce the consumer's effective choice drastically. Nevertheless, there is only very limited concern about public participation in the private sector, though the recent price increases have produced some public reaction. It is argued that the consumer need not purchase in the private sector, a feature not always present in relation to public services.

Public participation thus becomes a separate and special issue within the public sector. Formal decision-makers are often elected representatives and even where they are not the concept of public responsibility applies quite widely.

This implies, and ideally involves, a high degree of mutual communication and influence between governors and governed. It is the failure of that mutuality that is causing the present concern. Elections are mobilising fewer and fewer people and other forms of participation do not appear to be highly successful. Individuals are often not placed in a decisive consumer role, and areas of collective provision reveal the absence of any collective voice among the consuming publics. Without the devices and the underlying rationale of the private sector, public bodies must be concerned about participation.

This concern springs from several sources. *First, it is argued that participation improves the quality of decisions.* Both the public and the decision-makers benefit from such improvement, though they do not always agree about the form or the direction improvement should take. Optimal decisions vary for different decision-makers and for different publics. In economic terms there may be one unique best solution to a problem, but in the real political world there are many sub-optimal solutions several of which might be equally acceptable in pure economic terms. Thus participation may secure conformity to public wishes in spite of costs, or it may be a device which facilitates those in office taking decisions. It may increase the influence of some groups but not of others, indeed in many cases participation is now sought to modify the disproportionate influence of some groups within the present system. The key question concerns which goals are sought by increased participation and whether the techniques adopted achieve them.

A second argument for participation is found in the commitment to a democratic system of government. The theory which sustains our form of government rests on the opportunity for involvement and the widespread capacity to influence its decisions. There should be participation and response to it. It is clear that elections, certainly local ones, will not sustain that theoretical claim, nor in fact will mass participation in voluntary organisations. Improved participation would thus legitimise the present system of government, as well as giving a legitimacy to the particular decisions being made within the system. At present it is hardly credible for government to claim the support of the people for its policies in any but the most theoretical sense. Of course there is a risk present as well. Even among some advocates of increased participation there is an acceptance that limitations must be set and we must avoid the drift to indecision and anarchy which might follow.

The use of participation as a legitimising device at the particular level may be present in the 1968 Planning Act. Participatory opportunities are made mandatory by statute at various stages in the planning process and the Minister will regard their use as one criterion for judging the acceptability of ultimate plans.[1] The Minister thus declares participation to be necessary to his own acceptance of

---

[1] Town and Country Planning Act, 1968.

structure plans, but other side effects may also follow. Early participation, or even perhaps the mere opportunity to participate, may affect the content of plans, but equally it may make it more difficult for members of the public to object to ultimate plans. Participation, or the opportunities for it, may become yet one further form of cooption giving the appearance rather than the actuality of influence. It is the complicated relationship between participation and influence which creates the dilemma. Participation can be an empty exercise unless coupled with influence. While it may be a necessary condition to achieving influence it is by no means sufficient.

Whatever justification may be urged for increased participation, agreement among its many advocates is unlikely. Nor are its advocates necessarily in a majority. In local government, planners have been promoting participation (even without statutory pressure) but engineers and educationalists have not been so keen. Social workers often advocate participation, but many seem to regard it as cooperation with the voluntary sector and very few as giving clients and the public a voice in decisions.[2] Elected members also vary, many regarding (perhaps rightly) the demand for greater participation as a criticism of their performance. This was clear in the early reaction of some Liverpool councillors to the growth of local community councils. They resented their roles being usurped, though in most cases joined these organisations eventually and often played key roles within them. Where they adopted this course they occasionally used their position to forestall certain kinds of community action when local authority services were concerned. Among the public too there is variation. A few willingly participate, most do not. Motivation is often lacking, but the means and opportunities to participate are not widely available nor always appropriate. Each of these aspects is important if effective participation is to occur.

Three General Problems of participation—where, when and how?

Motivation and opportunity are closely tied up with the triple questions of where participation should occur, at what time and what techniques are appropriate.

Where—to participate does not refer to the physical location though that can be an important issue. Rather it refers to the level of decision at which participation ought to occur. Most obviously this can be seen in the new institutions of local government. Responsibility for many functions will be shared between the two levels and even where it is not there will be important indirect effects from one tier to another. Where this happens, will the second tier

---

[2] Report of the Committee on Local Authority and Allied Personal Social Services (Seebohm Report) (1968) Cmnd 3703, London: HMSO.

have to comply with the wishes of the first, or might those wishes be frustrated by the actions of lower tier governments? On the answers to such questions may rest decisions about where to engage in effective participation. If the former rule prevails then participation needs to be at county level, though there may be a possibility of a second veto point in the districts. The answer may of course lie in operations at both levels, though the motivations and the necessary skills to participate at each may be quite different.

More significant in my view, is a second distinction of level which may coincide with that just considered but which also occurs within single authorities. This is the distinction between policies and decisions.[3] The former may be conceived as broader in scope and more general in their implications. As such they create a probability that particular decisions will occur which coincide with the broad lines of policy. In education for example, one must distinguish between reorganisation of secondary education and the operation of a particular school. The former may dictate that all become Comprehensive, but this may result in widely varied practices in particular schools. None will have a selective intake (policy will not permit this) but they may stream classes or set subjects or institute some other arrangements for internal selective allocation. School level participation would not forestall reorganisation but it might affect detailed application.[4] The LEA would be the level of participation if one wished to fight for selection to be retained. Recognition of this distinction is important both to the creation of effective motivation and for the development of appropriate strategies and tactics of participation.

In practice the motivation to participate most often arises where the effects of action are felt directly and immediately. For most people this tends to involve detailed decisions and concentrates their interest at the school level in the example just quoted. Effective participation there will not be easy or straightforward, but the broad policy on non-selection will be completely out of range for most people. Frustration may follow for some of those participating, not because of their incapacity, but rather because of their level of operation. In addition, of course, low participation at the policy level means that involved elites dominate that sphere. Much planning is in fact policy-making and the new structure planning rules for participation, in seeking participation, seems to acknowledge the point being made here.

Whatever the level of participation, *when* to participate is equally important. Both the policy process and decision-making extend over time and the issue arises about when to involve the public. Constant involvement by the public is

---

[3] See for a treatment of this distinction; Alford, R.R. (1969) *Bureaucracy and Participation.* New York: Rand McNally.

[4] Of course school level pressure may induce the Secretary of State to omit a particular school from a general scheme, but this seems to have been unusual in fact.

obviously not possible, even decision-makers only participate occasionally.[5] Yet in its absence the timing of periodic involvement may be crucial. It may affect both the motivation to participate and the effect of that participation on the ultimate outcome. Early involvement usually means that the outcome is less apparent to large sections of the public, and motivation consequently limited. Equally it permits involvement before attitudes have hardened or options been considered and possibly rejected with consequent enhanced opportunities for impact. This conflict indicates one problem in timing public participation. Another problem arises when one considers the different aspects of policy and decision-making which occupy the time sequence. Early in the process options may be being invited and considered, a task which demands some skills and capacity on the part of individuals and groups. Later it may be a question of testing reaction to a particular selection of proposals. This stage does offer a possible veto power to those involved, but it is less easy to promote positive alternatives so late in the process. More importantly the capacity to respond depends on a different range of skills and capabilities, than the capacity to promote.

Current structure planning processes again offer an example. The legislation provides for participation at salient points during the preparation of plans, though not at the earliest phases. The first of these is when reports of survey are published which occurs after a good deal of work among the planners and others directly involved. This may be a realistic assessment of the possibilities of engaging the public, but it may also militate against an effective public contribution in the early formulation of ideas and priorities. In fact some structure plan teams have undertaken some pre-statutory consultation though it is too early as yet to tell whether this is an improvement on the legislation in terms of effective participation.

Besides the where and when of involvement, there is clearly a vital question about *how* it is to be generated and channelled. The present formal methods of participation—elections, open council meetings, available access to representatives and officials—do not seem to work, or at least not very effectively. The Liberal revival may indicate one basis for revitalising the conventional representative process but I do not think so.[6] It seems more to represent disillusion with the other parties and relies more on the transmission of party literature (very effectively done) than on the generation of large scale community involvement. Certainly the taking of office by the Liberals in places like Liverpool will test the credibility of the claim for community politics.

---

[5] The various stages of the decision process tend to involve different actors at different times. See, e.g. Friend, J.K. and Jessup, N. (1969) *Local Government and Strategic Choice*, London: Tavistock, for a discussion of such decision processes in an English local authority.

[6] The concept of "community politics" is presented as offering a basis for the widening of public participation and the effective operation of local political machinery.

But if the formal institutions do not work what substitutes might be employed? This is not the place for a catalogue of techniques. Suffice it to say that they must be related both to the level of activity involved and cater at the appropriate time. They must be based on the processes of policy and decision-making, but must also recognise the needs and capabilities of potential participants. If they are costly, we must ask who will pay and will there be strings attached to financing? If they demand high skills we must ask where the skills are to come from? Are they to be learned by participants or provided by advocates, and if the latter, will they have any additional implications? Often in the past the tendency has been for the public to have to conform to the needs and methods of decision-makers. Perhaps for the future we should seek to modify the latter in line with the needs and capabilities of the public.

One Underlying issue—communication

While where, when and how are three critical questions to ask in the context of improved participation, one theme underlies them all. Though it is not the only issue, effective communication lies at the core of the participatory problem. It is necessary to tell the public what is happening and what might happen if they are to be motivated to become involved. It is necessary to tell them where different decision-makers stand on issues if they are to give and withhold support in a representative system. Equally public views must be communicated to those in office if they are to be reflected in policies and decisions. Anticipated reactions too often pass in place of a real expression of public attitudes because there are few means for obtaining the latter. But if vertical communication in both directions is necessary, the need for horizontal communication among both public and decision-makers also has to be remembered. Division of the public into social or geographical units often serves to hide unity of interest. At best this means a reduction of public impact but at worst it may be a deliberate attempt to frustrate unity because of its implications. The same may be said of representatives and officials. Individualism and local concerns are often dominant in the former case, while professional and departmental isolation is all too common in the latter. Only when all these links are improved will effective participation be possible, though the result may well produce a clear need for compromise.

In terms of downward communication the problems are clear, though in some ways it is the most developed area. In many local authorities the council meeting or the public committee (not always common) provide the major source of information for the press and therefore the public. Observation suggests that neither offers the reporter, or the public in attendance, much opportunity for understanding the basis of policy or decision. Neither is usually the effective locus of decision so that at best the observer sees nothing more than a public rehearsal of a foregone conclusion. This is compounded by the shortage of space in most meeting rooms, by the absence of documentation available to the public, by the procedural devices designed to facilitate speedy meetings rather than to stimulate public interest, and by the incapacity of many members to make clear the basis of their argument or their decision. Many of these deficiencies could be remedied if the need was recognised, but effort should only be put into this if it is the appropriate location and timing for participation. This seems unlikely, unless one is merely seeking information about what has been decided. The enhanced communication of decisions might produce a reactive feedback in due course, but it would only have minor effects on the content of the decisions in question. Communication needs to be both more effective and earlier if the public are to have an opportunity to react before decisions are taken.

This is often interpreted as an argument for opening more committees to the public, circulating minutes earlier than before and so on. These may all be desirable but they do not tackle the key problem. It is not so much that decisions would come to be taken in sub-committees or party caucus, this is where many are taken now. It is that many are taken in departments by officials with committees exercising a merely formal role in approving them. It is these areas which have to be opened out and the ideas and activities within them which have to be communicated. This will call for a more outgoing attitude on the part of many people who currently operate away from public scrutiny, and the creation of channels of communication. We are not here dealing with meetings and other formal occasions which the public might attend. Rather we are concerned with day to day discussions, chairman-chief officer relationships, informal situations of many kinds, and increasingly with the professional and official aspects of the public sectors.

Communication from these situations is obviously not easy. Insight type journalism is one means of ventilating key issues but there is little evidence of its use. Indeed the role of the press, locally at any rate, leaves a large question mark over the creation of effective channels of communication.[7] Coverage of the key areas of decision listed above would call for journalistic resources in quantity and of high quality. It would also call for a willingness to publish information which resulted from such work, but which might be highly contentious. At present the local press seem unlikely to offer these services. Local government affairs, despite their obvious significance to so many people, enjoy a small and very conservative coverage. Campaign journalism is rare, but so too is the informed coverage which might enable others to see the need and opportunity for campaigns. The commercial pressures on newspapers and their other roles in the communication process may justify their present practices. If they do, then

---

[7] Cox, W.H. and Morgan, D.R. (1973). *Local Politics and the Press.* Cambridge: University Press, examines critically the role of the local newspaper in relation to local government.

some other vehicle is needed to fill the obvious gap in communication of vital information.

Local authority newspapers do not seem to do this. While they provide information which is useful to many people it is invariably of a routine kind. It is perhaps unrealistic to expect them to enter into more contentious areas inevitably offering ammunition to enemies as well as friends. The recent development of community newspapers in some areas reflects the frustration with the commercial press and goes some way towards providing the critical output which is required. Limited circulations, infrequent publication and the difficulty, once a critical stance has been adopted, in obtaining information, make their task difficult. They do however represent one breakthrough and given changed attitudes among officials they may grow into a much more powerful instrument. Perhaps another way would be the use of part of the commercial newspaper by groups and organisations to publicise information and attitudes. This might need to be subsidised, but would offer wide scope and a large audience.

While there is an obvious problem with such regular and permanent communication, there is also a problem with occasional ad hoc needs of this kind. Of course if the general system was better the problem would not arise. Education again provides an example of the problem. School reorganisation carried with it both a statutory and a practical need to consult with parents. In practice this meant special meetings being organised with speakers unused to the needs of such situations, unable in many cases even to use the offices of Parents' Associations for publicity because they did not exist. Information finally got home, but public consultation scarcely took place. Yet the meeting remains a major form of communication. Audiences of 200 are regarded as excellent, presumably on the assumption that two step communication reaches several thousands more. Even where it does, it is usually not the kind of information which facilitates much more than a very negative response. Many meetings are designed to communicate messages which the authorities wish to pass. Rarely are they designed to pass on the information necessary to an effective public response which could affect the policy or decision involved. Much the same is true of exhibitions and displays. This is not to decry the value of such action, indeed there is not enough of it. Rather it is to suggest its lack of relevance to some participatory needs.

If one can be critical about downward communication, how much easier is it to be critical about communication the other way. Of course people have access to elected members and officials, though precious few avail themselves of the opportunity provided.[8] When they do these channels are invariably seen as

---

[8] Committee on the Management of Local Government (The Maud Report) (1967). Volume III, London: HMSO, deals with various aspects of public awareness of, and contact with the local authorities.

dealing with the particular individual problem. This is of course important, but it seldom produces the policy change which a sequence of individual problems suggests might be necessary. Even within the narrower limit, these are channels which require the individual to display some competence and a good deal of tenacity if they are to be successfully exploited. Their failure is evident both in the number of individuals who continue to suffer where they should not and need not, and in the absence of policy development to deal with the general issues involved.

There are other channels as well. Organisations often have, and utilise, access to officials and members in order to press their collective points of view. These are often very effective and there is evidence that they are used as a source of information by many decision-makers. This in itself is good, but does raise questions about the internal dynamics of different organisations and the representative nature of their contribution. More importantly it leaves a major question mark over those who are not organised. Officials and members may be joiners of organisations, but the public are not nearly so gregarious in this formal sense. Public sector services evidence the advantage enjoyed by those who do tend to join organisations but extended participation is often designed to modify that advantage. More elaborate contact with those already organised will not achieve this. It is the non-joiners who need to be heard.

About lateral communication I need say very little. Among the public it is left to individual initiative and inter-communal ignorance is substantial. For the moment it seems that development in this sphere must wait until intra-communal awareness is increased. Collective self-consciousness is needed to motivate participation. How much it depends on recognising better off groups as reference points is a moot point. Among official and representative groups attempts are now being made to increase contacts. The present push towards corporate planning is the obvious evidence for such moves. How the various groups blend, and what the actual outcome of corporatism will be, remains to be seen. At present the fact that it is happening is the important thing, particularly for its bearing on any consequent pattern and timing of public participation.

Participation in practice: two examples from Merseyside

So far I have been looking at various aspects of participation in the public sector with a view to distinguishing key issues which may affect future development. It is important to recognise that communication will lie at the core of any effective development, but at the same time the question of where, when and how participation occurs should not be forgotten. I want now to look briefly at two developments in the Merseyside area which perhaps illustrate the points already made. These are interesting because they represent quite different methods being used at two entirely different levels in the decision-making structure.

The first concerns the appointment in Liverpool of Area Community Wardens (community development officers) and the attendant, though formally independent, growth of community councils in the city. (The comments which follow relate to the period up to the end of 1971 and a number of changes since then have altered the picture somewhat.)[9] Area Community Wardens were mainly employed by the local authority, being formally members of the education department, though in one case local authority funds were filtered through a voluntary agency instead. Their tasks were ill-defined, but embraced the whole gamut of 'community development'. Thus while one aspect of their work was directly related to the need for more effective public participation in public sector decisions, they saw other needs like self-help and integration as equally important. This left an ambiguity which militated against effective performance in some of their allotted roles. Local initiatives were developed, play groups organised, old people's clubs started, festivals held and so on. All were of benefit to some people within the local communities concerned, yet did not appear to touch fundamentally the capacity to affect decisions made by public authorities. Indeed it might be argued that they made the impact of those decisions more tolerable and thereby moderated any pressure for change.

Before commenting on this it may be worth saying something about the community councils which the Wardens often sponsored and regularly supported. These were locally based organisations serving varied sizes of population mainly in down-town areas or in the new peripheral council estates. Like the Wardens associated with them they also sought to fulfil a variety of needs which were not always reconcilable. Often it was under their auspices that play groups ran or festivals were held. The result was that they became potential spokesmen for the community, but did not often speak and then with a cautious voice. A conscious policy of accord with the local authority was adopted and this militated against taking up issues where conflict was highly probable. Of course, cases of conflict did arise, but they were infrequent enough to sustain the general rule that major effort was directed elsewhere.

Now it is true that neither Area Community Wardens nor Community Councils were devised simply to improve participation, though in both cases this might be seen as something more than a possible side benefit. The failure of this side benefit to emerge tells us something about how participation might need to be developed. Formal relationship with the local authority is clearly an important issue. Area wardens employed by the authority are not well placed to raise key criticism of council policy. Nor is Education the most strategic service from which to do so. The town clerk or chief executive would seem to provide a much

[9] This research was supported by a grant from the Social Science Research Council.

more satisfactory umbrella from under which to influence a range of departments. But perhaps it may be better not to be connected directly to the
authority at all. The benefit of independence probably outweighs the advantage
of inside knowledge. Certainly, officials involved in community councils were
often seen as having the latter, and the dependence of groups on them gave them
a strategic advantage within the group. Action was sometimes forestalled by such
knowledge. While this was often wise it effectively prevented the strength of
local feelings on some issues being communicated. The end result in any
particular case was probably no different, but a vital factor was possibly lost
from the broader policy context. In the case where an independent officer
worked in the voluntary sphere there was some evidence of greater militancy
though this might have been explained by other factors.

Organisationally a different question arises. Given their multiple goals it was
felt necessary that these councils should be set up as 'community' organisations.
Though there were problems of precise definition when boundaries were
considered, and the appropriate organisation scale is still not certain, the
principle of geographical organisation was clear. Yet the evidence is strong that
attachment to a locality seldom extends beyond a very narrow area, and that
shared concerns in urban areas are not always geographically based. The result in
participatory terms was salutory and important. The most obvious issues were
taken up (housing conditions and compulsory purchase for example) but many
others were not. Education seldom figured in discussions at all, perhaps because
there was no interest or because the organisation was inappropriate. Social
services seldom seemed to arise as objects for participatory involvement though
much self-help effort was devoted to this field. It seemed that the organisations
raised those issues for which they were the relevant vehicle, but that they were
unlikely to embrace other issues where participation is an equally great problem.
Perhaps problem oriented organisations would have been more appropriate.
These would coincide with people's interests and certainly reflect the way in
which decisions are presently made. If it is objected that such groups do not
engage enough people, then the answer must be that neither do community
groups. Community councils activated only small numbers of people, and
though this was a gain, it was obtained at considerable cost. Perhaps this would
have been better devoted to the creation and generation of more traditional
functional groups.

The second example I want briefly to consider involves the quite different
level of structure planning for greater Merseyside. This is policy making par
excellence and therefore raises a whole set of different questions. The whole
process has only just begun and there is a statutory need, and among some
planners a professional wish, to involve the public effectively. But as I have just
suggested this is not easy, even at the local level in relation to decisions which
might reasonably be seen by the public to be directly relevant. How much more
difficult then is structure planning where the perspective is 1980 and where

implementation depends on thousands of decisions to be taken by people not yet elected or appointed. Recognising the difficulty, the planners took a correct decision, I think, to consult as early as possible and in various ways. This avoided the criticism about consultation following rather than preceding the making of decisions, though it remains to be seen whether early involvement produces any final impact. The use of several methods insured a little against the failure of any one.

It is too early as yet to do full justice to all of these. Surveys of councillors and the general public were undertaken and are still being analysed. They provide information which would otherwise be missing and inevitably over-looked. But at the same time attitudes are not articulated at the policy level and are therefore difficult to incorporate into the policy process. There is a danger that having been voiced such opinions may not be translated, but it will be more difficult to object to ultimate plans because of the effort at formal consultation. This may be too pessimistic, but one awaits the later stages of the planning process with interest.

Another method used was to solicit the views of organised opinion. This was done largely in terms of functional organisations, though some were area based though not highly local. This suggests one occasion where functional organisa-tion would have been useful for public groups, though the salutary part of the exercise was the limited range of groups involved. While there are problems of relevance at this strategic level of planning, and the planners tried to seek out organisations, the numbers remained small. In effect a quite narrow band of opinion was sought, though it must be remembered that a random sample survey of households was also being mounted. Whether or not the planners might have done more, the points I want to stress here concern the responses of the groups who were consulted.

Most important is the issue of timing. In answer to when should they consult, the planners decided that it would be best to do so early in the process. Some groups shared that perception but many did not. They found the hypothetical nature of questions at such an early stage of development very difficult to cope with. In part because of habit, but also by preference, many would have preferred to be presented with plans at a later stage. They felt capable of reacting to proposals, whether negatively or positively, but not of formulating their own ideas de novo. For many groups then, early consultation is not satisfactory, or could only be so if they were given support and advocacy to assist in the preparation of their case. Among the groups who did respond, those with professional staff, or professional memberships, were most prominent. Also, it might be said, were those with a preventive goal in terms of public activity. Negative response is obviously easier than positive contribution. Promotional groups of various kinds did not seem to find it easy to reply.

Once again the full implications of this exercise will only become clear after further analysis. If I leave an impression of doubt about its quality and its success I do not mean to be unjust to the planners or to the organisations involved. This is a very difficult field and an honourable failure is better than no try at all.

Conclusions

Because of the need for condensation I have not done justice to these two Merseyside efforts and have perhaps stressed their negative features. If so this has been in order to lend weight to the need for a more rigorous examination of the processes of public decision as a necessary prelude to the development of means of participation. If we are to be serious about participation, and this includes participants possibly influencing decisions, then this is absolutely essential.

It is no use adopting a technique if the circumstances and the issue render it inappropriate. The public meeting may be a good device for transmitting messages to some selected public; it is not appropriate for the reasoned exchange necessary to complex decision-making. This does not mean that the latter cannot therefore involve the public in various ways. Decision processes could be opened to more scrutiny and officials could acknowledge their prominent role. The media could look more closely at such processes. Public participation might even occur at those stages. Liverpool tenants have been involved within the Housing department though not necessarily in the most influential places. Similarly Liverpool social services have begun to open new doors to more people. These are hopeful signs and I am sure are repeated elsewhere. Above all, the decision-makers are beginning to appreciate the need for participation and the capacity for it. The public pressure to be involved does not yet seem as great as the pressure to involve them. Perhaps we might then look to some of the key professionals for a change of disposition and a willingness to create opportunities for participation. Power will not easily be wrested from them. It would be interesting if they were to give it up.

PLANNING

PROBLEMS OF PROVISION
AND PLANNING FOR LEISURE

by J. L. CROMPTON
Loughborough Leisure Consultants.

The paper identifies and discusses a number of problems of leisure provision and planning which have confronted one organisation and its full-time team of 25 market researchers, managers, economists, architects and planners working exclusively in the recreation field, for public authorities, tourist boards, private developers and industrial organisations. The problems are discussed under three main headings: Political, Economic and Professional. The categorisation of problems is inevitably to some extent arbitrary, as is the choice of these particular words which are used in a generic rather than a specific sense, but since some of the problems are inter-related, to deal with them under these categories seemed the most expeditious way of focussing the discussion.

The first two categories—Political and Economic—relate to problems which are frequently beyond the control of the professional since he is not the formulator of policy or the decision-maker at that level. Nevertheless it is part of his executive task to educate the policy-makers to understand the full implications of any political or economic decision which they make.

Often the problems identified in relation to leisure provision are confined to Professional problems. The professional concentrates on these problems since he is more able to influence them. They lie within his sphere of decision-making. They are also generally more predictable, tangible and controllable, so that they are frequently easier to explore or resolve. However, it is our own experience that at the end of the day, when the major decisions to commit significant resources to any leisure project have to be made, it is the political and economic factors which decide the fate of the project rather than the professional factors. The integral worth of the project is obviously considered, but this is not the main criteria against which it is evaluated, no matter how comprehensive and rational the plan, or how logical and illustrative its presentation. This paper places some emphasis on the Political, Economic and Professional categories of problems since they are fundamental to the provision of any recreation facilities. Obviously political and economic problems can be examined at a macro or national level, but the comments in this paper are confined to experiences at the local level. If some of the points made in the discussion on specific problems at different parts of the paper appear contradictory, it is the inevitable result of discussing them in general terms when in reality every problem exists within its own unique context.

POLITICAL PROBLEMS

The minority situation in a local authority

Most of the decisions on the provision of leisure facilities in the public sector are taken by local councils who are rightly concerned about public opinion. Any particular public recreation project will cater for only a minority of people since even the most optimistic research shows that very low percentages of the population take advantage of any facilities provided, so that there is an inevitable built-in majority opposition to any recreation proposal put forward. Most projects will rely for their funding on the taxpayer in some form or other and it is difficult for a councillor to say 'yes' to any proposal which the majority of his constituents are likely to oppose.

There are always a number of other projects which would probably generate more popular and emotional public support, e.g. housing, hospital, welfare provision etc., and since there is no successful method available for quantitatively evaluating opportunity cost, the reticence of a councillor is understandable. The reticence is likely to be reinforced by initial ignorance of what is involved, since much leisure provision is relatively new and often outside the personal experience of local councillors, and the natural reaction to a lack of understanding is to play safe and say 'no'.

Thus from the outset any recreation project faces a severe uphill battle to win approval. The recreation professional, if he is convinced of the worth of his proposals and wants to see them translated into facilities, has got to 'sell' them to his council. This involves thoroughly researching the project and then presenting it with conviction, flair and imagination. Research findings are valuable in this 'selling' process because they help to provide a rational basis, but again it should be emphasised that in our experience research findings on their own, without the personal conviction and 'salesmanship' to back them up, are of limited value in getting a recreation project off the ground.

Obviously education and lobbying are valid means of approaching this uphill battle, but until there is a wider acceptance of a higher priority for leisure provision the problem will always be there. Even when a council does ultimately vote to support a leisure project it frequently does so tentatively, and with a restricted budget in order to minimise public criticism. When the council has had time to educate public opinion and accustom it to the new proposal, and when its members are sufficiently confident of their knowledge and experience of the envisaged facility that they can logically answer public criticism, they are frequently willing to commit increasing amounts of public resources to it, especially if it is a large scale project. Meanwhile, however, the architect will have started designing the project within the initial restrictive cost limits established by the council. As current building prices are increasing at the rate of 1½% per month the project cannot be redesigned every time more money is allocated to it, without incurring considerable extra capital costs. The result is badly designed buildings, which do not represent best value-for-money or optimum facilities, but reflect the change of brief given to the architect after the project was commissioned. Unfortunately many of the major recreation centres developed in this country reflect this process.

Prestige developments

After initial momentum has been created, local pride has often resulted in something more elaborate than had been originally envisaged. It is not economically viable to provide large facilities such as theatres or recreation complexes to serve small areas and the argument for providing more smaller facilities rather than a few large facilities, seems to be well supported by survey findings.

Although the catchment areas for different leisure facilities vary considerably according to the peculiar aspects of each facility, research studies have repeatedly shown how very small and local catchment areas are. The following are some typical examples of this:

60% of users of parks travelled less than half a mile, (Law 1972)
43% of indoor bowls players came from within 2 miles of the Centre, (Loughborough Recreation Planning Consultants Ltd Report 1971a: 1972a)
56% of squash players travelled less than 2 miles to play, (Loughborough Recreation Planning Consultants Ltd Report 1972b)
70% of sports hall users travelled less than 3 miles, (D.o.E. 1971)
50% of theatre audiences travelled less than 5 miles, (Haverhill Theatre Study Report, London Borough of Haverhill 1966).
Membership rates fell from 28% for residents within a quarter mile radius of the nearest public library to 6% for residents over 2 miles away, (Luckham 1971)

Obviously these figures show the usage of facilities in their existing locations and scales so that the percentages are probably much higher than they would be if optimum locations and scales of facilities had been adopted. Many other examples could be cited, but whatever facility is considered one feature of the catchment areas stands out—namely that these are much smaller than were anticipated prior to the above researches. Regional theatre productions (Haverhill Theatre Study Report (1966); Mann, P.H. (1969); Newcastle on Tyne Theatre

Survey (1969); Loughborough Recreation Planning Consultants Ltd Report (1971b)) national sports centres like Crystal Palace, and activities such as squash, whose participants travel almost exclusively by car still attract basically local audiences and participants, (Loughborough Recreation Planning Consultants Ltd Report 1972b).

Despite the trend suggested by these research studies, popular emphasis in leisure provision is still on the large centralised projects rather than on smaller scattered facilities. In a recent survey made of fifty metre swimming pools in this country, (Loughborough Recreation Planning Consultants Ltd Report 1973) most of the pools showed a net annual loss in excess of £100,000 and since their capital cost was generally around one million pounds, the obvious question is perhaps why did they not build 10 smaller pools each costing £100,000? This type of provision is unlikely to be less economic, indeed it seems logical to expect such pools to generate greater total usage figures, because of the increased convenience to users.

This advantage in providing several small facilities instead of one large one seems to be especially relevant in the 'green fields' situation of a New Town. In such cases, emphasis still seems to be on providing major facilities. They are likely to be provided before the necessary threshold population to support each and make it viable is available and therefore will require large financial subsidy initially. Further, if there is delay in building a centre until the threshold population arrives, there will be no facilities in the town and the situation will be conducive to 'new town blues'. It would seem to be a much sounder proposition to provide small facilities at the local level in phase with the population build-up and on a small scale appropriate to the neighbourhood level threshold population. Some of these facilities could be in temporary buildings, e.g. inflatables which have a 10-15 year life span and cost only 30% of the cost of traditional buildings. They could be replaced by permanent buildings when the sizes of the population justify large expenditures.

There is no doubt that the large project brings much prestige to the community, its council members, the architect concerned, and the manager who will operate it when it is completed. This is possibly one factor which has contributed to the present tendency. Other factors are a lack of awareness of the alternatives; lack of professional advice from officers trained or experienced in recreation; shortage of appropriate land; government reorganisation, the effects of which are discussed later; opportunity planning—a 'now-or-never' situation; and the hard political struggle involved. The implication of this latter factor is that only one political battle has to be fought rather than ten, for if ten be the optimum number of small facilities then there is a danger that only three may be constructed because of continued political debate, election changes in council personnel or changes in the economic climate.

Local government reorganisation

The two years pending reorganisation were a major source of impetus for the provision of leisure facilities, because many councils felt that if they did not provide facilities their community may not have adequate recreation facilities for many years to come. New larger councils may see their priorities elsewhere. The primary way adopted by a local authority to raise money has been to sell a piece of land to a developer and to use the income to finance a major recreation facility before the local authority loses its identity to the new authority. The rationale for this has been that the land belongs to the local community and the council wants to see all the benefits from its sale go to the local community and not elsewhere, under the new authority. There has also been an awareness that any losses that may be incurred by any of these major facilities would be spread over the new larger authority so that the local taxpayers would not have to bear this full cost, but would achieve maximum benefits from the facility of having it on their doorstep.

This transitional stage is probably not representative of the way in which leisure provision will be provided in the future, and it is possible that exclusive emphasis on the large-scale project will give way to a more balanced scale of provision when reorganisation is implemented.

The 'sheep' attitude

One of the major faults in planning is the tendency to follow what has gone before and to justify a new project on the grounds 'it works at x'. This results in early errors in concept, policy and execution being repeated and magnified. This paper discusses two of them: dual use and joint provision and 'honey-pots'.

Dual use and joint provision

This concept has become synonymous for much that is supposed to be good in recreation planning. The school uses the facilities in the day time hours and the community uses them in the evenings, at weekends and during vacations. This sounds very logical and many people and bodies now seem to be firmly 'hitched on to this particular bandwagon'. The local politicians are pleased because they feel able to supply the community with adequate leisure facilities at minimum cost through sharing the financial outlay with the education authority thus apparently making very efficient use of the taxpayer's 'pound'. Unfortunately, joint provision is frequently an inadequate compromise which involves the local community in a significant financial outlay with most of the benefits of the arrangement going to the education authority.

The following points are frequently relevant, but often not considered. On the basis of the school using the facilities exclusively when it is in session and the community for the remaining time, the community and not the school is the majority user of the facilities in the ratio of at least 2:1 over a period of a full year. Nevertheless the facilities are frequently controlled by the education authorities. If they were controlled, managed and programmed by the community, the education authority could have priority access during certain times when community use is minimal. This would represent a complete reversal of the typical management arrangement currently in force. Defining distinct demarcation times of use for the school and for the community is very inflexible and likely to lead to the facilities being under-utilised for considerable periods.

Pressures for increased use of educational investment are growing. These pressures could lead to secondary schools operating for the full 12 months period and for a 12 or 14 hour day with children attending on a shift basis and having staggered vacations. Such educational systems are now common practice in the United States. Increased use of facilities by the education authority must mean a decrease in access to any education facilities by the community.

Nationally 25% of the nation's male manual workers are shift workers (Gretton 1971) and in some communities this figure is substantially higher. Shift workers are likely to seek access to leisure facilities during the day time. Further, exclusive day time use by the school prevents use by housewives and the working population during lunch times. Often, planners assume that there is no demand from housewives and the working population for use of facilities during the working week. This assumption is unsound.

Joint provision is undoubtedly an eminently sensible solution in some areas, e.g. rural districts, but it should not be blindly pursued, since blanket coverage with joint provision projects does not meet the requirement for community leisure provision.

Honey-pots'

'Honey-pot' theory states that if an intensive area, e.g. a country park, is created, it will take considerable pressure off those outdoor recreation areas, particularly the National Parks, which are meant to offer a 'wilderness' experience, or which are already overcrowded. Fifteen years ago in California, it was recognised that this was not a valid assumption, since when State Parks were supplied at intermediate points in an attempt to reduce the pressure and congestion of the National Parks of the Sierra (e.g. Yosemite, Sequoia, etc.) they simply stimulated an increased demand and they were immediately heavily used, thus contributing nothing to easing the congestion problems of the National Parks. Similar experiences have occurred in this country. For instance the designation of the Forest of Bowland as a country park was hoped to take some pressure off the Lake District; but while Bowland has been very popular it appears to have served only to stimulate more of the population to take an interest in the Lake District.

Lack of insistence on quality

There are many examples which could be cited but this paper chooses sports centres that illustrate the point. We, as a nation, have had ten years' experience of designing sports centres and yet with few exceptions, the centres that have more recently been built are fundamentally the same as the earlier centres, in philosophy, concept and design. A book on the subject of Sports Centres was published by the National Playing Fields Association (Perrin 1966) having been written and researched by an architect after a small number of sports centres had been completed. Since this was a new field and few architects have had experience in it the 'sheep' attitude prevailed. Planners and architects invariably copied the suggestions in the book (which are most helpful in themselves though like any basic text they are invariably limited in scope and development) instead of using them as examples and as a basis on which to develop their own ideas on how their briefs should be interpreted. This situation is being reinforced by clients who have a predetermined view of what a sports centre should look like from having visited one or two of them, and being anxious to conform in order to minimise any public criticism. This must have been one of the most sterile areas of architectural development in recent years, during which the potential for innovation and improvement has been high.

The design of some leisure facilities has become so stereotyped that centres are now being constructed through standardised building systems. This encourages the spread of basic buildings, lacking in imagination, excitement and that ingredient of atmosphere which is so critical in leisure facilities.

When a decision is made to go out for dinner, since the quality of the food is probably similar in half-a-dozen restaurants, the ultimate choice is usually determined by the 'atmospheres' of the various alternatives. This is synonymous with quality in a leisure centre, and failure to try to create an atmosphere is a weakness in most of our present recreation planning. If people are to be attracted to facilities, we have to draw them from the numerous home-centred leisure activities available. The main constraint on their participating and making use of facilities may not be time, income, mobility, population, education or whatever; often the main constraint is the potential quality of the experience being offered. Commercial operators have learned this lesson and the public sector needs to quickly follow.

This is one reason, for example, that private country clubs are proving very successful commercial investments, while recreation centres which frequently offer the same basic facilities continue to lose money.

If a facility is not going to be of a high quality—interpreted as above—doubts should be expressed on whether it should be provided at all. High quality does not imply gold-plated finishes, it implies creating the 'right' atmosphere which will be conducive to a successful recreational experience. For example, there are high quality and low quality adventure play-grounds. The problem at present is that we do not think 'quality', we only think 'facilities, full-stop'.

Public participation

In nearly all our public projects attempts have been made to initiate 'participation' in planning. This is a popular theme, and participation is now required by statute before any structure plan will be accepted. But how is public participation to be defined? How do we achieve it? Many papers have been written about it and sociologists have emphasised how important it is to obtain involvement in order to minimise alienation and anomie, but when one is concerned with planning a scheme for a leisure project for a town of say 60,000 people, how does one achieve participation? The writer and his colleagues have been involved in the following actions seeking participation.

(a) Public meetings at which the proposals have been explained to those present and feed-back received. In one case an attendance as high as 300 was attracted which most people who have tried such meetings would consider to be a successful meeting. But can the involvement of 0.5% of the town's population be considered successful participation, and can commenting on existing plans rather than formulating their own plans be considered to be effective participation?

(b) Addressing the leaders of all the groups in the community at a series of meetings; but is this not likely to create an unrepresentative lobby group that will provide an unreliable indicator of public opinion?

(c) Exhibitions in a town centre location, e.g. library or town hall, lasting a period of a week, during which a representative has been constantly on duty to explain the proposals. Visitors have been invited to write their comments, anonymously if they wish, and place them in a sealed box for consideration.

(d) Extensive local press coverage with full explanations and graphics of proposals, inviting readers to comment or contribute ideas.

It is recognised that none of these represent participation in its ideal sense. Some people have suggested going onto the street corners from the outset and getting the population to draw their own plans or to select from a wide range of alternatives. But this is hardly likely to be acceptable particularly because (a) the proposed leisure facilities may be beyond the experience of the people being invited to participate; and (b) the long period of survey and gestation involves a significant delay, and with building prices rising consistently at the rate of 1½% a month over the last two years, the delay would mean curtailing the range of facilities or even abandoning the project.

In the light of our experiences we are tending to doubt whether participation in any form beyond the level of information dissemination and public relations can be achieved, and we feel we are still dependent on the empathy of the recreation planner with the needs of all the various socio-economic, age and ethnic groupings.

ECONOMIC PROBLEMS

Commercial investment

Attraction of private money into the leisure field is often an emotive issue. Private enterprise represents a valuable part of the total spectrum of resources available to supply leisure facilities. There is an unfortunate tendency in the recreation field for people to discourage and be suspicious of the motives of private enterprise involvement. This is probably a hang-over from the days when recreation was looked upon as 'welfare' provision to be provided because it was good for you, rather than because it was enjoyed. By definition the private enterprise recreation project is consumer-oriented and provides the people with what they want, since if it does not, it does not survive. 'If people are prepared to pay for it, it must be good' is not necessarily a valid aphorism since this could be claimed by the heroin pusher, but if it brings no disbenefits or diseconomies to society then it can be whole-heartedly and enthusiastically encouraged. Certainly on the basis of the writer's recent experiences in a number of theme pleasure parks in the United States, it is believed that the imagineering and presentation of the parks offered children stimulation, considerable enjoyment, and memorable experiences. Those antagonistic towards commercial projects on principle are surely in danger of wanting to impose their own values on others rather than allowing people to have maximum choice and freedom to make their own value decisions. Private enterprise invests in the leisure field for three main reasons:

(a) to earn money
(b) to improve their image which may be increasingly of concern; e.g. the gravel extractors are now proudly flaunting their new respectability as providers of water recreation and beautifiers of the landscape. Hence a recent advertisement in 'The Times' (1973) was headlined 'We create water for pleasure' and ended with 'So next time you see the familiar orange trucks and plant of—at work in Britain, remember—we don't

just supply building materials for steelworks, roads, docks, houses, bridges and power stations. We build lakes, leafy banks, water-meadows, lakeside restaurants—and so actually leave things better than we found them'.

(c) To gain bargaining power with a public authority i.e. 'I will provide this leisure facility for you if you will let me build my offices, warehouses or whatever, elsewhere in the town'. The primary motivating factor is undoubtedly to earn money and it is this which possibly rankles with some people in the leisure field, for they see this as exploitation. However, after having been closely involved with commercial developments for a number of private developers we can confirm that it is extremely difficult to convince them to invest in leisure facilities. If they know they can obtain 15% or 20% return or considerable capital appreciation on their offices, warehouses or whatever, at minimum risk, why should they invest in the high risk leisure market in which it is very difficult to achieve this level of return?

Commercial leisure developments are an important part of the total leisure spectrum because:

(a) They serve minority tastes which would otherwise rate a low priority in the public sector, e.g. golf courses, hotels.

(b) They are innovative and prepared to try something new, e.g. ten-pin bowls.

(c) The facilities are provided at no cost to the community whereas publicly provided facilities usually require subsidies out of taxes.

(d) They establish high standards in design and management terms since in a competitive situation they are forced to provide a high quality service or go out of business.

(e) They can initiate large scale projects requiring large amounts of capital which could not be justified on the taxpayers budget because of the risk involved, e.g. Aviemore Centre,[1] Merrie England,[2] South Coast Marina,[3].

(f) They cater for the 'non-establishment' recreations such as bingo.

(g) They provide a source of capital, through such mechanisms as lease-back for public projects, which would otherwise not get off the ground.

---

[1] Highland Tourist (Cairngorm Development) Ltd.

[2] Mecca and Grand Metropolitan Hotels.

[3] Royal Insurance, National Westminster Bank, E.M.I. and Brighton Corporation.

The recreation field can only gain by encouraging private enterprise to invest and should bury its conservative feelings that somehow it is not appropriate to make money out of recreation.

Operational costs

Often financial considerations of a project are confined to resolving of how to raise the capital to get the facility off the ground when the important question should be, 'If we build this facility what are the operational cost implications?' If the facility is likely consistently to lose money, doubts should be examined about implementation being justified when only a minority of taxpayers will use it, often a relatively privileged minority, and yet all taxpayers will have to pay for any loss. There may seem to be no justification for the poorer groups having to support financially the recreational enjoyment of the wealthier groups.

During a recent visit to an American university, the writer was shown round a new $25 million Arts Centre which included five theatres and concert halls. It was run by one of the members of the theatre department as an extra-curricular activity and was used primarily for student lectures because the university could not afford to staff or to provide productions which would use it. It had been donated by an oil-millionaire who had not at any stage considered its operational costs, and so this magnificant complex now stands empty and unused.

Co-ordination between agencies

Co-ordination between different agencies especially between education and local authorities on the provision of capital money for joint schemes creates another problem. The education authority's planning has to be done so far in advance that its budgets are relatively inflexible, so that all chances of 'opportunity planning' are foregone and the vital variable of political climate cannot be considered. Obviously whenever two agencies are involved co-ordination problems are inevitable, but the problem needs some consideration for it is causing us to lose some leisure facilities.

PROFESSIONAL

Market research

The need for relevant market research to determine what people want is a fundamental requisite before any major project or plan proceeds, but much of our leisure provision is still built on the basis of intuition. This is inadequate. So often when we are first approached by a local authority we are told "we want a—with this, this and this in it, this is your brief, tell us how much you can provide it for". This 'back of the envelope' brief, thought out and written up by someone who has seen something similar elsewhere, is frequently the foundation from which a project develops. Part of the problem lies with the inherent nature of 'recreation'. Everyone indulges in some form of recreation and thus considers himself an expert and well-qualified to determine precisely what is needed.

This is an irresponsible basis from which to indulge in the spending of public money, and certainly few businessmen would contemplate spending high sums of money without detailed market research from the outset.

The first question which must be asked when somebody states: 'We want/need a . . . . . .' is 'How do you know there is a demand for it?' Invariably the answer is either 'Because town Y has one' or 'Because we have a catchment area of X thousand people, which is sufficient to sustain one'. Both these intuitive answers are inadequate.

Population characteristics in terms of age, sex, social group, purchasing power of the community, recreational habits and interests, communication systems and potential and actual mobility of the population are widely different from one town to another. The only way in which a recreation project can be justified is on the basis of a carefully detailed analysis of the market demand. Frequently the term 'feasibility study' is used for this initial research, yet seldom in such a study is market demand analysed on an accurate quantitative basis. Assessment of the likely use of facilities, the capital cost of constructing the facilities, the cost of operating them, and the likely income from their use should be essential features of every feasibility study and no project, publicly or privately financed, should be allowed to proceed until this basic work has been completed, discussed and debated.

In the field of recreation we must learn the lesson which has been painfully learned in the field of commerce: we must become 'market-oriented' rather than 'product-oriented'.

To provide a facility first and then hope the people will come and use it is the wrong way to approach the problem, and it makes the job of attracting customers much harder than it need be. The logical way of planning is to analyse first the demand in order to discover, create and arouse consumer needs, and then to build the most appropriate facility to satisfy those needs.

The objectives should be to discover the potential customers in number and type, not to build an arbitrary facility which then has to be sold irrespective of what the customer really requires. The service should begin with the customer and his needs not with the construction of the facility. When the needs have been delineated and quantified it is then time to develop the project with the knowledge and confidence that it is the most appropriate facility.

Interdisciplinary teams

Once a decision has been taken to proceed, the production of the facility lies usually almost exclusively in the hands of the architect. The client, i.e. the council, is a layman, and their professional officers frequently lack expertise in this new field which is outside their sphere of recognised expertise, so they are generally satisfied to accept the architect's guidance.

The architect is not usually trained to have an understanding of the specialised needs of the recreation-user, nor is he trained in management. There is a need for the provision of facilities to be undertaken by an interdisciplinary team so that the market researcher and recreation manager are incorporated into, and recognised as an integral part of, the design team.

The architect can be preoccupied with the appearance of the building rather than its functional appearance. In many cases this preoccupation has resulted in unsuitable and often unnecessarily expensive materials being used; inappropriate sizes of rooms and fittings and dispositions of rooms and spaces being recommended; and most common of all, the management of the facility being ignored. All these factors contribute to the high running costs of facilities.

The largest item of expenditure in the running of a recreation facility will be wages and salaries. These are likely to account for between 60 and 75% of total running costs. In order to make the centre economically viable the number of personnel required to operate the facility must be kept to a minimum, and to do this it is necessary to build in management control at the design stage. The general architect has had little training or experience in this specialised aspect, and frequently he does not consider this element when developing his design.

Having to learn to work together is likely to be painful to both recreation manager/planner and architect at the outset. It takes a period of time and several projects before the architect fully appreciates the nature of the contribution he can expect from the recreation professional. Similarly it takes the recreation professional some time before he learns the appropriate time at which the architect needs particular information and direction, for if he provides the information too late either the architect is involved in abortive work and has to retrace his steps and delay the project, with all the cost implications such a measure has, or alternatively the input is disregarded and the scheme is sub-optimal.

Management personnel

Good management is required in order to make leisure facilities effective and financially sound. There is a shortage of experienced personnel in the recreational field at managerial level. In the public sector reorganisation of local government has given impetus to recreation, with the grouping together of recreation and amenity services under one directorate and senior appointments are being made in the £5,000 to £9,000 salary range. The senior positions in these departments are, however, in some cases being occupied by people with little insight into recreation and leisure and little previous experience of it. Several of the new Recreation Departments will be headed by men whose previous jobs were in other spheres of public service who have proved they have administrative ability, but planning and managing recreation facilities are based on a unique technology calling for particular management training and skills.

Thus if recreation planning and management is to be done well in the future, there are large numbers of people at the senior level who will require training, and if we are to make efficient use of scarce resources, the provision of this training is an urgent task.

Location

Location of facilities is frequently not considered. It is usually a case of 'a site is available there, so let's do this leisure project there'. This is the decision and so the project proceeds on that site. Again, no businessman would do this. Marks & Spencer wait until the right site is available before they open up a store in a new location. Burton's insist on a corner site and will not open up until one becomes available. They are very conscious of the importance of accessibility and awareness.

Despite the anticipated continued increase in travel by private car, public transport is the main means of transport for many people to any facility not within walking distance. It seems logical that those who are on or near a public transport route are more likely to use facilities than those who are not. Further, if it is necessary to change vehicles this will act as a discouragement. It is possible that, because of supplies of petrol becoming less plentiful, the use of private cars will decrease. This would add to the desirability of building leisure facilities near to routes of public transport.

If we do not know that something exists, we will obviously not go to visit it or see it. The only way of learning of the existence of any attraction is to hear about it, see it or see a reference to it. Generally, as far as most leisure facilities are concerned, because they are not essential to our material needs, the extent to which we actively seek to find out what exists is limited. Most knowledge about leisure facilities, particularly in urban areas, derives directly from other more essential activities. This means that very much more is generally known about facilities in central areas than in outer fringes of urban areas.

Taking the specific case of the Green Belt around London, remarkably few people living in London know very much about what is available and worth visiting within the Green Belt. Even in the outer fringes of the urban areas, people tend to know more about the existence of facilities in both the central area and the inner sector along their approach routes to the centre. This is presumably the result of seeing them when travelling to the City centre for work or shopping, or by coming into contact with other people who have seen them. Maw and Cosgrove's (1972) work (Leisure Model Unit of the Built Environment Research Group, Polytechnic of Central London) at Swiss Cottage illustrated the significance of the 'awareness' factor in limiting a catchment area. It was noticed that the effective demand level was not concentrically distributed around the centre, but was concentrated in the north-west sector leading away from Central London. This could not be accounted for by the intervening competition of other swimming pools, nor the varying population character-istics—in fact, it corresponded with the car, bus and tube routes of people travelling from outer areas to Central London who saw the Centre, or the name Swiss Cottage in the case of the tube traveller, when passing.

These factors of accessibility and awareness must be critically examined before deciding to make a major investment in leisure facilities. They are primary considerations to commercial leisure operators and yet are frequently ignored in the public sector. We accept that there must be a large element of opportunity planning (i.e. providing facilities when and where the opportunity presents itself or risk that those facilities be delayed or abandoned). But the market research must still be done, and basic planning rules such as accessibility and awareness must be obeyed, if optimum facilities are to be provided.

Cost of available land in the central areas is obviously a deterrent to the provision of facilities in these areas, but this can be surmounted, by offering developers a site with planning permission to build offices, shops, flats, etc. but only on the condition that they include a number of recreation facilities which the town requires in the development.

Demand

This is a problem which has been repeatedly tackled and it is basic to recreation planning. There is a real need to identify the size and nature of latent demand. This identification does not lend itself easily to research since it involves a before-and-after type study with appropriate control groups, so that a study period of a number of years and a fairly substantial budget are required. Nevertheless, we really do need some guidance on factors influencing demand, since much of our present demand forecasting is based on careful analogy and relevant interpolation, but we have no real knowledge of the latent demand effect.

Over the last ten years since the ORRRC (1962) reports were published there has been considerable emphasis on the description of and relationship between, the elements of consumer constraint, T.I.M.P.E. (time, income, mobility, population & education) and recreation participation. Now there is probably a general realisation that while at one level these elements may offer some general constraint, it is the variables of accessibility, awareness and quality which are really the fundamental constraints, and we need to know much more about their influence and effect on recreation participation. Again these variables are much more difficult to control, explore and evaluate than the T.I.M.P.E. factors, but hopefully researchers will direct some attention towards them.

There must be concentration on the collection of data, and development of a methodology we can use in the field to estimate demand, and not on the development of models which require so much data to operate that they become redundant because time and money are not available to produce the data.

We need to carry out considerable research in order to be able to suggest what kinds of leisure provision are required for older people. The union at the Chrysler Motor Company in the U.S.A. is this year seeking an earlier retirement with higher pensions from the company, which if the union is successful will mean that some Chrysler employees will retire at 50. We need similar work to determine what type of leisure provision to provide for the low socio-economic groups and what kind of management and marketing approaches are needed to encourage such people to participate.

Relevant research

Most of the current research work being done is contributing towards better planning of leisure facilities. There is an increased awareness of the fundamental problems (e.g. what people want; catchment areas; profiles of users and non-users etc.) and many efforts are geared towards solving these problems.

However, there is a danger that as more and more educational institutions become involved in the leisure field the research they do becomes less relevant, more introverted and less communicative. Over the past ten years in the United States, this trend has been very noticeable. The ORRRC, reports generated the initial momentum which started the research bandwaggon rolling, and as the years have passed the published research has been less and less relevant to the practical recreation planner working in the field.

The emergence of specialist research journals in the leisure field seems to have intensified this trend with people anxious to publish in order to further their academic careers rather than to assist in resolving practical problems. As a generalisation this is obviously open to criticism, but there is no doubt that many American researchers in recreation appear to be primarily concerned with establishing internal validity of their research rather than with its external validity, i.e. its applications. This has produced a preoccupation with minor irrelevancies, obscure statistics and jargon which may lend to themselves good research design, but also a reluctance to approach major problems.

References

C.C.P.R. (1968). Crystal Palace Survey—some preliminary results. Unpublished Report.

DEPARTMENT OF THE ENVIRONMENT (1971). *Indoor Sports Centres.* Sports Council Study No. 1. London: H.M.S.O.

GRETTON, J. (1971). The hours we work. *New Society,* January.

LAW, S. et al (1972). Surveys of the use of open spaces—Volume 2. Greater London Council Department of Planning and Transportation Strategy Branch.

LONDON BOROUGH OF HAVERHILL (1966). Haverhill Theatre Study— Unpublished Report.

LOUGHBOROUGH RECREATION PLANNING CONSULTANTS LTD REPORT (1971a). Research study on Shaws Bridge Indoor Bowls Centre (unpublished).

LOUGHBOROUGH RECREATION PLANNING CONSULTANTS LTD REPORT (1971b). Survey at Chichester Hall County Antrim (in Association with the N. Ireland Arts Council); Unpublished Report.

LOUGHBOROUGH RECREATION PLANNING CONSULTANTS LTD REPORT (1972a). Research study on eleven indoor bowls centres (unpublished).

LOUGHBOROUGH RECREATION PLANNING CONSULTANTS LTD REPORT (1972b). Research study on seven squash centres (unpublished).

LOUGHBOROUGH RECREATION PLANNING CONSULTANTS LTD REPORT (1973). Research study on 300 indoor swimming pools. Unpublished Report.

LUCKHAM, B. (1971). *The Library in Society.* London: The Library Association.

MANN, P.H. (1969). The provincial audience for Drama, Ballet and Opera, a survey in Leeds. Department of Sociological Studies, University of Sheffield.

MAW, R. & COSGROVE, D. (1972). Assessment of demand for Recreation—a modelling approach. Working paper 2/72. Leisure Model Unit of the Built Environment Research Groups. Polytechnic of Central London.

NEWCASTLE-on-TYNE CITY PLANNING DEPARTMENT (1969). *Theatre Survey,* unpublished Report.

OUTDOOR RECREATION RESOURCES REVIEW COMMISSION (1962). Washington D.C.

PERRIN, G. (1966). *Sports Halls.* London: National Playing Fields Association (Reprinted in 1972 and renamed Recreation Centres).

'THE TIMES' NEWSPAPER, July 27th 1973.

PLANNING

DESIGNING FOR LEISURE

by B. GILLINSON Architect,
Gillinson, Barnett and Partners, Leeds.

It is only in recent years, because of the increasing complexity of designing for leisure, that architects have in some cases begun to specialise in this field. More than half the architectural profession are employed in central or local government or their agencies and many work in specific industries. The remainder are in private practices or teaching.

With the surge of interest in the wide field of building for leisure, a small number of medium and large practices have now gained broad experience designing a range of buildings and planning projects in the field of leisure activities.

Sponsorships for these projects have come from either private enterprise for 'entertainment' buildings or more generally from local authorities, sometimes with Sports Council backing for sports complexes.

Apart from straightforward dimensional physical requirements and formal sets of recommendations for swimming pools, the assembling of briefs for the architects has generally been the province of entrepreneurs or committees acting with often the sparsest information as to the true social needs of the society intended to be served by the project.

The interest now being shown by psychologists and other social scientists in this field is thus encouraging to the design professions who have been building 'hopefully', sometimes quite successfully, but without adequate assessment of the correctness of the assumptions inherent in their designs.

Architects and their related design professions who have become interested and involved in this field must have a full understanding of what is meant by the definition 'leisure'. Although this may have been covered in previous chapters it is proper that, as an architect, my understanding of the subject is stated. Most forms of professional work are by their nature, a form of leisure activity. My endeavouring to write this chapter on a Sunday afternoon is a form of leisure activity. The line between work and leisure must blur for those fortunate minority who 'enjoy' and are fulfilled by their work.

By the nature of the organisation of our society, it seems, that the majority of people are able to derive little personal satisfaction or fulfilment from their work. Their leisure activities often become the means of fulfilment, and their work merely the agency which enables the attainment of leisure.

The development of our society points to a situation whereby a person's status in that society may well be measured by the nature of their leisure rather than by their work activity. This will probably lead to a future pattern whereby the entrepreneurial and the professional will continue to 'work' long hours whilst the majority of people in the non-fulfilling occupations will gradually work fewer hours per week with a consequent steady increase in their leisure time. This time availability will lead to a demand for more leisure facilities of a higher standard.

Thinking educationalists understand the need to teach children to develop their interest in leisure as at least an equally important facet of their lives as their work.

Of course not all leisure activities need special places or buildings. Listening to the gramophone or radio, watching television or reading are straightforward 'leisure' activities. Going for a walk or riding a cycle in the country are equally straightforward leisure pursuits requiring no special facilities other than the important, if obvious necessity, to retain and develop the countryside as a recreational area and overcome the conflicts now developing between the city dweller, with increased mobility and time, and the farming community. It would seem, however, from what little research information is available, that the majority, the broad mass of people, are gregarious by nature and require a wide range of community buildings and facilities of both the types traditionally or historically provided by public authorities and private enterprise.

In Britain, it has become customary for the leisure activity of swimming to be catered for by local authorities with substantial financial subsidies. Many social-cum-leisure facilities have been provided by the entrepreneur who seeks to profit by providing parks and buildings to suit the tastes of people at the time. These types of provision will continue to be needed even though the providers may not restrict themselves to traditional areas. It is surely only historical accident that these examples are catered for in the way they are. Our limited research shows quite a different situation existing in other countries.

In the 1960's, by which time my firm had a considerable number of leisure building projects in the pipeline, there was so little information available that we set up a leisure research and development unit. The prime objectives were to endeavour to find out about real needs and the best and most economical way of providing for them. In some ways we bit off more than we could chew, particularly so in respect of our attempts to find out people's real needs.

It is in this field that the social scientist can, and it is to be hoped will, come to the aid of the architect and the other creative decision-makers working in this field.

The work of the social scientist can either be a creative 'aid' or it can detail the quandaries already facing the architect and divide him from his objectives by a new and obscure jargon which can be used as a marvellous instrument of evasion.

Methodology can warn us of pitfalls but it will not help us conceive new ideas. It tells us how to test hypotheses but not how to arrive at them. In other words, when the social sciences are used as alternatives rather than as an aid to creative design, the consequences can be unfortunate.

The social scientist can most aid the architect by researching in as great a depth as possible the real needs and means of fulfilling the aspirations of the mass of people in our modern industrialised society. By analysing data in such a way, he can provide a basic 'brief' of these needs related to population densities and regional characteristics, but not overlooking adequate provisions for minorities within communities. The information provided must be presented in a clear form and be free of the sort of jargon so often used by architects—perhaps even more than by sociologists. By a *basic* 'brief', I mean a list of requirements with some sort of order or priority, bearing in mind that most people or groups want more than they are prepared to pay for or can afford.

The architects and designers need practical help from the social science professions in the carrying out of surveys of the use of the buildings recently completed or coming into use at the present time. The use of existing leisure facilities is insufficiently researched and documented in ways which are of practical value to the professionals who have to actually 'turn out the goods'.

Social research is, and has been, carried out by many individuals and groups at universities, but where are we to turn to find set out in relatively simple and easily interpretable terms the likely needs of a quickly changing society?

The social scientist should not overlook the many restraints within which the building and environmental designer must work—these are many and include town planning and building regulations, fire regulations, insurance, transportation, landscaping and even basic problems like the provision of services.

We certainly do not want a schedule of rooms, or even a catalogue of activities and the physical means to provide for them. We have enough of that information as a result of our own recent practical research. Perhaps the knowledge we seek is not, and cannot be made available by social and user research. People and tastes are changing too rapidly, in which case we should pursue our current theories to the ultimate in design and put into our structures as much flexibility as the restraints of normal building practice permits. We would then rely on the results of research studies carried out regularly and in some depth on our completed projects, in an effort to learn from experience and develop by trial and error. Not only buildings, but also management must have a flexible approach to cater quickly for changing tastes and needs.

The social research effort is urgent however, and feed-back on the schemes completed in the early 70's needs to come through quickly in order to correct any wrong assumptions in the large number of projects in the pipeline or under construction in Britain at the present time.

If it is accepted that the more leisured society of the future will need and demand the right facilities, then how are these to be provided?

Thinking in terms of the U.K., the private sector in general apart from a few specialised fields, has been slow to seize opportunities. Many primary financial sources, however, are at last beginning to realise that in the field of leisure there is the potential for a major 'growth' industry. Local authorities too, in many cases, are beginning to appreciate that their obligations can, and should, properly extend beyond the supply of basic services and education, and include leisure provision for the community.

How the resources can be found is outside my brief, but clearly if society as a whole wants the provisions to be made then it will obtain them either by paying at the door, or by annual memberships or a combination of both, or alternatively by voting a slice of their taxes, whether national or local to be expended on the facilities they want provided.

The solutions might often be found in a marriage between state or local government (supplying the sport and recreational facilities) and private investment (financing the more glamorous and perhaps more profitable facilities).

Turning to a consideration of types of facility, it might be useful to mention briefly the background to the 'popular' leisure centre in terms of modern history. The precedent for the idea of the really large enclosure for a leisure building was the 'Crystal Palace', erected in 1857 in Hyde Park, London. Built originally as an exhibition hall it was later taken down and re-assembled in south London as a general entertainment building. It is perhaps to be regretted now that when, for the centenary in 1951, it was decided to have the 'Festival of Britain', that the opportunity was not taken to build a contemporary equivalent. The best example of an equivalent building of our time was the centrepiece, 'Megastructure', at the Osaka Expo in 1971 in Japan. This was a wonderful example of flexible use—grand scale leisure architecture.

It is really more appropriate to talk of a leisure environment rather than just a leisure building because the field of provision must extend from the small community centre to the largest 'leisure park'.

National Wildlife parks or areas of particularly scenic beauty are of course physically the largest category and will increase in importance, but a new phenomena, the 'commercial' leisure park, for which Disneyland in California was the precedent and pacemaker, will become commonplace.

Those who have not seen Disneyland may feel a repugnance for the 'dream world' idea, but few who do pay a visit will fail to be impressed by the sheer commitment of the idea, the very high standard and 'quality' of the whole thing, plus the cleanliness and order.

With 10 years of increasing success with Disneyland on 250 acres, the Disney Company used all their experience so gained to develop in Florida a 'Disney World', but this time on 43 square miles!

Disneyland last year saw 7 million visitors, the incomplete Disneyworld expected 10 million in its first year.

There have been developed in the U.S.A. over recent years, a number of 'theme parks', and some of these have very impressive attendance figures which prove that they fill a real leisure need.

On a smaller scale in Britain the stately houses attract very large numbers of visitors and those properly in the leisure business such as Beaulieu and Woburn are following to a large extent, the American theme park idea.

One down in scale from the leisure park is the Regional Leisure Centre. This will often, and certainly in Britain, be associated with the sea-side. These centres already exist all over the world. In more amenable climates than ours, they can and do work successfully with little architecture, other than the provision of accommodation in the form of hotels and housing, with open air swimming pools, restaurants and bars. Bearing in mind the difficulty presented by the climate in Britain, it has become necessary to find solutions for the provision of recreation and leisure which protect from the weather. The idea of a large seaside solarium was thought out in 1964, by a Manx architect, J. Phillips Lomas, and my practice was concerned with him in the construction of Summerland at Douglas. This scheme was enormously successful but the terrible fire which occurred there in 1973 will inevitably hold back similar projects elsewhere for some time. A large structure on the same theme was carried out at about the same time in Japan. Both of these were successful and very popular. Leisure centres do not rely on the availability of spectator events, but try to provide a controlled environment for the holidaymaker. Whilst with easier travelling, many people go abroad for a holiday, it is still a fact that only 58% of all the population take a holiday away from home at all, and only 16% in fact go abroad. There is already an enormous investment in existing facilities at British resorts which cannot easily be abandoned. Thus, many of the more enlightened seaside authorities are investigating the possibility of providing large covered areas. It is fair to say that there are still difficulties in financing these projects and in order to do so it is necessary to prepare very detailed financial studies which examine the visitor population and its economic characteristics, and to arrive from this at a reasonably accurate decision as to the right combination of activities which will be desirable and commercially viable for a particular situation. Only when such a study has been done, is it possible to look at the architectural problems involved in providing a suitable building or buildings for the activities suggested. It is necessary these days for an architect involved in this field to understand the various methods of finance available to his client, to know the effect of possible landlord and tenant relationships relating to this financing, to know the relative popularity and profitability of all the activities and to sort these out and accommodate them in reasonably favourable and properly inter-related spaces.

As mentioned earlier, flexibility is vitally important but can be very costly to achieve. The simile of the spatial concept of a large fully equipped TV studio is perhaps the best example one can suggest for an ideal leisure area. A large space with moveable walls and crammed with sophisticated electronics.

Another group of architects called Archigram have designed a scheme which is at present being constructed underground at Monte Carlo. This is a very mature solution to the idea of a huge flexible leisure resort. The key to the success of this as yet unfinished project, will I feel sure, be an imaginative management. This comment must apply to any large leisure project; unless it is managed with intelligence and imagination it is likely to fail.

The next category I will talk about is the purely commercial development. In the U.K. these are exemplified by the Bristol Centre. This was erected in the mid 60's for Mecca Ltd and comprises within one huge building a whole range of commercial leisure activities. Similarly in the Merrion Centre, Leeds, which is a large commercial office centre and shopping precinct, there is also incorporated a whole range of leisure activities from cinemas and dance halls to night clubs and a bowling alley.

Many new central area developments are now following the trend set by the Merrion Centre, in incorporating facilities for leisure activities; for example the Arndale Centre in Poole, which contains a local authority run sports centre as an adjunct to an enclosed shopping centre.

More recent interesting projects at present under construction include a scheme my firm have designed at Brownlow Hill in Liverpool, opposite the Adelphi Hotel, which contains discotheque, restaurant, a large bier hall, 3 cinemas—all in one complex. There is no doubt as to the popular appeal of these entertainment centres. The certainty of this is the fact that purely commercial organisations are prepared to invest large amounts of capital in building them.

An example of a large local authority sponsored regional centre is the scheme my firm have designed for Sunderland Corporation and now under construction. We were commissioned in December 1970 to undertake a leisure and recreational feasibility study of the Sunderland region, as a result of which proposals have been made for an exciting central leisure complex to be operated by the Corporation on commercial lines. Not surprisingly, Sunderland is similar to most large towns and cities in the U.K. in that provision for leisure generally is hopelessly inadequate both for existing and future demand. Existing swimming pools, for example, cater mainly for competitive swimming when in fact the overwhelming demand is for recreational swimming. Thus the new complex will go some way towards satisfying the high latent demand for leisure in the area.

The importance of leisure in the community becomes more and more apparent each year, until, like Sunderland, it achieves a most prominent position in the heart of the community—in the middle of the town centre.

The third and smallest type of leisure building is the neighbourhood centre. This is the most common but we do not yet have them in sufficient numbers. They need to be sited centrally serving a population of between 40,000 and

80,000 people. In this category, in one complex we have swimming pools, sports halls, community centres, dance and bingo halls, evening classes, in short, all the activities carried out by people on a repetitive pattern for social reasons.

These centres should be sited close to the other neighbourhood central activities, shopping, schools etc. One of the outstanding examples of a flexible solution to this problem is Van Kligeren's Dronten Agora (AD 7/69). With the complete lack of any social facilities within this new town, in Holland, he reproduced the environment of the Italian market square to suit the Dutch climate. It is a place of great charm and informality, and Van Kligeren's subsequent work at Lelystad will be watched with interest.

British examples of neighbourhood leisure centres nearly, or already completed include those at Huddersfield, Bletchley and Rotherham. All of these combine variously, swimming pools, sports halls, squash courts, indoor bowling, together with bars and discotheques. The scheme at Rotherham designed by my firm includes one of the first of two 'fun swimming pools' built indoors in the world. A similar pool we have designed is now operating at Whitley Bay, Northumberland.

It has been assumed for many years by local authorities that swimming pools must be a loss on the rates. The reasons for this are interesting. There is, as mentioned before, this tradition that we will swim for health reasons and not particularly enjoy it, and for that we must pay no more than 10p. This type of price structure was based upon much simpler pool designs, with much less sophisticated plant, and lower standards of hygiene. For instance a typical pool of the early 1900's would have no filtration system, the pool would be completely drained and refilled on Saturdays and Wednesdays. Mondays and Thursdays were called freshwater days, and adults were charged 4p including towels. Tuesdays and Fridays the charge was 2p for obvious reasons. Costs and standards have climbed since those days without a corresponding rise in charges, and yet for social reasons local authorities have refused to charge more. There are two ways of tackling this problem. One way is to reduce the capital cost of the swimming pool, and the D.O.E., Technical Unit for Sport, have produced their documents, design notes Nos 1 and 2, explaining how this can be done. Their designs have a minimum of accommodation based upon an analysis of existing pools throughout the country. The cost per square foot of their pools is very similar to most other modern pools in that the lower capital cost is achieved by planning the smallest possible spaces for everything. The resultant pools will be rather sterile, but they will certainly be loved by the Amateur Swimming Association whose priorities are for rectangular racing pools. But the competition type swimmers represent only 7% of the total swimming public and the other 93% need something very different.

The alternative method of tackling the problem is by designing a different type of pool altogether. The average Majorca Hotel operator knows more about what people really want and he provides it. Perhaps if a little more is spent on the pool by providing a more varied and interesting water environment, then more people will attend and it will be possible to have slightly higher entrance charges, thereby making the scheme more viable. Some of the best examples of such leisure pools are at resort hotels like that of the Acapulco Hilton. Free shape, palm trees, waterfalls, bridges, paddling areas and plenty of lounging spaces all round. The British invented wave making machinery before the Second World War and yet it was the Germans and Japanese who realised their potential and installed them. So let us provide a little more fun in our pools and attract a new kind of swimmer who perhaps for the improved facility will pay more at the door. In fact, the current enthusiasm for such things as foreign travel, pop festivals, voluntary work in underdeveloped countries, the live entertainment cabaret clubs and eating out, all indicate a desire for experience, and our leisure facilities in general must match this need and not be dull.

While this may be a general consideration, it is obviously not the only one. Age for example, may also be an important factor to consider. In provision for the under 25's, sport is of great importance and poses a real problem since there is a limit to the acreage of open space that we can devote to the active sports, especially in the areas where it is most needed, in large conurbations.

The 25 to 39 age group is the one with the highest growth rate. By the year 2000 there will be 18 million more people in this age group. Traditionally, this age group consists of married people with children, and although the number of children will be fewer on average than today and the marriage tradition may have altered in some way, the family unit seems likely to stay more or less the same. This means that we have to cater for those units rather than for individuals, so the trend must be towards larger family centres where there is a large selection of things to do for all ages and which contains a well fitted-out creche properly staffed to accommodate the really young children.

The 40+ group has the next to the lowest predicted growth rate of 2.6 million. Most of us will probably retire at a lower age than the statutory 65 for men and 60 for women, and perhaps will live slightly longer on average than today so that we will have a lot of leisure time to fill. It is therefore important that we learn to face this fact and we educate ourselves during our working life to appreciate and to use this increased leisure. So there must be more leisure facilities to suit that age group, bowls, fishing, foreign travel, garden centres and open space.

Other factors besides age, will also be of importance, but here I return to the point of enlisting the help of the social scientists, many of whom are now interested in this field of study.

SUBJECT INDEX

199

AUTHOR INDEX

201